The Michigan Guidelines on the International Protection of Refugees

Published in the United States of America by
Michigan Publishing
Manufactured in the United States of America

DOI: http://doi.org/10.3998/mpub.11478533

ISBN 978-1-60785-525-5 (hardcover)
ISBN 978-1-60785-527-9 (e-book)
ISBN 978-1-60785-526-2 (open-access)

An imprint of Michigan Publishing, Maize Books serves the publishing needs of the University of Michigan community by
making high-quality scholarship widely available in print and online. It represents a new model for authors seeking to share
their work within and beyond the academy, offering streamlined selection, production, and distribution processes. Maize
Books is intended as a complement to more formal modes of publication in a wide range of disciplinary areas.
fulcrum.org/maizebooks

Contents

Preface

The complexity of refugee law is often daunting.

Both the internationally agreed definition of refugee status and the unique catalog of rights to which refugees are entitled are routinely invoked by millions of persons in search of protection. Advocates, officials, judges and others charged with applying the standards set by the UN's Convention relating to the Status of Refugees ("Refugee Convention") must give meaning to often ambiguous but unquestionably important norms, knowing that an error can literally have life and death consequences.

Yet despite its routine invocation and critical importance, refugee law sadly stands alone as the only body of international human rights law that lacks an independent and authoritative supervisory body. The normative void created by our collective failure to establish a mechanism charged with resolving interpretive ambiguity is both confusing for refugees (who must try to identify and reach a state sympathetic to their particular case) and problematic for states (which understandably fear the distortion of refugee flows in response to any perceived liberality). As the Full Federal Court of Australia observed,

> It is desirable that obligations of the host states under an instrument such as the Convention be consistently interpreted in order that there be uniformity of approach not only as to host state rights and obligations, but also as to the derivative legal position of refugees thereunder.[1]

Our best hope of achieving this uniformity of approach in an inherently imperfect environment was identified nearly two decades ago by the British House of Lords:

> . . . [A]s in the case of other multilateral treaties, the Refugee Convention must be given an independent meaning . . . without taking colour from distinctive features of the legal system of any individual contracting state. In principle, there can only be one true interpretation of a treaty . . .
>
> In practice it is left to national courts, faced with the material disagreement on an issue of interpretation, to resolve it. But in doing so, it must search, untrammelled by notions of its national legal culture, for the true autonomous and international meaning of the treaty.[2]

---

1   *NBGM v. Minister for Immigration and Multicultural and Indigenous Affairs*, [2006] FCAFC 60 (Aus. FFC, May 12, 2006).
2   *R. v. SSHD, ex parte Adan and Aitseguer*, [2001] 2 WLR 143 (U.K. House of Lords, Dec. 19, 2000).

Embracing this imperative, the University of Michigan's Program in Refugee Law was established 20 years ago with a commitment to furthering a truly transnational approach to international refugee law. A key part of our mission has been to bring scholarly acumen to bear on the meaning of both refugee status and refugee rights, and to do so in a way that draws on and supports the efforts of judges and others who must wrestle with how best to identify the "true autonomous and international meaning" of refugee law.

To this end, we established the *Colloquium on Challenges in International Refugee Law* and produced the first *Michigan Guidelines on the International Protection of Refugees* in 1999. Each of the eight sets of *Guidelines* reproduced in this volume has resulted from a uniquely rigorous process in which in-house faculty and external experts worked with senior Michigan Law School students to design and implement a research program relating to a single, cutting-edge and difficult issue of refugee law. Over the course of 18 months, relevant jurisprudence and scholarship from around the world were sifted, analyzed, and organized by sequential groups of students, resulting in a comprehensive background study (each of which has been published in the *Michigan Journal of International Law*). A small number of highly qualified external experts—including scholars, advocates, officials, judges, and a high-level observer from the UNHCR—have then been invited to respond in writing to the study, leading to the formulation of a detailed plan for discussion and debate on the most difficult questions raised. The panel of external experts then met jointly with the student contributors for three days of guided intensive reflection and debate in Ann Arbor, over the course of which *Michigan Guidelines* were drafted by consensus.

The Michigan Colloquium process is not, of course, the only mechanism seeking to remedy the normative voids of the Refugee Convention.[3] It is, however, unique in several respects. The first is the depth and intensity of the 18-month collaborative research enterprise that has informed each Colloquium debate. The second is the requirement that no Guidelines are issued without the agreement of *all* expert and student contributors—an extraordinarily demanding standard given the real diversity of views and backgrounds of those participating, but critical to ensuring the integrity of the project. Third and most relevant to this volume, the Michigan process has from its inception been committed to producing tightly framed, succinct Guidelines that can be readily understood and drawn upon by those engaged in the cut and thrust of making protection decisions on the ground.

Over the course of two decades, the Colloquium has produced Guidelines that address five of the most difficult issues of refugee status—what is the meaning of a "well-founded fear"; when may refugee status be denied on grounds of an "internal protection alternative"; how is the causal connection to a Convention ground to be assessed; when is a risk fairly said to be for reasons of "political opinion"; and under what circumstances are persons believed to have violated rules of international criminal law to be excluded from refugee status? In addition, Guidelines have also been issued on three critical aspects of refugee rights—when may a refugee be required to seek protection in a country not of his or her choosing; to what extent is a refugee entitled to undertake employment or other economic activity; and what is the scope of a refugee's right to freedom of movement, both between states and within the asylum country? We have been gratified that judicial and other decision-makers around the world have so frequently engaged with our analysis of these important questions, giving rise to precisely the thoughtful give and take that a robust interpretive dialog requires.

---

3 Of particular importance, the United Nations High Commissioner for Refugees (UNHCR) has more recently embarked on a comparable enterprise, issuing its first *Guidelines on International Protection* in 2002.

To celebrate its 20ᵗʰ anniversary, the University of Michigan's Program in Refugee and Asylum Law chose to translate the full set of eight *Michigan Guidelines on the International Protection of Refugees*—initially released in both English and French—into three additional languages: Arabic, Russian, and Spanish. With the able assistance of the University of Michigan Press, we are disseminating 1500 copies of the five-language compendium of the *Guidelines* to libraries and experts around the world, as well as making it available to all online.

The work of adjudicating refugee status and rights will never be simple: the world is too often a messy place in which it will always be challenging to apply legal norms to quickly changing facts and to reconcile the needs of those compelled to flee to the capacity and legitimate concerns of asylum states. Our hope is nonetheless that by sharing this collective analysis of more than one hundred Colloquium participants on some of the most intractable issues of refugee law we may make the interpretive process at least a bit less daunting.

James C. Hathaway
James E. and Sarah A. Degan Professor of Law
Founding Director, University of Michigan Program in Refugee and Asylum Law
Ann Arbor, Michigan
March 2019

Acknowledgments

The existence of the Michigan Guidelines on the International Protection of Refugees is very much due to the support of Jane and Ron Olson, whose generous gift funded the establishment of the Program in Refugee and Asylum Law at the University of Michigan Law School in 1998. But for their vision, the Colloquium on Challenges in International Refugee Law and the resultant Guidelines would never have happened. I am ever grateful to them.

A series of deans of the University of Michigan Law School—Jeffrey Lehman, Evan Caminker, and Mark West—have sustained and encouraged the Program over the last two decades, allowing it to becomes the world's most comprehensive program in international and comparative refugee law.

The Michigan Guidelines themselves are the product of more than one hundred brilliant contributors—academics, judges, officials, research scholars, and most especially JD and LLM students at Michigan Law. Their dedication and commitment to creative thinking and their determination to find and articulate common ground on difficult questions has been nothing short of extraordinary. Particular mention should be made of the marvelous collaboration with the United Nations High Commissioner for Refugees (UNHCR), which has sent a high level observer to engage thoughtfully at each Colloquium; of the chairing of several colloquia by the incomparable Rodger P.G. Haines, QC ONZM; and of Professor Pene Mathew's dynamic interim directorship of the Program during my 2008–2010 leave of absence, including organization of the 5th Colloquium on the right to work.

The Guidelines were immediately issued in French, thanks to the hard work of Professors Jean-Yves Carlier, Luc Leboeuf, and Jack Mangala. Additional translations for this volume have been contributed by Reham Hussain (Arabic), Karina Sarmiento (Spanish), Julia Zelvenska (Russian), and Trusted Translations. I am immensely grateful to each of these brilliant and committed scholars and linguists for the care they took to ensure the truly global reach of the Guidelines.

Maureen MacGlashan kindly took time from an already overtaxed schedule to prepare a careful and comprehensive index to the full set of Michigan Guidelines, making it possible for the first time to draw issue linkages among them. She is quite simply the guru of indexers.

At the University of Michigan Law School, my colleagues Bridgette Carr, Barbara Garavaglia, and Monica Hakimi provided crucial support and endorsements for the Michigan Guidelines process. I have also been very lucky to work with Michigan Publishing to produce this compendium, and thank Jason Colman, Senior Associate Librarian, and Lauren Stachew, Digital Publishing Coordinator, for their commitment to quality and accessibility.

Last—but most definitely not least—I thank Julia Fedeson, my trusted and devoted executive assistant. Julia has both coordinated the Colloquium process over the years and overseen the production of this volume. She is in every sense the model of a committed and careful manager. Her unstinting generosity of spirit and determination to leave no stone unturned in supporting not just me, but everyone involved in the Colloquium and resultant Guidelines projects, mean the world to me.

JCH

THE MICHIGAN GUIDELINES ON THE INTERNAL PROTECTION ALTERNATIVE (1999)

In many jurisdictions around the world, 'internal flight' or 'internal relocation' rules are increasingly relied upon to deny refugee status to persons at risk of persecution for a Convention reason in part, but not all, of their country of origin. In this, as in so many areas of refugee law and policy, the viability of a universal commitment to protection is challenged by divergence in state practice. These Guidelines seek to define the ways in which international refugee law should inform what the authors believe is more accurately described as the 'internal protection alternative.' It is the product of collective study of relevant norms and state practice, debated and refined at the First Colloquium on Challenges in International Refugee Law, in April 1999.

LES RECOMMANDATIONS DE MICHIGAN SUR L'ALTERNATIVE DE PROTECTION INTERNE

De nombreuses juridictions de par le monde font de plus en plus usage des notions de « fuite interne » ou de « réinstallation interne » pour refuser le statut de réfugié à certaines personnes qui risquent une persécution pour l'un des motifs conventionnels dans une partie, mais non la totalité, de leur pays d'origine. Il en résulte des pratiques étatiques dont la divergence, ici comme dans de nombreux autres domaines du droit des réfugiés, met en cause le caractère universel de l'obligation de protéger. Ces recommandations entendent préciser la mesure dans laquelle le droit international des réfugiés devrait encadrer ce que nous considérons comme étant mieux qualifié par les mots « alternative de protection interne ». Elles sont le résultat d'une étude commune sur les normes et pratiques des États, dont les résultats ont été débattus et affinés à l'occasion du premier colloque sur les défis du droit international des réfugiés organisé en avril 1999.

LAS DIRECTRICES DE MICHIGAN SOBRE LA ALTERNATIVA DE PROTECCIÓN INTERNA

En muchas jurisdicciones de todo el mundo, se recurre cada vez más a las reglas de "huida interna" o "reubicación interna" para denegar la condición de refugiado a personas en riesgo de persecución por un motivo de la Convención en parte de su país de origen, pero no en la totalidad del mismo. En este sentido, como en tantas áreas del derecho y la política de refugiados, la viabilidad de un compromiso universal de protección se ve desafiada por la divergencia en la práctica estatal. Estas directrices buscan definir las formas en que el derecho internacional de los refugiados debería informar lo que los autores creen que se describe con más precisión como la "alternativa de protección interna". Es el producto del estudio colectivo de las normas pertinentes y la práctica estatal, debatido y perfeccionado en el Primer Coloquio sobre Desafíos en el Derecho Internacional de los Refugiados, en abril de 1999.

THE ANALYTICAL FRAMEWORK

1. The essence of the refugee definition set out in Art. 1(A)(2) of the 1951 Convention relating to the Status of Refugees ('Refugee Convention') is the identification of persons who are entitled to claim protection in a contracting state against the risk of persecution in their own country. This duty of state parties to provide surrogate protection arises only in relation to persons who are either unable to benefit from the protection of their own state, or who are unwilling to accept that state's protection because of a well-founded fear of persecution.

LE CADRE ANALYTIQUE

1. L'objectif premier de la définition du réfugié telle que consacrée par l'article 1, A, §2, de la Convention relative au statut des réfugiés (« la Convention ») consiste à identifier les personnes qui ont droit à une protection au sein d'un des États parties, en raison du risque de persécution auquel elles font face dans leur pays d'origine. L'obligation des États parties d'accorder une protection se substituant à celle du pays d'origine n'existe qu'à l'égard des individus qui soit ne peuvent pas bénéficier de la protection de leur pays, soit ne veulent pas s'en réclamer en raison d'une crainte fondée de persécution.

EL MARCO ANALÍTICO

1. La esencia de la definición de refugiado establecida en el artículo 1 (A)(2) de la Convención de 1951 sobre la Condición de los Refugiados ("Convención de Refugiados") es la identificación de personas que tienen derecho a reclamar protección en un estado contratante frente al riesgo de persecución en su propio país. Este deber de los estados partes de brindar protección sustitutiva surge solo en relación con las personas que no pueden beneficiarse de la protección de su propio estado o no están dispuestas a aceptar la protección de ese estado debido a un temor fundado de persecución.

2. It therefore follows that to the extent meaningful protection against the risk of persecution is genuinely available to an asylum-seeker, Convention refugee status need not be recognized.

2. Il en résulte que si et dans la mesure où une protection réelle est effectivement accessible au demandeur d'asile dans son pays d'origine, le statut de réfugié au sens de la Convention ne doit pas lui être reconnu.

2. Por lo tanto, se deduce que, en la medida en que una protección significativa contra el riesgo de persecución esté realmente disponible para un solicitante de asilo, no es necesario reconocer la condición de refugiado de la Convención.

دليل ميشيغان الإرشادي حول استخدام الحماية الداخلية كبديل للحماية الدولية

МИЧИГАНСКИЕ РЕКОМЕНДАЦИИ ПО АЛЬТЕРНАТИВЕ ВНУТРЕННЕЙ ЗАЩИТЫ

تشهد الكثير من الأنظمة القانونية بالعالم زيادة في الاعتماد على ما يمكن تسميته بـ "الانتقال الداخلي" أو "إعادة التوطين الداخلية" كأساس لرفض منح صفة اللجوء لأشخاص يتعرضون لخطر الاضطهاد بسبب عرقهم أو دينهم أو جنسيتهم أو انتمائهم إلى فئة اجتماعية معينة أو آرائهم السياسية، وذلك في حالة ما إذا كان هؤلاء الأشخاص يتعرضون للاضطهاد في أحد أقاليم دولتهم الأصلية ولكن ليس في جميع أقاليم هذه الدولة. وقد نتج عن انتشار هذا التطبيق القانوني، ضمن العديد من الاتجاهات والممارسات الأخرى في قانون اللاجئين الدولي والسياسات التطبيقية المتعلقة به، الكثير من المشاكل والتحديات التي تواجه التزام الدول الموقعة على الاتفاقية بتحقيق حماية عالمية للاجئين. ويزيد من هذه التحديات التفاوت الكبير بين ممارسات الدول الموقعة على الاتفاقية عند تطبيق القانون الدولي للاجئين. ويهدف هذا الدليل إلى تقديم مساهمة قانونية لما نراه أفضل قراءة ممكنة لمفهوم "بديل الحماية الداخلي" وفقاً لقواعد القانون الدولي للاجئين. وقد تم تخصيص الدورة الأولى من سلسلة ورش العمل حول مشاكل تطبيق القانون الدولي للاجئين، التي نُظمت في أبريل 1999، لعمل مناقشات جماعية مستفيضة للكثير من المبادئ والممارسات التي تتبناها الدول المختلفة المتعلقة بقوانين اللاجئين. وقد أثمر هذا المجهود الجماعي كما أسلفت الإشارة عن هذا الدليل.

В юридической практике многих стран мира, такие опирающиеся на Конвенцию критерии как «бегство в границах государства» и «перемещение в границах государства», все чаще используются как основание для отказа в предоставлении статуса беженца лицам, находящимся под угрозой преследования в одном из регионов, но не на всей территории государства гражданской принадлежности указанных лиц. Здесь, как и во многих других сферах законодательства и политики, относящихся к проблемам беженцев, реализация международных обязательств по защите беженцев осложняется расхождениями в практике отдельных государств. Данные *Рекомендации* стремятся определить те направления, по которым международное законодательство о беженцах должно информировать о том, что, как полагают авторы, может быть более точно названо «альтернативой защиты внутри страны, гражданами которой являются беженцы».

Указанные *Рекомендации*, являющиеся результатом совместных исследований соответствующих норм и практики разных государств, обсуждались и уточнялись в апреле 1999 года на Первом коллоквиуме по проблемам международного законодательства о беженцах.

إطار العمل التحليلي

АНАЛИТИЧЕСКАЯ ОСНОВА

1. إن جوهر تحديد صفة اللاجئ، كما ورد بالمادة الأولى (فقرة أ، رقم 2) من الاتفاقية الدولية للاجئين الصادرة عام 1951 والخاصة بتحديد صفة اللاجئين، ينصرف على وجه الخصوص إلى كافة الأشخاص الذين يحق لهم طلب اللجوء في أحد الدول الأطراف بالاتفاقية، في حالة تعرض هؤلاء الأشخاص لخطر الاضطهاد في دولهم الأصلية. وينصرف واجب الدول الأطراف في الاتفاقية بتقديم الحماية إلى أحد الحالتين الآتيتين: إما أن يكون الأشخاص طالبو اللجوء غير قادرين على الحصول على الحماية من دولهم الأصلية أو إذا كان هؤلاء الأشخاص غير راغبين في الحصول على حماية دولهم الأصلية بسبب توافر خوف له ما يبرره من الاضطهاد.

1. Суть определения понятия «беженец», приведенного в статье 1(A)(2) Конвенции 1951 года о статусе беженцев («Конвенция о беженцах») заключается в определении категории лиц, имеющих право просить защиты от угрозы преследования в стране проживания в одном из государств-участников соглашения. Обязанность государств предоставить суррогатную защиту возникает только по отношению к лицам, которые либо не могут воспользоваться защитой государства их гражданской принадлежности, либо не желают принять эту защиту в силу вполне обоснованных опасений преследования.

---

2. وفي هذا السياق، فإنه يمكن التسليم برفض منح صفة اللجوء فقط إذا تم التأكد من أنه يمكن توفير بديل حماية داخلية معقولة لطالب اللجوء من خطر الاضطهاد توفراً حقيفياً.

2. Отсюда следует, что в случае, если необходимая защита от риска преследования действительно доступна искателю убежища, в признании статуса беженца в соответствии с Конвенцией нет необходимости.

3. Both the risk of persecution and availability of countervailing protection were traditionally assessed simply in relation to an asylum-seeker's place of origin. The implicit operating assumption was that evidence of a sufficiently serious risk in one part of the state of origin could be said to give rise to a well-founded fear of persecution in the asylum-seeker's 'country.' Contemporary practice in most developed states of asylum has, however, evolved to take account of regionalized variations of risk within countries of origin. Under the rubric of so-called 'internal flight' or 'internal relocation' rules, states increasingly decline to recognize as Convention refugees persons acknowledged to be at risk in one locality on the grounds that protection should have been, or could be, sought elsewhere inside the state of origin.

3. Traditionnellement, tant le risque de subir une persécution que l'accessibilité à une protection étaient évalués eu égard à l'endroit dont le demandeur d'asile était originaire. Il était implicitement présumé que la preuve d'un risque suffisamment sérieux dans une partie du pays d'origine suffirait à établir l'existence d'une crainte fondée de persécution au sein du « pays » du demandeur d'asile. Les pratiques contemporaines, dans la plupart des États aux systèmes d'asile les plus développés, ont toutefois évolué. Ces pratiques tiennent compte des variations régionales dans l'existence du risque au sein du pays d'origine. Sous l'appellation générale de « fuite interne » ou de « réinstallation interne », les États ont de plus en plus souvent refusé de reconnaître le statut de réfugié aux personnes risquant une persécution dans une partie de leur pays d'origine, au motif que la protection aurait dû, ou pourrait, être recherchée ailleurs au sein de leur pays d'origine.

3. Tanto el riesgo de persecución como la disponibilidad de protección compensatoria tradicionalmente se evaluaban simplemente en relación con el lugar de origen de un solicitante de asilo. La suposición implícita vigente era que la evidencia de un riesgo suficientemente grave en una parte del país de origen podía dar lugar a un temor fundado de persecución en el "país" del solicitante de asilo. Sin embargo, la práctica contemporánea en la mayoría de los estados de asilo desarrollados ha evolucionado para tener en cuenta las variaciones de riesgo por región en el interior de los países de origen. Bajo la rúbrica de las llamadas reglas de "huida interna" o "reubicación interna", los estados se niegan cada vez más a reconocer como refugiados de la Convención a personas que se sepa que se encuentran en riesgo en una determinada localidad, alegando que se podría haber brindado, o se podría brindar, protección en otra región dentro del país de origen.

4. In some circumstances, meaningful protection against the risk of persecution can be provided inside the boundaries of an asylum-seeker's state of origin. Where a careful inquiry determines that a particular asylum-seeker has an 'internal protection alternative,' it is lawful to deny recognition of Convention refugee status.

4. Dans certaines circonstances, une protection réelle contre le risque d'être persécuté peut exister au sein du territoire du pays d'origine d'un demandeur d'asile. Lorsqu'il résulte d'un examen attentif d'une demande d'asile que le demandeur bénéficie d'une « alternative de protection interne », le statut de réfugié conventionnel peut lui être refusé sans violer la Convention.

4. En algunas circunstancias, se puede brindar una protección significativa contra el riesgo de persecución dentro de los límites del estado de origen de un solicitante de asilo. Si mediante una investigación profunda se determina que un determinado solicitante de asilo dispone de una "alternativa de protección interna", es lícito denegar el reconocimiento de la condición de refugiado en virtud de la Convención.

5. A lawful inquiry into the existence of an 'internal protection alternative' is not, however, simply an examination of whether an asylum-seeker might have avoided departure from her or his country of origin ('internal flight'). Nor is it only an assessment of whether the risk of persecution can presently be avoided somewhere inside the asylum-seeker's country of origin ('internal relocation'). Instead, 'internal protection alternative' analysis should be directed to the identification of asylum-seekers who do not require international protection against the risk of persecution in their own country because they can presently access meaningful protection in a part of their own country. So conceived, internal protection analysis can be carried out in full conformity with the requirements of the Refugee Convention.

5. Examiner s'il existe une « alternative de protection interne » conforme à la Convention n'implique pas uniquement de vérifier si le demandeur d'asile aurait pu éviter de quitter son pays d'origine (« fuite interne »). De même, il ne s'agit pas uniquement de vérifier si le risque de persécution peut actuellement être évité dans une autre partie du pays d'origine (« relocalisation interne »). Déterminer s'il existe une « alternative de protection interne » suppose plutôt d'identifier les demandeurs d'asile qui n'ont pas besoin d'une protection internationale contre le risque de persécution existant dans leur pays d'origine, parce qu'ils peuvent actuellement bénéficier d'une protection effective dans une partie de leur pays d'origine. Ainsi même, l'examen de l'existence d'une alternative de protection interne est pleinement conforme aux exigences de la Convention.

5. Sin embargo, una investigación legal sobre la existencia de una "alternativa de protección interna" no es simplemente un examen de si un solicitante de asilo podría haber evitado abandonar su país de origen ("huida interna"). Tampoco es solo una evaluación de si en la actualidad el riesgo de persecución puede evitarse en algún lugar del interior del país de origen del solicitante de asilo ("reubicación interna"). En cambio, el análisis de la "alternativa de protección interna" debe apuntar a identificar solicitantes de asilo que no requieran protección internacional frente al riesgo de persecución en su propio país en ese momento por tener la posibilidad de recibir un nivel de protección significativo en una parte de su propio país. De esta manera, el análisis de protección interna puede llevarse a cabo de plena conformidad con los requisitos de la Convención de Refugiados.

3. وقد جرت العادة سابقاً في الدول الموقعة على الاتفاقية على البحث في السياق الواقعي لدولة طالب اللجوء الأصلية عند تقييم هذه الدول لمدى توافر خطر الاضطهاد وأيضاً مدى توافر بديل الحماية الداخلي الفعال. وقد كان هذا المنطق يقوم على افتراض أساسي هو إن مجرد توافر دليل على وجود خطر جسيم بوقوع الاضطهاد في أحد أقاليم دولة الطالب الأصلية يكفي لإثبات أن الخوف المعقول الموجود لدى الطالب له ما يبرره. لكن مؤخراً بدأت ممارسات الكثير من الدول في الاختلاف. وبدلاً من الاكتفاء بوجود خطر الاضطهاد ضد طالب اللجوء في إقليم واحد بدولته الأصلية، بدأت الدول المتقدمة في منح الحماية للاجئين وقبول الملاذ في عمل دراسات أعمق تبحث فيها مدى توافر الخطر وتباينه في الأقاليم المختلفة للدولة الأصلية لطالب اللجوء قبل منحه صفة اللجوء. وبدأت الكثير من هذه الدول في رفض منح صفة اللجوء لأشخاص كثيرين يتعرضون للاضطهاد في أحد أقاليم دولهم الأصلية إذا ثبت إن هؤلاء الأشخاص يمكنهم الحصول على حماية في أقاليم أخرى لدولهم الأصلية. ولجأت هذه الدول الموقعة على الاتفاقية في أخذ هذا الاتجاه تحت مسمى "الانتقال الداخلي" أو "إعادة التوطين الداخلية."

3. Риск преследования, равно как и наличие компенсирующей защиты от него, обычно оценивались по отношению к стране, гражданами или жителями которой являются искатели убежища. Исходным рабочим предположением было то, что доказательства вполне обоснованного риска преследований в одной из частей страны могли рассматриваться как причина для вполне обоснованных опасений преследований во всей «стране», гражданином или жителем которой является искатель убежища. Однако в настоящее время практика предоставления убежища в большинстве развитых стран изменилась: стали приниматься во внимание региональные особенности риска преследований в странах, гражданами или жителями которых являются вышеупомянутые лица. Используя критерии «бегства в границах государства» или «перемещения в границах государства», развитые страны все чаще отказывают в предоставлении статуса беженца согласно Конвенции лицам, в отношении которых было признано, что им угрожает опасность в одном из регионов, на основании того, что эти лица могли бы или должны были бы искать защиты в других регионах страны.

4. بالطبع فإن هناك بعض الظروف التي يمكن أن تشهد توفير حماية معقولة لطالب اللجوء – الذي يتعرض للاضطهاد – داخل حدود دولته الأصلية. ولذلك، يعتبر رفض منح صفة اللاجئ، لشخص ما يمارسة قانونية وشرعية، طالما سبق قرار الرفض تحقيقاً وبحثاً متأنياً نتج عنه التأكد من أن طالب اللجوء يمكنه الحصول على الحماية الداخلية كبديل.

4. При некоторых обстоятельствах, необходимая защита от угрозы преследования может быть предоставлена в границах государства, гражданами или жителями которого являются искатели убежища. В случае, когда тщательное расследование показывает, что у лиц, претендующих на получение убежища, имеется возможность получить «альтернативную защиту в границах государства, гражданами или жителями которого они являются», отказ в признании статуса беженца в соответствии с Конвенцией считается правомочным.

5. ولكي يكون التحقيق حول مدى توافر الحماية الداخلية كافياً بطريقة قانونية لا يجب أن يقتصر هذا التحقيق على مجرد عمل بحث بسيط حول إمكانية تجنب طالب اللجوء مغادرة دولته الأصلية من الأصل، أو البحث في مدى استطاعة طالب اللجوء تجنب الاضطهاد إذا انتقل إلى إقليم آخر من أقاليم دولته الأصلية. لكن البحث القانوني الكافي حول مدى توافر الحماية الداخلية يجب أن يتركز بالأساس على البحث في حالات طالبي اللجوء الذين لا يتطلبون حماية دولية من خطر تعرضهم للاضطهاد لأنهم يستطيعون الحصول على حماية معقولة داخلية في أحد أقاليم دولهم الأصلية. وبهذا المنطق، فإن التحقيق في مدى توافر الحماية الداخلية يكون قد تم بالتماهي مع متطلبات وغايات الاتفاقية الدولية للاجئين.

5. Юридическое исследование наличия «альтернативной защиты внутри страны» является, однако, не просто проверкой возможности искателей убежища избежать выезда из страны. Это расследование не является и только оценкой возможности избежать риска преследования в настоящий момент где-либо на территории государства, гражданами или жителями которого являются искатели убежища. Напротив, анализ «альтернативной защиты внутри страны» должен быть направлен на идентификацию искателей убежища, не нуждающихся в предоставлении международной защиты от преследований в их родной стране, поскольку в настоящее время они могут получить достаточную защиту в каком-либо из регионов государства, гражданами или жителями которого они являются. При такой трактовке, анализ наличия защиты в границах государства может быть проведен в полном соответствии с требованиями Конвенции о статусе беженцев.

6. We set out below a summary of our understanding of the circumstances under which refugee protection may lawfully be denied by a putative asylum state on the grounds that an asylum-seeker is able to avail himself or herself of an 'internal protection alternative.' Our analysis is based on the requirements of the Refugee Convention, and is informed primarily by the jurisprudence of leading developed states of asylum. No attempt is made here to address the additional limitations on removal of asylum-seekers from a state's territory that may follow from other international legal obligations, or from a given state's domestic laws. In particular, state parties to the Organization of African Unity's *Convention governing the specific aspects of refugee problems in Africa* have obligated themselves to protect not only Convention refugees, but also persons at risk due to '. . . external aggression, occupation, foreign domination or events seriously disturbing public order *in either part or the whole* of [the] country of origin or nationality . . . (emphasis added)."

6. Nous résumons ci-après les circonstances, telles que nous les entendons, dans lesquelles le statut de réfugié peut être refusé par un État auprès duquel l'asile est sollicité, en conformité avec la Convention, au motif que le demandeur d'asile pourrait bénéficier d'une alternative de protection interne. Notre analyse est fondée sur les exigences de la Convention et repose essentiellement sur la jurisprudence des principaux pays d'asile parmi les pays développés. L'objectif n'est pas ici d'examiner d'autres obstacles, à l'expulsion des demandeurs d'asile, qui pourraient résulter d'obligations de droit international, ou de législations nationales spécifiques. En particulier les États parties à la Convention de l'Organisation de l'unité africaine (OUA, devenue Union africaine, UA, en 2002) régissant les aspects propres aux problèmes des réfugiés en Afrique sont tenus non seulement de protéger les réfugiés au sens de la Convention, mais également les personnes obligées de quitter leur résidence habituelle « . . . du fait d'une agression, d'une occupation extérieure, d'une domination étrangère ou d'événements troublant gravement l'ordre public *dans une partie ou dans la totalité* de son pays d'origine ou du pays dont elle a la nationalité . . . (nous soulignons) ».

6. A continuación presentamos un resumen de nuestra comprensión de las circunstancias bajo las cuales un supuesto estado proveedor de asilo puede negarse legalmente a proteger a refugiados bajo el argumento de que un solicitante de asilo puede valerse de una "alternativa de protección interna". Nuestro análisis se basa en los requisitos de la Convención de Refugiados y se basa principalmente en la jurisprudencia de asilo de los principales estados desarrollados. Aquí no se pretende abordar las limitaciones adicionales para expulsar a solicitantes de asilo del territorio de un estado que puedan derivarse de otras obligaciones legales internacionales, o de las leyes nacionales de un determinado estado. En particular, los estados partes de la *Convención que regula los aspectos específicos de los problemas de los refugiados en África* de la Organización para la Unidad Africana se han comprometido a proteger no solo a los refugiados de la Convención, sino también a las personas en riesgo debido a "(. . .) agresión externa, ocupación, dominación extranjera o eventos que perturben seriamente el orden público *en cualquier parte o en todo* [el] país de origen o nacionalidad (. . .) (énfasis añadido)".

7. More generally, state parties are under no duty to decline recognition of refugee status to asylum-seekers who are able to avail themselves of an 'internal protection alternative.' Because refugee status is evaluated in relation to conditions in the asylum-seeker's *country* of nationality or former habitual residence, and because no express provision is made for the exclusion from Convention refugee status of persons able to avail themselves of meaningful internal protection, state parties remain entitled to recognize the refugee status of persons who fear persecution in only one part of their country of origin.

7. De manière générale, les États parties à la Convention n'ont pas l'obligation de refuser la reconnaissance du statut de réfugié aux demandeurs d'asile qui pourraient bénéficier d'une « alternative de protection interne ». Étant donné que le statut de réfugié est évalué en fonction de la situation dans *le pays* de nationalité ou de résidence habituelle du demandeur d'asile, et qu'aucune disposition expresse de la Convention ne prévoit l'exclusion du statut de réfugié conventionnel de ceux qui peuvent bénéficier d'une protection interne effective, les États parties à la Convention conservent leur droit de reconnaître le statut de réfugié aux demandeurs d'asile qui ne craignent une persécution que dans une partie de leur pays d'origine.

7. En términos más generales, los estados partes no tienen la obligación de denegar el reconocimiento de la condición de refugiado a los solicitantes de asilo que puedan recurrir a una "alternativa de protección interna". Debido a que la condición de refugiado se evalúa en relación con las condiciones en el *país* de nacionalidad o antigua residencia habitual del solicitante de asilo, y debido a que no se prevé expresamente excluir de la condición de refugiado de la Convención a personas que puedan beneficiarse de un nivel de protección interna significativo, los estados partes siguen teniendo derecho a reconocer la condición de refugiado de personas que teman ser perseguidos en una sola parte de su país de origen.

6. نقدم في السطور التالية ملخصاً لفهمنا الجماعي للظروف المشتركة حول الظروف التي يعتبر فيها رفض دولة ما لمنح صفة اللجوء لأحد الأشخاص بمثابة رفض قانوني، وذلك إذا كان هذا الرفض يستند على حقيقة إن طالب أو طالبة اللجوء يستطيع تأمين الحماية الداخلية كبديل لنفسه أو لنفسها. ونعتمد في تحليلنا هذا على ما نعتقد أنه فهم معقول ومنصف لمتطلبات الاتفاقية الدولية لشؤون اللاجئين، ويعتمد هذا التحليل على دراسة متأنية للعديد من الأنظمة القانونية لكثير من الدول الرائدة في منح الحماية والملاذ للاجئين. وتجدر الإشارة هنا إلى أننا لم نتعرض في هذا التحليل إلى القيود الواردة في الدول الموقعة على الاتفاقية وخاصة تلك المتعلقة بحالات نقل بعض الأشخاص من طالبي اللجوء من أقاليم دول معينة لأسباب لا تتعلق بتطبيق الاتفاقية الدولية لشؤون اللاجئين، ولكن بناءً على التزامات دولية قانونية أخرى على هذه الدول أو بناءً على التزامات نابعة من القوانين الوطنية. وعلى وجه الخصوص يذكر إن الدول الأعضاء بمنظمة الوحدة الأفريقية كانوا قد أصدروا اتفاقية خاصة لتحكم الجوانب المختلفة لمشاكل اللاجئين في أفريقيا. ووفق هذه الاتفاقية قد التزم الدول الأعضاء ليس فقط بحماية الأشخاص طالبي اللجوء وفقاً للتعريف والمتطلبات الواردة في الاتفاقية الدولية للاجئين عام 1951، لكنهم وسعوا من الحماية التي يمكن أن يقدموها وقد أقروا أنهم يشملون بالحماية كل الأشخاص الذين يتعرضون لأخطار بسبب ". . . العدوان الخارجي أو احتلال أو سيطرة أجنبية أو بسبب أي أحداث جسيمة تهدد النظام العام سواء وقع ذلك في جزء من أو في كافة أقاليم بلد المنشأ أو بلد الجنسية. . . ." التي ينتمي إليها طالب اللجوء (تمت إضافة التشديد السابق).

7. وبصفة عامة يمكن اعتبار إن الدول الموقعة على الاتفاقية ليست ملتزمة وليس عليها أي واجب قانوني برفض منح صفة اللجوء لطالبي اللجوء الذين يستطيعون تأمين الحماية الداخلية كبديل لأنفسهم. وعلى ذلك نعتقد إن الدول الأطراف في الاتفاقية الدولية لشؤون اللاجئين يظلوا ملتزمين بمنح صفة اللجوء لكل هؤلاء الأشخاص الذين يتعرضون للاضطهاد في إقليم واحد من أقاليم دولة المنشأ أو الجنسية. نقول ذلك لأننا نرى إن تقدير منح صفة اللجوء هو عملية شاملة ينبغي أن يراعى فيها بحث الظروف الموضوعية لدولة المنشأ لطالبي اللجوء أو مكان إقامتهم، كما انه يذكر إن الاتفاقية الدولية لشؤون اللاجئين لم يرد بها إلزام صريح يقرر بأنه يجب رفض منح صفة اللجوء لطالبي اللجوء الذين يمكنهم تأمين حماية داخلية لأنفسهم.

6. Ниже будет представлено краткое изложение нашего понимания обстоятельств, при которых может быть отказано в предоставлении статуса беженца государством убежища на основании того, что искатели убежища могут получить «альтернативную защиту внутри страны». Наш анализ основан на требованиях Конвенции о беженцах и опирается, главным образом, на судебную практику ведущих развитых стран убежища. Здесь не делается попытки коснуться дополнительных ограничений в отношении выдворения лиц, ищущих убежища, с территории государства-предоставителя убежища, которые могут вытекать из других международных правовых обязательств или из внутреннего законодательства данного государства. В частности, государства-участники Конвенции Организации африканского единства, определяющей особые аспекты проблем беженцев в Африке, обязались защищать не только конвенционных беженцев, но также и лиц, которым угрожает опасность из-за «внешней агрессии, оккупации, иностранного господства или событий, серьезно нарушающих общественный порядок *в какой-либо части или во всей* стране происхождения или гражданства . . . (курсив наш)».

7. В более широком смысле, государства-участники отнюдь не обязаны отказывать в признании статуса беженца лицам, которые могут воспользоваться «альтернативой внутренней защиты». Поскольку статус беженца рассматривается с учетом условий в стране гражданства или постоянного проживания в прошлом лица, ищущего убежища, и поскольку не существует выраженных условий об исключении из-под действия Конвенции лиц, которые могут воспользоваться существенной внутренней защитой, государства-участники Конвенции вправе признавать статус беженца в отношении и тех лиц, которые опасаются преследований только в одной части страны происхождения.

GENERAL NATURE AND REQUIREMENTS OF 'INTERNAL PROTECTION ALTERNATIVE' ANALYSIS

8. There is no justification in international law to refuse recognition of refugee status on the basis of a purely retrospective assessment of conditions at the time of an asylum-seeker's departure from the home state. The duty of protection under the Refugee Convention is explicitly premised on a prospective evaluation of risk. That is, an individual is a Convention refugee only if she or he would presently be at risk of persecution in the state of origin, whatever the circumstances at the time of departure from the home state. Internal protection analysis informs this inquiry only if directed to the identification of a present possibility of meaningful protection within the boundaries of the home state.

EXIGENCES GÉNÉRALES RELATIVES À L'ANALYSE AFIN DE DÉTERMINER S'IL EXISTE UNE « ALTERNATIVE DE PROTECTION INTERNE »

8. Rien ne justifie, en droit international, que le statut de réfugié soit refusé sur le fondement d'une analyse purement rétroactive des conditions qui existaient au moment où le demandeur a quitté son pays d'origine. L'obligation d'octroyer une protection telle que consacrée par la Convention est explicitement fondée sur une évaluation prospective du risque. Cela signifie qu'il suffit qu'un individu risque une persécution dans son pays d'origine pour qu'il soit réfugié au sens de la Convention, quelles que soient les conditions qui prévalaient lors de son départ. Dans ce cadre, l'analyse afin de déterminer s'il existe une « alternative de protection interne » n'est pertinente que si elle vise à identifier les possibilités actuelles de bénéficier d'une protection effective au sein du pays d'origine.

NATURALEZA GENERAL Y REQUISITOS DEL ANÁLISIS DE LA "ALTERNATIVA DE PROTECCIÓN INTERNA"

8. No existe ninguna justificación en el derecho internacional para denegar el reconocimiento de la condición de refugiado sobre la base de una evaluación puramente retrospectiva de las condiciones en el momento en que un solicitante de asilo parte de su país de origen. El deber de protección bajo la Convención de Refugiados se basa explícitamente en una evaluación prospectiva del riesgo. Es decir, la Convención reconoce a un individuo como refugiado solo si actualmente estaría en riesgo de ser perseguido en su país de origen, independientemente de cuáles sean las circunstancias en el momento de la partida del país de origen. El análisis de protección interna informa esta investigación solo si apunta a identificar una posibilidad actual de brindar un nivel de protección significativo en el interior del país de origen.

9. Because this prospective analysis of internal protection occurs at a point in time when the asylum-seeker has already left his or her home state, a present possibility of meaningful protection inside the home state exists only if the asylum-seeker can be returned to the internal region adjudged to satisfy the 'internal protection alternative' criteria. A refugee claim should not be denied on internal protection grounds unless the putative asylum state is in fact able safely and practically to return the asylum-seeker to the site of internal protection.

9. Étant donné que l'analyse visant à déterminer s'il existe une alternative de protection interne se réalise lorsque le demandeur d'asile a déjà quitté son pays d'origine, la possibilité de bénéficier d'une protection effective dans le pays d'origine n'existe que si le demandeur d'asile peut être renvoyé vers la région de son pays d'origine qui lui offre une « alternative de protection interne ». Une demande d'asile ne devrait être refusée au motif qu'il existe une alternative de protection interne que si l'État qui examine la demande est effectivement en mesure de renvoyer le demandeur en toute sécurité vers la région de son pays d'origine où il bénéficie d'une protection interne.

9. Debido a que este análisis prospectivo de la protección interna ocurre en un momento en que el solicitante de asilo ya ha dejado su país de origen, en la actualidad existe una posibilidad de protección significativa dentro del estado de origen solo si el solicitante de asilo puede ser enviado a la región interna que se ha declarado que cumple con los criterios de "alternativa de protección interna". No se debe denegar una solicitud de refugio por motivos de protección interna a menos que el supuesto estado proveedor de asilo de hecho pueda, de manera segura y práctica, enviar al solicitante de asilo al sitio capaz de brindar protección interna.

ОБЩИЙ АНАЛИЗ И АНАЛИЗ ТРЕБОВАНИЙ, ПРЕДЪЯВЛЯЕМЫХ К «АЛЬТЕРНАТИВЕ ВНУТРЕННЕЙ ЗАЩИТЫ»

8. لا يوجد أي مسوغ أو مبرر في القانون الدولي لرفض منح صفة اللجوء لأحد الأشخاص على أساس عمل تقييم بصفة رجعية للأوضاع والظروف التي أحاطت بوقت مغادرة هذا الشخص لبلاده. فواجب تقديم الحماية طبقاً للاتفاقية الدولية يعتمد بصفة صريحة على تقييم الأوضاع والمخاطر التي تهدد طالب اللجوء في المستقبل.* وعلى هذا الأساس يجب اعتبار شخص ما لاجئاً وفقاً للاتفاقية الدولية إذا كان هذا الشخص يتعرض لخطر حال يوجد في بلد المنشأ، وذلك بغض النظر عن الظروف التي أحاطت بطالب اللجوء وقت مغادرته لهذه الدولة. ومن هذا المنطلق، يعتبر تطبيق إطار "الحماية الداخلية"** متماشياً مع غايات ومنطق الاتفاقية الدولية وفقاً للإطار السابق، أي فقط إذا تم هذا التحليل بالتركيز على مدى توافر الحماية الداخلية كبديل مقبول داخل الدولة الوطنية لطالب اللجوء في وقت إجراء هذا التحليل.

* أي إن التقييم يجب أن يكون بصفة استشرافية وليس بصفة رجعية (المترجم للعربية).

** طوال السطور التالية ينصرف استخدام تطبيق تحليل " البديل الحمائي الداخلي" إلى قيام الدولة التي نظر طلب اللجوء بالتحقيق في مدى توافر الحماية الداخلية كبديل مقبول في بلد طالب اللجوء (المترجم للغة العربية).

8. В международном законодательстве нет оправдания для отказа в признании статуса беженца на основании исключительно ретроспективной оценки ситуации на момент отъезда лица, ищущего убежища, из страны, гражданином или постоянным жителем которой он является [далее - страна происхождения]. Обязанность предоставления защиты в соответствии с Конвенцией о беженцах основывается исключительно на оценке потенциального риска в будущем. Это значит, что вышеназванное лицо является конвенционным беженцем только в том случае, если ему в настоящее время угрожает опасность преследования в стране происхождения, какими бы ни были обстоятельства на момент отъезда из нее. При изучении фактов, анализ состояния внутренней защиты принимается во внимание только в том случае, когда он направлен на выявление имеющейся в настоящее время возможности предоставления существенной защиты в пределах страны происхождения.

9. والمنطق السديد يقول انه لا توجد أي جدوى من عمل تحليل " الحماية الداخلية " إذا كانت عودة طالب اللجوء سالماً إلى بلاده ممكنة، وإذا لم يكن من الممكن فعلاً توافر هذا البديل في وقت إجراء التحقيق الخاص به، أخذاً في الاعتبار إن إجراء هذا التحقيق يتم بالفعل في لحظة يكون قد غادر فيها طالب اللجوء بلاده بالفعل، كما أن هذا التحليل كما أسلفت الإشارة يجب أن يتسم بالطبيعة الاستشرافية.

9. Поскольку анализ внутренней защиты происходит в тот момент, когда лицо, ищущее убежища, уже покинуло свою страну, существующая в настоящее время возможность существенной защиты в указанной стране имеется только в том случае, если лицо, ищущее убежища, может быть возвращено во внутренний регион страны, удовлетворяющий критериям «альтернативы внутренней защиты». Ходатайство об убежище не должно отклоняться на основаниях внутренней защиты, кроме как в том случае, когда государство-предоставитель убежища в действительности и фактически может безопасно вернуть лицо, ищущее убежища, к месту предоставления внутренней защиты.

10. Legally relevant internal protection should ordinarily be provided by the national government of the state of origin, whether directly or by lawful delegation to a regional or local government. In keeping with the basic commitment of the Refugee Convention to respond to the fundamental breakdown of state protection by establishing surrogate state protection through an interstate treaty, return on internal protection grounds to a region controlled by a non-state entity should be contemplated only where there is compelling evidence of that entity's ability to deliver durable protection, as described below at paras. 15-22.

10. La protection interne qui peut être prise en considération sans violer la Convention devrait en principe émaner des autorités du pays d'origine, qu'elles agissent directement ou indirectement par le biais d'une autorité régionale ou locale subordonnée. Conformément aux exigences fondamentales de la Convention, qui entend pallier les graves défaillances d'un État en instaurant une protection subsidiaire, émanant d'autres États conformément à un traité conclu entre États, le retour d'un demandeur d'asile au motif qu'il existe une alternative de protection interne au sein d'une région contrôlée par une entité non étatique ne devrait être envisagé que s'il existe des preuves convaincantes de la capacité de cette entité à offrir une protection durable, telle que définie ci-après dans les paragraphes 15 à 22.

10. La protección interna legalmente relevante normalmente debería ser provista por el gobierno nacional del país de origen, ya sea en forma directa o mediante la delegación legal a un gobierno regional o local. De acuerdo con el compromiso básico de la Convención de Refugiados de responder al colapso fundamental de la protección estatal mediante el establecimiento de protección estatal sustituta a través de un tratado interestatal, el regreso por motivos de protección interna a una región controlada por una entidad no estatal debería contemplarse solo cuando existan pruebas convincentes de la capacidad de esa entidad de brindar protección duradera, como se describe más adelante en los párrafos 15 a 22.

---

11. The evaluation of internal protection is inherent in the Convention's requirement that a refugee not only have a well-founded fear of being persecuted, but also be 'unable or, owing to such fear, [be] unwilling to avail himself of the protection of [her or his] country.'

11. L'évaluation de l'existence d'une alternative de protection interne est inhérente à l'exigence conventionnelle selon laquelle un réfugié ne doit pas seulement éprouver une crainte fondée d'être persécuté, mais doit en outre « ne (. . .) (pas pouvoir) ou, du fait de cette crainte, ne (. . .) (pas vouloir) se réclamer de la protection de ce pays ».

11. La evaluación de la protección interna es inherente a la exigencia de la Convención de que un refugiado no solo tenga un temor fundado de ser perseguido, sino que también sea "incapaz o, debido a ese temor, no (esté) dispuesto a acogerse a la protección de (su) país".

---

12. The first question to be considered is therefore whether the asylum-seeker faces a well-founded fear of persecution for a Convention reason in at least some part of his or her country of origin. This primary inquiry should be completed before consideration is given to the availability of an 'internal protection alternative.' The reality of internal protection can only be adequately measured on the basis of an understanding of the precise risk faced by an asylum-seeker.

12. La première question consiste donc à déterminer si le demandeur d'asile éprouve une crainte fondée de subir une persécution pour l'un des motifs conventionnels, dans au moins une partie de son pays d'origine. Cette question fondamentale devrait trouver une réponse avant qu'une « alternative de protection interne » ne soit envisagée. La réalité de la possibilité de bénéficier d'une protection interne ne peut être évaluée adéquatement que si le risque précis auquel un demandeur d'asile est confronté a fait l'objet d'une évaluation préalable.

12. Por lo tanto, la primera pregunta que se debe plantear es si el solicitante de asilo presenta un temor fundado de persecución por un motivo reconocido por la Convención en al menos una parte de su país de origen. Esta averiguación primaria debe completarse antes de considerar la disponibilidad de una "alternativa de protección interna". La realidad de la protección interna solo puede medirse adecuadamente sobre la base de una comprensión del riesgo preciso que enfrenta un solicitante de asilo.

10. يعتبر الحماية الداخلية – ذو الصلة – قانونياً في حالة أن يتم تنفيذه عن طريق إجراءات عادية بواسطة الحكومة الوطنية لدولة المنشأ، أو بواسطة ممثلية حكومية إقليمية أو محلية ترتبط بالحكومة المركزية بطريقة قانونية. وفي ضوء الالتزام الواقع على جميع الدول الأطراف بالاتفاقية الدولية والمترتب على حالات انهيار الحماية الأساسية التي تقدمها الدول للاجئين، يمكن إعادة أي شخص إلى بلاده الأصلية على أساس توافر الحماية الداخلية كبديل فقط إذا كانت هناك أدلة قوية تؤكد إن دولة هذا الشخص قادرة على توفير الحماية المستمرة له، وذلك كما سيتم الشرح بالتفصيل في الفقرات من 15 إلى 22.

10. Юридически адекватная внутренняя защита обычно должна предоставляться центральным правительством страны происхождения, как напрямую, так и путем законного поручения этой функции региональным или местным властям. В соответствии с основным обязательством Конвенции о беженцах, заключающемся в необходимости реагировать на фундаментальный развал государственной защиты путем предоставления суррогатной государственной защиты в рамках межгосударственного соглашения, возвращение на основаниях внутренней защиты в регион, контролируемый негосударственным образованием, должно рассматриваться как возможность только при наличии неоспоримых доказательств способности этого образования предоставить надежную и долговременную защиту, о чем говорится ниже в пунктах 15-22.

---

11. ينبغي أن يتم تقييم مدى توافر الحماية الداخلية كبديل بالتوافق مع المتطلبات التي حددتها الاتفاقية والخاصة بمنح صفة اللجوء، وذلك ليس فقط لكل شخص لديه خوفاً معقولاً من التعرض للاضطهاد، ولكن أيضاً " لا يستطيع، أو لا يريد بسبب استمرار الخوف من الاضطهاد، أن يستظل بحماية بلد جنسيته."

11. Оценка внутренней защиты органически вытекает из требования Конвенции о том, что беженец не только должен иметь вполне обоснованные опасения стать жертвой преследования, но и «не может или не желает вследствие таких опасений пользоваться защитой [своей] страны».

---

12. ولذلك فأن أهم الأسئلة التي يجب أن تطرح قبل غيرها أثناء إجراء التحقيق حول مدى توافر " الحماية الداخلية " هو السؤال التالي: هل لدى طالب اللجوء خوفاً مبرراً من التعرض للاضطهاد لأحد الأسباب التي حددتها الاتفاقية الدولية، في إقليم واحد على الأقل من أقاليم دولة المنشأ أم لا؟ ويجب الوصول إلى إجابة لهذا السؤال الأول قبل البحث في السؤال الثاني حول مدى توافر " الحماية الداخلية." والمنطق يُحتم إثارة السؤال الأول قبل السؤال الثاني، والسبب في ذلك أنه لا يمكن الجزم بتوافر درجة مقبولة يمكن تقديرها أو قياسها لواقع الحماية الداخلية، بدون أن يفهم المُحقق بدقة أولاً طبيعة الخطر الذي يواجه طالب اللجوء.

12. Поэтому первый вопрос, который должен быть рассмотрен, заключается в следующем: имеет ли лицо, ищущее убежища, вполне обоснованные опасения стать жертвой преследования по одному из конвенционных признаков, по крайней мере, в одном из регионов страны происхождения. Ответ на этот вопрос должен быть дан до начала изучения возможности «альтернативы внутренней защиты». Реальность внутренней защиты может быть адекватно оценена только на основании понимания конкретной опасности, угрожающей лицу, ищущему убежища.

13. Assessed against the backdrop of an ascertained risk of persecution for a Convention reason in at least one part of the country, the second question is whether the asylum-seeker has access to meaningful internal protection against the risk of persecution. This inquiry may, in turn, be broken down into three parts:

(a) Does the proposed site of internal protection afford the asylum-seeker a meaningful 'antidote' to the identified risk of persecution?

(b) Is the proposed site of internal protection free from other risks which either amount to, or are tantamount to, a risk of persecution?

(c) Do local conditions in the proposed site of internal protection at least meet the Refugee Convention's minimalist conceptualization of 'protection'?

13. La seconde question, qui doit être évaluée après l'identification du risque de persécution pour un motif conventionnel dans au moins une partie du pays d'origine, consiste à déterminer si le demandeur d'asile a accès à une protection interne effective contre le risque de persécution. Cette analyse peut elle-même se dérouler en trois parties:

(a) Est-ce que le lieu, envisagé comme alternative de protection interne, garantit au demandeur d'asile un « antidote » adéquat face au risque de persécution qui a été identifié?

(b) Est-ce que le lieu, envisagé comme alternative de protection interne, n'implique pas que le demandeur soit soumis à d'autres risques qui constituent ou sont équivalents à des persécutions?

(c) Est-ce que les conditions de vie dans le lieu, envisagé comme alternative de protection interne, rencontrent au moins la « protection » minimale établie par la Convention de Genève?

13. Evaluado el contexto de un riesgo comprobado de persecución por un motivo contemplado en la Convención en al menos una parte del país, la segunda pregunta es si el solicitante de asilo tiene acceso a una protección interna significativa frente al riesgo de persecución. Esta investigación, a su vez, se puede dividir en tres partes:

(a) ¿El sitio de protección interna propuesto sirve como un "antídoto" significativo para el riesgo identificado de persecución al solicitante de asilo?

(b) ¿El sitio de protección interna propuesto está libre de otros riesgos que representen un riesgo de persecución o equivalgan a uno?

(c) Las condiciones locales en el sitio de protección interna propuesto, ¿cumplen al menos con la conceptualización minimalista de "protección" de la Convención de Refugiados?

14. Because this inquiry into the existence of an 'internal protection alternative' is predicated on the existence of a well-founded fear of persecution for a Convention reason in at least one region of the asylum-seeker's state of origin, and hence on a presumptive entitlement to Convention refugee status, the burden of proof to establish the existence of countervailing internal protection as described in para. 13 should in all cases be on the government of the putative asylum state.

14. Étant donné que l'évaluation de l'existence d'une alternative de protection interne suppose que le demandeur d'asile éprouve une crainte fondée de subir la persécution pour un motif conventionnel dans au moins une région de son pays d'origine et, donc, qu'il pourrait bénéficier du statut de réfugié conventionnel, la charge de la preuve de l'existence d'une alternative de protection interne, telle que décrite au paragraphe 13, devrait dans tous les cas reposer sur les autorités qui examinent la demande d'asile.

14. Debido a que esta investigación sobre la existencia de una "alternativa de protección interna" se basa en la existencia de un temor fundado de persecución por un motivo contemplado en la Convención en al menos una región del estado de origen del solicitante de asilo, y por lo tanto, en un derecho presunto a la condición de refugiado en virtud de la Convención, la carga de la prueba para determinar la existencia de protección interna compensatoria como se describe en el párrafo 13 en todos los casos debe recaer en el gobierno del supuesto estado de asilo.

THE FIRST REQUIREMENT: AN 'ANTIDOTE' TO THE PRIMARY RISK OF PERSECUTION

15. First, the 'internal protection alternative' must be a place in which the asylum-seeker no longer faces the well-founded fear of persecution for a Convention reason which gave rise to her or his presumptive need for protection against the risk in one region of the country of origin. It is not enough simply to find that the original agent or author of persecution has not yet established a presence in the proposed site of internal protection. There must be reason to believe that the reach of the agent or author of persecution is likely to remain localized outside the designated place of internal protection.

LA PREMIÈRE EXIGENCE: L'« ANTIDOTE » FACE AU RISQUE ORIGINEL DE PERSÉCUTION

15. Premièrement, l'« alternative de protection interne » suppose que le demandeur d'asile puisse se rendre en un lieu où il n'aura pas une crainte fondée de subir la persécution pour l'un des motifs conventionnels, qui a donné lieu à un besoin de protection par rapport à sa région dans son pays d'origine, n'existe pas. Il n'est pas suffisant d'établir que l'agent ou l'auteur de la persécution originelle ne se trouve pas encore dans le lieu suggéré au titre d'alternative de protection interne. Il faut également des motifs raisonnables de penser que la zone d'influence de l'agent ou de l'auteur de la persécution ne s'étendra probablement pas au lieu désigné comme alternative de protection interne.

EL PRIMER REQUISITO: UN "ANTÍDOTO" PARA EL RIESGO DE PERSECUCIÓN PRINCIPAL

15. En primer lugar, la "alternativa de protección interna" debe ser un lugar en el que el solicitante de asilo ya no se enfrente al temor fundado de persecución por un motivo contemplado en la Convención que haya dado lugar a su presunta necesidad de protección frente al riesgo en una región del país de origen. No basta simplemente descubrir que el agente original o el autor de la persecución aún no ha establecido una presencia en el sitio de protección interna propuesto. Debe haber razones para creer que es probable que el alcance del agente o autor de la persecución permanezca fuera del sitio de protección interna designado.

13. فإذا انتهى المُحقق من التأكد من أن طالب اللجوء يتعرض للاضطهاد أو يخشى خطر الاضطهاد لأحد الأسباب التي حددتها الاتفاقية في أحد أقاليم دولة المنشأ على الأقل، فإنه يمكنه الانتقال إلى التحقيق التفصيلي في مدى توافر الحماية الداخلية. ويمكن تقسيم البحث في هذا السؤال الأخير إلى ثلاثة أسئلة فرعية:

أ. هل يمكن أن يقدم المكان المُقترح لتقديم الحماية الداخلية حماية فعالة قادرة على صد ومقاومة (antidote) خطر الاضطهاد الذي يواجه طالب اللجوء؟
ب. هل يتمتع المكان المُقترح لتقديم الحماية الداخلية بالضمانات الكافية التي تجعله هو نفسه أمناً من خطر الاضطهاد؟
ج. هل توفر الظروف والشروط المحلية الخاصة بهذا الموقع المتطلبات الدنيا للحماية كما حددتها الاتفاقية الدولية للاجئين؟

13. Второй вопрос, который оценивается исходя из установленной угрозы преследования по одному из конвенционных признаков по меньшей мере в одной из частей страны, заключается в том, имеет ли лицо, ищущее убежища, доступ к получению существенной внутренней защиты от угрозы преследования. Изучение этого вопроса, в свою очередь, можно разделить на три части:

a) Может ли предложенное место внутренней защиты предоставить лицу, ищущему убежища, существенное «противоядие» от установленной угрозы преследования?
b) Отсутствуют ли в предложенном месте внутренней защиты такие факторы, которые либо приравниваются к угрозе преследования, либо равносильны ей?
c) Соответствуют ли местные условия в предложенном месте внутренней защиты хотя бы тому минимальному понятию «защиты», которое предусмотрено в Конвенции о беженцах?

14. يقع عبء إثبات وجود الحماية الداخلية كبديل وفقاً للأوصاف التي حددتها الفقرة 13 على الدولة التي تبحث طلب اللجوء وتقترح الحماية الداخلية. والسبب في ذلك إن البحث في الحماية الداخلية هو خطوة تعقب التأكد من وجود خوف له ما يُبرره لدى طالب اللجوء بأنه معرض للاضطهاد لأحد الأسباب التي حددتها الاتفاقية. ومعنى التحقق من ذلك أولاً أن منح صفة اللجوء قد أصبح حقاً مُفترضاً لطالب اللجوء، سيما بعد أن تأكدت الدولة التي تبحث طلب اللجوء أن طالب اللجوء مُعرض للاضطهاد فعلاً. ومعنى أن تقترح هذه الدولة تنفيذ نقل هذا الشخص وفقاً الحماية الداخلية كبديل، أنها تريد أن " تتخلص " من تنفيذ هذا الحق المُفترض لهذا الشخص، بالحصول على صفة اللجوء. وذلك ما يُبرر وقوع عبء الإثبات على هذه الدولة.

14. Так как это рассмотрение существования «альтернативы внутренней защиты» основано на существовании вполне обоснованных опасений стать жертвой преследования по одному из конвенционных признаков, по крайней мере, в одном из регионов страны происхождения лица, ищущего убежища, и, следовательно, на презумпции права на получение статуса беженца в соответствии с Конвенцией, обязанность доказать факт существования эффективной внутренней защиты, о которой говорится в пункте 13, должна во всех случаях лежать на властях потенциальной страны убежища.

الشرط الأول
أن يتوافر بالمكان المُقترح حماية فعالة قادرة على صد ومقاومة خطر الاضطهاد الذي يواجه طالب اللجوء
15. يجب أولاً أن يتوافر الحماية الداخلية في مكان حيث لا يشعر فيه طالب اللجوء بأي خوف مبرر بوقوع الاضطهاد لأحد الأسباب التي حددتها الاتفاقية الدولية. وهذا الخوف هو المُبرر الذي دفع هذا الشخص من الأصل للبحث عن حماية. وذلك مثلاً، لا يكفي لاعتبار هذا المكان المُقترح بديلاً أمناً من الاضطهاد القول بأن الجهة القائمة بالاضطهاد لا توجد في هذا المكان في وقت البحث في مدى توافر وجود هذا البديل. لكن ينبغي أن تكون هناك أسباب معقولة للاعتقاد بأن الشخص أو الجهة القائمة بالاضطهاد لن يستطيعوا الوصول إلى هذا المكان، وأنهم سوف يظلون بعيداً عنه.

ПЕРВОЕ ТРЕБОВАНИЕ: «ПРОТИВОЯДИЕ» ОТ ОСНОВНОЙ УГРОЗЫ ПРЕСЛЕДОВАНИЯ

15. Во-первых, «альтернатива внутренней защиты» должна быть местом, в котором лицо, ищущее убежища, больше не будет испытывать вполне обоснованные опасения стать жертвой преследования по одному из конвенционных признаков, который вызвал его предположительную потребность в защите в одном из регионов страны происхождения указанного лица. Недостаточно будет просто установить, что изначальный агент или субъект преследования пока еще не появился в предложенном месте внутренней защиты. Необходимо иметь основание полагать, что пределы досягаемости агента или субъекта преследования, скорее всего, останутся локализованными за пределами назначенного места внутренней защиты.

16. There should therefore be a strong presumption against finding an 'internal protection alternative' where the agent or author of the original risk of persecution is, or is sponsored by, the national government.

16. Pour cette raison, il devrait exister une forte présomption selon laquelle il n'existe pas d'« alternative de protection interne » lorsque le risque originel de persécution émane des autorités nationales, ou d'un agent ou auteur que ces autorités soutiennent.

16. Por lo tanto, debe haber una fuerte presunción contra la búsqueda de una "alternativa de protección interna" cuando el agente o autor causante del riesgo original de persecución es, o está patrocinado por, el gobierno nacional.

THE SECOND REQUIREMENT: NO ADDITIONAL RISK OF, OR EQUIVALENT TO, PERSECUTION

17. A meaningful understanding of internal protection from the risk of persecution requires consideration of more than just the existence of an 'antidote' to the risk identified in one part of the country of origin. If a distinct risk of even generalized serious harm exists in the proposed site of internal protection, the request for recognition of refugee status may not be denied on internal protection grounds. This requirement may be justified in either of two ways.

LA SECONDE EXIGENCE: L'ABSENCE D'UN RISQUE SUPPLÉMENTAIRE DE SUBIR UNE PERSÉCUTION OU DES ACTES ÉQUIVALENTS

17. Une évaluation rigoureuse de l'existence d'une alternative de protection interne face à un risque de persécution implique de ne pas se limiter à établir s'il existe un « antidote » face au risque identifié par rapport à une partie du territoire du pays d'origine. S'il existe un risque distinct, ou même généralisé, d'atteintes graves là où il existerait une alternative de protection interne, la demande de reconnaissance du statut de réfugié ne peut pas être refusée pour ce motif. Cela se justifie pour deux raisons.

EL SEGUNDO REQUISITO: AUSENCIA DE RIESGO ADICIONAL DE PERSECUCIÓN O EQUIVALENTE AL MISMO

17. Una comprensión significativa de la protección interna frente al riesgo de persecución implica considerar algo más que la simple existencia de un "antídoto" para el riesgo identificado en una parte del país de origen. Si existe un claro riesgo de daños graves, incluso generalizados, en el sitio de protección interna propuesto, la solicitud de reconocimiento de la condición de refugiado no podrá denegarse por razones de protección interna. Este requisito puede justificarse de dos maneras.

18. First, the asylum-seeker may have an independent refugee claim in relation to the proposed site of internal protection. If the harm feared is of sufficient gravity to fall within the ambit of persecution, the requirement to show a nexus to a Convention reason is arguably satisfied as well. This is so since but for the fear of persecution in one part of the country of origin for a Convention reason, the asylum-seeker would not now be exposed to the risk in the proposed site of internal protection.

18. Premièrement, le demandeur d'asile pourrait avoir une raison distincte de solliciter la qualité de réfugié par rapport au lieu envisagé au titre d'alternative de protection interne. Si l'atteinte crainte est suffisamment grave pour pouvoir être qualifiée de persécution, l'exigence de démontrer un lien avec un motif conventionnel est également satisfaite. En effet, s'il n'existait pas de crainte fondée de subir de persécution dans une région du pays d'origine en raison d'un motif conventionnel, le demandeur d'asile ne serait pas exposé à un risque de subir une persécution là où une alternative de protection interne est proposée.

18. En primer lugar, el solicitante de asilo puede tener una solicitud de refugio independiente en relación con el sitio de protección interna propuesto. Si el daño que se teme puede ser lo suficientemente grave como para caer dentro del ámbito de la persecución, el requisito de mostrar un nexo con una razón contemplada en la Convención también podría ser suficiente. Esto es así ya que, de no ser por el temor a la persecución en una parte del país de origen por un motivo contemplado en la Convención, el solicitante de asilo no estaría ahora expuesto al riesgo en el sitio de protección interna propuesto.

16. Поэтому необходимо наличие весомой презумпции против установления «альтернативы внутренней защиты» в тех случаях, когда агентом или субъектом изначальной угрозы преследования является центральное правительство страны, либо же оно является ее инициатором.

16. ولا يمكن قبول أي الحماية الداخلية كبديل على الإطلاق مثلاً إذا كانت الجهة القائمة بتوجيه الاضطهاد هي جهة تخضع لإشراف ورعاية الحكومة الوطنية. ويعتبر الاعتقاد بتوافر الحماية الداخلية في مثل هذه الظروف أمراً غير منطقي وغير قانوني.

ВТОРОЕ ТРЕБОВАНИЕ: ОТСУТСТВИЕ ДОПОЛНИТЕЛЬНОЙ УГРОЗЫ СТАТЬ ЖЕРТВОЙ ПРЕСЛЕДОВАНИЯ ИЛИ ЕЁ ЭКВИВАЛЕНТА

17. Существенное понимание внутренней защиты от угрозы преследования требует принимать во внимание нечто большее, чем наличие «противоядия» от риска, установленного в одной из частей страны происхождения. Если в предложенном месте внутренней защиты существует отчетливо проявляющаяся угроза хотя бы потенциально существенного ущерба, ходатайство о признании статуса беженца не может быть отклонено на основании наличия внутренней защиты. Это требование может быть обосновано одним из двух способов.

الشرط الثاني
عدم وجود خطر اضطهاد آخر أو خطر آخر يرقى لمرتبة الاضطهاد

17. لا يكفي مجرد توافر الحماية الداخلية كبديل لطالب اللجوء ضد خطر الاضطهاد في أحد أقاليم دولة المنشأ على الأقل للقول بأنه ثمة الحماية الداخلية كبديل مقبول قانوناً. فلا يعتبر رفض منح صفة اللجوء مُبَرَّراً على أساس توافر الحماية الداخلية كبديل إذا كان مكان البديل المُقترح يشهد أخطاراً أخرى منظورة بإيذاء طالب اللجوء، ولو اتسمت هذه الأخطار بالصفة العمومية. ويرجع الأساس القانوني للحكم الوارد في هذه الفقرة إلى أحد المُبررين التاليين (كما هو موضح في الفقرتين التاليتين).

---

18. Во-первых, лицо, ищущее убежища, может иметь независимые притязания на статус беженца в отношении предложенного места внутренней защиты. Если ожидаемый вред имеет настолько серьезный характер, что может быть приравнен к преследованию, то требование доказательства причинной связи с конвенционным признаком тоже может считаться соблюденным. Дело обстоит таким образом потому, что, если бы не опасение стать жертвой преследования в одной из частей страны происхождения согласно основанию Конвенции, лицо, ищущее убежища, в настоящее время не подвергалось бы опасности в предложенном месте внутренней защиты.

18. أولاً، غالباً ما يقدم طالب اللجوء طلبه بغض النظر عن المكان المقترح كالحماية الداخلية كبديل. وفي كل الحالات، فإن مجرد وجود خوف من إيذاء يتسم بدرجة من الجسامة الكافية التي يتحقق بها وجود الاضطهاد، فإن هذا الإيذاء أصبح يرقى من الناحية القانونية لمرتبة الاضطهاد، وذلك طالما إن هذا "الاضطهاد" يقع لأحد الأسباب التي حددتها الاتفاقية الدولية. وبناء على ذلك، فإن مجرد اتسام الحماية الداخلية ذاته بخطر محقق يعتبر بمثابة اضطهاد (أي اضطهاد آخر)، فإن هذا الأمر يوفر أحد اشتراطات منح صفة اللجوء، وهي قيام اضطهاد بأحد أقاليم دولة المنشأ لطالب اللجوء.

19. Second, the legal duty to avoid exposing the asylum-seeker to serious risk in the place of internal protection may be derived by reference to the Refugee Convention's Art. 33(1), which requires state parties to avoid the return of a refugee '. . . in any manner whatsoever to the frontiers of territories where his life or freedom would be threatened . . .' for a Convention reason. Where the intensity of the harms specific to the proposed site of internal protection (such as, for example, famine or sustained conflict) rises to a particularly high level, even if not amounting to a risk of persecution, an asylum-seeker may in practice feel compelled to abandon the proposed site of protection, even if the only alternative is return to a known risk of persecution for a Convention reason elsewhere in the country of origin.

19. Deuxièmement, l'article 33, §1ᵉʳ, de la Convention de Genève pourrait impliquer une obligation légale de ne pas exposer un demandeur d'asile à un risque sérieux là où une alternative de protection interne est envisagée, étant donné qu'il interdit aux États parties d'expulser ou de refouler « . . . de quelque manière que ce soit, un réfugié sur les frontières des territoires où sa vie ou sa liberté serait menacée . . . » en raison d'un des motifs conventionnels. Lorsque l'atteinte risquée là où il existerait une alternative de protection interne atteint une certaine intensité, par exemple en raison d'une famine ou d'un conflit persistant, le demandeur se verra en réalité contraint de quitter les lieux pour retourner là où il éprouve une crainte fondée de persécution pour un motif conventionnel.

19. En segundo lugar, el deber legal de evitar exponer al solicitante de asilo a un riesgo grave en el lugar que brindaría protección interna puede evocarse haciendo referencia al artículo 33 (1) de la Convención de Refugiados que exige que los estados partes eviten el regreso de un refugiado "(. . .) de cualquier manera a las fronteras de los territorios donde su vida o libertad estarían amenazadas (. . .)" por un motivo contemplado en la Convención. Cuando la intensidad de los daños específicos del sitio de protección interna propuesto (como, por ejemplo, hambruna o conflicto continuo) se eleva a un nivel particularmente alto, incluso si no representa un riesgo de persecución, un solicitante de asilo en la práctica puede sentirse obligado a abandonar el sitio de protección propuesto, incluso si la única alternativa es regresar a un riesgo de persecución conocido por un motivo contemplado en la Convención en otro lugar del país de origen.

THE THIRD REQUIREMENT: EXISTENCE OF A MINIMALIST COMMITMENT TO AFFIRMATIVE PROTECTION

20. The denial of refugee status is predicated not simply on the absence of a risk of persecution in some part of the state of origin, but on a finding that the asylum-seeker can access internal protection there. This understanding follows from the *prima facie* need for international refugee protection of all asylum-seekers whose cases are subjected to internal protection analysis. If recognition of refugee status is to be denied to such persons on the grounds that the protection to which they are presumptively entitled can in fact be accessed within their own state, then the sufficiency of that internal protection is logically measured by reference to the scope of the protection which refugee law guarantees.

LA TROISIÈME EXIGENCE: UN ENGAGEMENT MINIMAL DE GARANTIR UNE PROTECTION EFFECTIVE

20. Le refus de reconnaître le statut de réfugié ne peut résulter de la seule absence de risque de subir une persécution dans une partie du pays d'origine, mais suppose également que le demandeur d'asile puisse accéder à une protection interne. Cette exigence résulte du besoin de protection *prima facie* des demandeurs d'asile pour lesquels une alternative de protection interne est envisagée. Si le statut de réfugié leur est refusé au motif que la protection à laquelle ils ont potentiellement droit est en réalité accessible dans leur pays d'origine, alors cette protection interne doit nécessairement être évaluée en fonction de l'étendue de la protection garantie par le droit des réfugiés.

EL TERCER REQUISITO: EXISTENCIA DE UN COMPROMISO MINIMALISTA CON LA PROTECCIÓN AFIRMATIVA

20. La denegación de la condición de refugiado se basa no solo en la ausencia de un riesgo de persecución en alguna parte del estado de origen, sino también en la constatación de que allí el solicitante de asilo puede beneficiarse de protección interna. Esta comprensión se deriva de la necesidad *prima facie* de protección internacional para refugiados de todos los solicitantes de asilo cuyos casos estén sujetos a un análisis de protección interna. Si se niega el reconocimiento de la condición de refugiado a dichas personas argumentando que la protección a la que presuntamente tienen derecho se puede recibir en su propio estado, la suficiencia de esa protección interna se mide lógicamente por referencia al alcance de la protección que garantiza la legislación sobre refugiados.

19. ثانياً، يرجع الواجب الواقع على الدول الموقعة على الاتفاقية بعدم إعادة طالب اللجوء إلى مكان يُفترض فيه انه بديلاً كافياً للحماية الداخلية، يرجع هذا الواجب إلى الالتزام القانوني الواقع على الدول الأطراف بالاتفاقية الدولية لشؤون اللاجئين، والنابع من المادة 33 الفقرة الأولى من الاتفاقية الدولية. وتحظر هذه المادة على أي دولة " طرد أو رد اللاجئ بأية صورة إلى الحدود أو الأقاليم حيث تكون حياته أو حريته مهددتان بسبب عرقه أو دينه أو جنسيته أو انتمائه إلى فئة اجتماعية معينة أو بسبب آرائه السياسية." فطالما توفر خطر جسيم في المكان المُفترض أن يقدم الحماية اللازمة (ولو لم يمثل ذلك اضطهاداً، مثل أخطار المجاعة أو النزاع المسلح)، فإن طالب اللجوء الحق في اختيار عدم العودة لبلاده في هذا المكان، طالما إن البديل الوحيد الذي أصبح في متناول هذا الشخص هو العودة إلى مكان آخر يتعرض فيه للاضطهاد في أحد أقاليم دولة المنشأ.

19. Во-вторых, юридическое обязательство не подвергать серьезной угрозе лицо, ищущее убежища, в месте внутренней защиты, следует из ссылки на статью 33(1) Конвенции о статусе беженцев, которая не позволяет государствам-участникам «. . . никоим образом высылать или возвращать беженцев на границу страны, где их жизни или свободе угрожает опасность . . .» согласно Конвенции. В случае, когда степень ущерба, существующего в предложенном месте внутренней защиты (например, голод или длительный конфликт) возрастает до особенно высокого уровня, даже если она и не достигает уровня угрозы преследования искатель убежища, на практике может быть вынужден покинуть предложенное место защиты, даже если единственной альтернативой будет возвращение к месту наличия угрозы преследования по одному из конвенционных признаков где-либо еще в стране происхождения.

الشرط الثالث

وجود حد أدنى للالتزام بتوفير حماية "إيجابية" فعالة

20. يستند الجوهر الأساسي لرفض منح صفة اللجوء على أساس إيجاد الحماية الداخلية كبديل على الإمكانية الفعلية لوجود هذا البديل وعلى ضمان أن يصل طالب اللجوء اليه. وبالتالي فإن مكمن البحث هنا ليس هو مدى غياب وقوع اضطهاد في أحد أقاليم دولة المنشأ من عدمه، ولكن هو مدى توفر الحماية البديلة من عدمه. ويجد الحكم السابق أساسا له في حقيقة أن توفر حماية دولية للاجئين تعتبر هي الهدف والمطلب الأول لكل لاجئ معرض لأن يطبق عليه تحليل " الحماية الداخلية." هذه الحقيقة التي تعتبر من الوهلة الأولى (prima facie) عند البحث في تقديم حماية دولية للاجئين. والمنطق يقول إن رفض طلبات اللجوء كبديل "مُفترض" يجب أن يتم بالمقارنة النسبية وبالقياس على نطاق وحجم الحماية التي تضمنها القوانين الدولية للاجئين. ومدى كفاءة الحماية التي يقدمها البديل ينبغي أن يقاس وفقاً للمعايير والقوانين الدولية وليس شيء أخر.

ТРЕТЬЕ ТРЕБОВАНИЕ: СУЩЕСТВОВАНИЕ МИНИМАЛЬНЫХ ОБЯЗАТЕЛЬСТВ ПО ПРЕДОСТАВЛЕНИЮ ЗАЩИТЫ

20. Отказ в статусе беженца обусловлен не просто отсутствием угрозы преследования в какой-либо части страны происхождения, но также и установлением того, что лицо, ищущее убежища, может получить там доступ к получению внутренней защиты. Это понимание исходит из первоначальной потребности в международной защите всех лиц, ищущих убежища, чьи заявления подвергаются анализу с точки зрения внутренней защиты. Если в признании статуса беженца таким лицам может быть отказано на основании того, что защита, на которую они якобы имеют право, может в действительности быть доступной им в пределах их собственного государства, тогда достаточность внутренней защиты логически соизмеряется с масштабом защиты, гарантированной правом в области беженцев.

21. Good reasons may be advanced to refer to a range of widely recognized international human rights in defining the irreducible core content of affirmative protection in the proposed site of internal protection. In particular, one might rely on the reference in the Refugee Convention's Preamble to the importance of '. . . the principle that human beings shall enjoy fundamental rights and freedoms without discrimination.' Yet the Refugee Convention itself does not establish a duty on state parties to guarantee all such rights and freedoms to refugees. Instead, Arts. 2-33 establish an endogenous definition of the rights and freedoms viewed as requisite to '. . . revise and consolidate previous international agreements relating to the status of refugees and to extend the scope of and *the protection accorded by* such instruments . . . (emphasis added).' These rights are for the most part framed in relative terms, effectively mandating a general duty of non-discrimination as between refugees and others.

21. Il existe de sérieux arguments pour considérer que diverses obligations de droit international des droits de l'homme doivent être prises en considération pour identifier la substance minimale de la protection effective qui doit exister là où l'alternative de protection interne est envisagée. En particulier, le préambule de la Convention relative au statut des réfugiés souligne l'importance « du principe (. . .) (selon lequel) les êtres humains, sans discrimination, doivent jouir des droits de l'homme et des libertés fondamentales ». Toutefois, la Convention n'impose pas, en tant que telle, aux États parties de garantir ces droits et libertés aux réfugiés. Les articles 2 à 33 établissent une définition autonome des droits et libertés considérés comme nécessaires pour « réviser et (. . .) codifier les accords internationaux antérieurs relatifs au statut des réfugiés et (. . .) étendre l'application de ces instruments et la protection qu'ils constituent pour les réfugiés ». Ces droits sont principalement définis en des termes relatifs et reviennent à consacrer un principe général de non-discrimination entre les réfugiés et les autres personnes.

21. Se pueden presentar buenas razones para referirse a una gama de derechos humanos internacionales ampliamente reconocidos al definir el contenido básico irreductible de la protección afirmativa en el sitio de protección interna propuesto. En particular, uno puede confiar en la referencia en el Preámbulo de la Convención de Refugiados sobre la importancia de "(. . .) el principio de que los seres humanos deben gozar de los derechos y las libertades fundamentales sin discriminación". Sin embargo, la propia Convención de Refugiados no establece el deber de los estados partes de garantizar todos esos derechos y libertades a los refugiados. En cambio, los artículos 2 a 33 establecen una definición endógena de los derechos y libertades considerados como un requisito para "(. . .) revisar y consolidar acuerdos internacionales previos relacionados con la condición de los refugiados y ampliar el alcance de *la protección acordada por* tales instrumentos (. . .) (énfasis añadido)". La mayoría de estos derechos se enmarca en términos relativos, creando una obligación efectiva general de no discriminación entre los refugiados y los demás individuos.

22. At a minimum, therefore, conditions in the proposed site of internal protection ought to satisfy the affirmative, yet relative, standards set by this textually explicit definition of the content of protection. The relevant measure is the treatment of other persons in the proposed site of internal protection, not in the putative asylum country. Thus, internal protection requires not only protection against the risk of persecution, but also the assimilation of the asylum-seeker with others in the site of internal protection for purposes of access to, for example, employment, public welfare, and education.

22. Pour cette raison, les conditions de vie là où une alternative de protection interne est envisagée devraient au minimum répondre aux standards de protection impératifs, bien que relatifs, définis explicitement par le texte de la Convention. À cette fin, le traitement des autres personnes là où l'alternative de protection interne est envisagée, et non au sein de l'État où l'asile est sollicité, constitue la référence pertinente. L'alternative de protection interne suppose donc non seulement une protection contre la persécution, mais également l'assimilation du demandeur d'asile aux autres personnes vivant là où il existe une protection, en ce qui concerne par exemple l'accès au marché de l'emploi, à l'assistance publique et à l'éducation.

22. Por lo tanto, como mínimo las condiciones en el sitio de protección interna propuesto deben satisfacer los estándares afirmativos, aunque relativos, establecidos por esta definición del contenido de la protección, explícita en forma textual. La medida relevante es el tratamiento de otras personas en el sitio propuesto de protección interna, no en el supuesto país de asilo. Por lo tanto, la protección interna no solo exige protección frente al riesgo de persecución, sino también la asimilación del solicitante de asilo con otros en el sitio de protección interna a los efectos de acceder, por ejemplo, al empleo, al bienestar público y la educación.

21. وعندما نقول إن المعايير الدولية ينبغي أن تكون هي الأساس الوحيد الذي يمكن في ضوئه تقييم مدى كفاءة الحماية التي يقدمها البديل المُقترح فإن المقصود بذلك هو الحد الأدنى الذي لا يقبل التجزئة لحقوق الإنسان، كما هو معترف بها عالمياً. وعلى وجه الخصوص، ينبغي أن نتذكر هنا ديباجة الاتفاقية الدولية الخاصة بشؤون اللاجئين التي أكدت على مبدأ أن "جميع البشر يجب أن يتمتعون بالحقوق والحريات الأساسية بلا أي تمييز." وبالرغم من إن الاتفاقية الدولية لم تفرد حصراً خاصاً توضح به ماهية الحقوق والحريات الأساسية التي يجب أن تلتزم بتوفيرها الدول الأطراف، لكنها قد قدمت ما يمكن تسميته بالتعريف الداخلي المُرتبط (endogenous definition) لمثل هذه الحقوق في المواد من 2 إلى 33 من الاتفاقية. فقد قررت الاتفاقية إن الدول الأطراف عليها واجب "مراجعة كافة المعاهدات الدولية المتعلقة بشؤون اللاجئين، وأن توسع من نطاق الحماية الواردة بالاتفاقية الدولية وفقاً لهذه التعهدات السابقة كلما كان ذلك محل من الواقع (تمت إضافة التشديد)". وينبغي أن نتذكر هنا أيضاً للقول بأن كافة هذه الحقوق يجب أن يتم تعريفها بطريقة نسبية في الواقع. والمعيار الأساسي الحاكم هنا ـ فيما يتعلق بالبحث في هذه الصورة النسبية ـ لضمان تطبيق نزيه لها هو واجب كل دولة المتمثل في عدم التفرقة بين اللاجئين وغير اللاجئين.

21. Существенные причины могут быть указаны для того, чтобы сослаться на широко признанные международные права человека при определении не поддающегося сокращению базового содержания позитивной защиты в предложенном месте получения внутренней защиты. В частности, можно сослаться на Преамбулу Конвенции о беженцах о важности «. . . принципа, согласно которому все люди должны пользоваться основными правами и свободами без какой бы то ни было в этом отношении дискриминации». Однако сама по себе Конвенция о беженцах не устанавливает обязательства государств-участников гарантировать беженцам все права и свободы. Вместо этого статьи со 2-й по 33-ю устанавливают свои собственные определения прав и свобод, которые рассматриваются как необходимые для того, чтобы «. . . пересмотреть и объединить заключенные ранее международные соглашения о статусе беженцев и расширить область применения этих договоров и *предоставляемую таковыми защиту* . . . (курсив наш)». Эти права главным образом сформулированы в соотносительных выражениях и по существу устанавливают общую обязанность по недопущению дискриминации как беженцев, так и других лиц.

22. وبناء على ما سبق، فإنه للقول بأن الحماية الداخلية بديل كافٍ، يُشترط أن يُوفر هذا المكان حماية حقيقية تتوافق مع المعايير الدولية، حتى بمعناها النسبي كما سبقت الإشارة. ولكن قبل كل شيء فإن هذا الحد الأدنى من الحقوق الكافي للحماية يجب أن يتم تعريفه وفقاً للنص الصريح الوارد في الاتفاقية الدولية، مع الأخذ في الاعتبار أن غالبية الحقوق يتم تعريفها بطريقة نسبية. والمعيار الحاكم والأساسي هنا للقول بتوافر كفاية الحماية هو أن يلقى طالب اللجوء نفس المعاملة والاحترام للحقوق الذي يتلقاه غير اللاجئين في هذا المكان ذاته (وليس في الدولة التي تبحث طلب اللجوء وتقترح الإعادة وفقاً لسياسة الحماية الداخلية). وباختصار، وبناء على ما سبق، فإن المفهوم الإيجابي للحماية المطلوبة في مكان الحماية الداخلية يتجاوز بكثير مجرد توفير حماية للشخص طالب اللجوء من غير الاضطهاد، ولكن ينصرف هذا المفهوم بالإضافة إلى ما سبق إلى ضرورة إدماج طالب اللجوء في هذا المكان، بما يتضمنه ذلك من حصوله على كافة الخدمات والحقوق التي يتلقاها المواطنين من غير اللاجئين في نفس المكان، مثل الحق في التعليم والحصول على وظيفة والحصول على الرعاية الاجتماعية، على سبيل المثال لا الحصر.

22. Поэтому, как минимум, условия в предложенном месте внутренней защиты должны удовлетворять позитивным, но все же относительным нормам, установленным этим явно выраженным в тексте определением содержания защиты. Существенным критерием здесь является обращение с другими лицами в предложенном месте внутренней защиты, а не в потенциальной стране убежища. Таким образом, внутренняя защита требует не только защиты от угрозы преследования, но также и ассимиляции лица, ищущего убежища, в месте получения внутренней защиты, например, в целях трудоустройства, доступа к социальному обеспечению и образованию.

'REASONABLENESS'

23. Most states that presently rely on either 'internal flight' or 'internal relocation' analysis also require decision-makers to consider whether, generally or in light of a particular asylum-seeker's circumstances, it would be 'reasonable' to require return to the proposed site of internal protection. If the careful approach to identification and assessment of an 'internal protection alternative' proposed here is followed, there is no additional duty under international refugee law to assess the 'reasonableness' of return to the region identified as able to protect the asylum-seeker.

LE CARACTÈRE « RAISONNABLE »
23. La plupart des États qui vérifient si une « fuite interne » ou une « relocalisation interne » serait envisageable exigent également des autorités en charge de la détermination du statut de réfugié qu'elles évaluent si, de manière générale ou compte tenu du profil spécifique du demandeur d'asile, il serait « raisonnable » d'exiger qu'il retourne dans la région où il pourrait bénéficier d'une protection. Si les modalités d'évaluation et d'identification d'une « alternative de protection interne » telles que proposées ici sont rigoureusement suivies, il n'est pas indispensable d'évaluer en plus le « caractère raisonnable » du retour vers la région où le demandeur d'asile pourrait bénéficier d'une protection.

"CARÁCTER RAZONABLE"
23. La mayoría de los estados que actualmente confían en el análisis de "huida interna" o "reubicación interna" también solicitan que los responsables de tomar decisiones consideren si, en general o a la luz de las circunstancias particulares de un solicitante de asilo, sería "razonable" exigir el regreso al sitio propuesto para brindar protección interna. Si se sigue el enfoque cuidadoso para la identificación y evaluación de una "alternativa de protección interna", como se propone aquí, no existe un deber adicional bajo la ley internacional de refugiados para evaluar la "el carácter razonable" del regreso a la región identificada como capaz de proteger al solicitante de asilo.

---

24. Assessment of the 'reasonableness' of return may nonetheless be viewed as consistent with the spirit of Recommendation E of the Conference of Plenipotentiaries, that the Refugee Convention '. . . have value as an example exceeding its contractual scope and that all nations . . . be guided by it in granting so far as possible to persons in their territory as refugees and who would not be covered by the terms of the Convention, the treatment for which it provides.'

24. L'évaluation du « caractère raisonnable » du retour constitue toutefois une exigence cohérente avec l'esprit de la Recommandation E de la conférence de plénipotentiaires, selon laquelle la Convention relative au statut des réfugiés « aura valeur d'exemple, en plus de sa portée contractuelle, et (. . .) (. . .) incitera tous les États à accorder dans toute la mesure du possible aux personnes se trouvant sur leur territoire en tant que réfugiés et qui ne seraient pas couvertes par les dispositions de la Convention, le traitement prévu par cette Convention ».

24. Sin embargo, la evaluación del "carácter razonable" del regreso puede considerarse en línea con el carácter de la Recomendación E de la Conferencia de Plenipotenciarios, que la Convención de Refugiados "(. . .) tendrá valor como ejemplo que exceda su alcance contractual y que todas las naciones (. . .) se guíen por ella al otorgar, en la medida de lo posible, a las personas presentes en su territorio como refugiados y que no estarían amparados por los términos de la Convención, el tratamiento que garantiza".

PROCEDURAL SAFEGUARDS

25. Because the viability of an 'internal protection alternative' can only be assessed with full knowledge of the risks in other regions of the state of origin (see paras. 15-16), internal protection analysis should never be included as a criterion for denial of refugee status under an accelerated or manifestly unfounded claims procedure.

LES GARANTIES PROCÉDURALES
25. Étant donné que la viabilité d'une « alternative de protection interne » ne peut être évaluée que moyennant une connaissance complète des risques existant dans d'autres régions du pays d'origine (voy. supra, §§15 à 16), l'analyse visant à déterminer s'il existe une alternative de protection interne ne devrait jamais être réalisée dans le cadre d'une procédure dite d'examen accéléré ou d'une procédure appliquée à une demande dite manifestement non fondée (procédure de recevabilité ou d'admissibilité).

GARANTÍAS PROCESALES
25. Debido a que la viabilidad de una "alternativa de protección interna" solo puede evaluarse con pleno conocimiento de los riesgos en otras regiones del estado de origen (ver párrafos. 15-16), el análisis de protección interna nunca debe incluirse como un criterio para denegar la condición de refugiado en virtud de un procedimiento de reclamación acelerado o manifiestamente infundado.

مدى المعقولية

٢٣. تتطلب معظم الدول التي تلجأ إلى تحليل الحماية الداخلية (بإعادة النقل أو إعادة التوطين الداخليين) من مُتخذي القرار فيها بالنظر في كافة الظروف المعينة المتعلقة بطالب اللجوء، وخاصة بالنظر في مدى معقولية اشتراط أو طلب إعادة هذا الشخص إلى موقع للحماية في بلده الأصلي. وفي حالة تطبيق المنظور السابق ـ الذي تم شرحه في السطور السابقة ـ الحماية الداخلية كبديل، بما يشتمله من ضمانات، فإنه لا توجد التزامات أو واجبات إضافية تقع على عاتق الدولة باحثة طلب اللجوء ـ تتعلق بالبحث في مدى معقولية إعادة طالب اللجوء إلى موقع حمائي داخلي.

«РАЗУМНОСТЬ»

23. Большинство государств, которые в настоящее время прибегают к анализу факта «бегства внутри страны» или «перемещения внутри страны», одновременно требуют от лиц, принимающих решение, рассматривать вопрос о том, насколько в целом или с учетом обстоятельств конкретного искателя убежища, было бы «разумным» требовать от него возвращения к предполагаемому месту внутренней защиты. Если скрупулезно следовать предложенному здесь подходу к выявлению и оценке «альтернативы внутренней защиты», отпадет дополнительная обязанность, вытекающая из международного законодательства о беженцах, оценивать «разумность» возвращения в регион, признанный как место, где лицо, ищущее убежища, может получить защиту.

---

٢٤. أي تقييم لمدى معقولية إعادة طالب اللجوء إلى الحماية الداخلية كبديل يجب أن يكون متسقاً ومتماشياً مع روح التوصية الخامسة من المؤتمر الدبلوماسي التحضيري للاتفاقية الدولية للاجئين، والتي جاء فيها "إن هذه الاتفاقية يجب النظر اليها بما يتجاوز قيمتها التعاقدية ونطاق الالتزامات القانونية الضيقة على الدول الأطراف، أي بالنظر إلى القيم التي تحملها؛ فيجب النظر إلى ما تحمله من غايات، وان يكون المرشد العام في تطبيقها هو الرغبة الصادقة في منح أكبر قدر من الأشخاص صفة اللجوء، حتى ولو لم يكونوا مشتملين برعاية الاتفاقية."

24. Несмотря на это, оценка «разумности» возвращения может считаться соответствующей духу Рекомендации E Конференции полномочных представителей, согласно которой Конвенция о беженцах «. . . представляет ценность как пример документа, имеющего более широкое значение, и что все страны . . . должны руководствоваться ею в максимальной степени при предоставлении предусмотренного ею обращения с лицами, находящимися на их территории в качестве беженцев, и теми лицами, которые не подпадают под действие Конвенции»

ضمانات إجرائية

٢٥. لا يمكن رفض منح صفة اللجوء استناداً إلى أخطاء أو مسائل إجرائية محضة ـ مثل وجود طلب لا يستند إلى أدلة كافية مثلاً ـ عند تطبيق تحليل "الحماية الداخلية." والسبب في ذلك إن كفاية هذا التحليل يرتبط ارتباطاً وثيقاً وبصفة أساسية بوجود تحقيق شامل ومعرفة بكافة الأخطار المُتحققة والمتوقعة في دولة الطالب الأصلية (أنظر فقرات ١٥ و١٦).

ПРОЦЕДУРНЫЕ ГАРАНТИИ

25. Поскольку жизнеспособность «альтернативы внутренней защиты» может быть оценена только при полной осведомленности об угрозах в других регионах в стране происхождения (см. пункты 15-16), анализ внутренней защиты ни в коем случае не должен быть включен в качестве критерия для отказа в статусе беженца в рамках ускоренной процедуры или процедуры отказа по явно необоснованным заявлениям.

26. To ensure that assessment of the viability of an 'internal protection alternative' meets the standards set by international refugee law, it is important that the putative asylum state clearly discloses to the asylum-seeker that internal protection is under consideration, as well as the information upon which it relies to advance this contention. The decision-maker must in all cases act fairly, and in particular ensure that no information regarding the availability of an 'internal protection alternative' is considered unless the asylum-seeker has an opportunity to respond to that information, and to present other relevant information to the decision-maker.

26. Afin de garantir que la procédure visant à déterminer s'il existe une « alternative de protection interne » rencontre les standards du droit international des réfugiés, il est essentiel que l'État où l'asile est sollicité informe le demandeur d'asile qu'une alternative de protection interne pourrait exister, et qu'il lui communique les informations sur lesquelles il se fonde pour aboutir à cette conclusion. L'autorité responsable de la détermination du statut de réfugié doit, dans tous les cas, agir avec loyauté et, en particulier, s'assurer qu'aucun élément relatif à l'existence d'une « alternative de protection interne » ne soit examiné sans donner au demandeur d'asile l'occasion d'y répondre et de présenter, le cas échéant, d'autres éléments pertinents.

26. Para garantizar que la evaluación de la viabilidad de una "alternativa de protección interna" cumpla con los estándares establecidos por el derecho internacional de refugiados, es importante que el supuesto estado proveedor de asilo le revele claramente al solicitante de asilo que se está considerando la opción de la protección interna, así como la información sobre la cual se basa para avanzar con este argumento. El responsable de tomar decisiones debe actuar de manera justa en todos los casos y, en particular, asegurarse de que no se tenga en cuenta información sobre la disponibilidad de una "alternativa de protección interna" a menos que el solicitante de asilo tenga la oportunidad de responder a esa información y de presentar otra información relevante ante el responsable de tomar la decisión.

These Guidelines reflect the consensus of all the participants at the First Colloquium on Challenges in International Refugees Law, held at Ann Arbor, Michigan, USA, on April 9–11, 1999.

James C. Hathaway
Colloquium Convener
University of Michigan

Philip Rudge
Colloquium Chairperson
University of Michigan

Deborah Anker
Harvard University

Jean-Yves Carlier
Université de Louvain-la-Neuve

Rodger P.G. Haines, Q.C.
University of Auckland

Lee Anne de la Hunt
University of Cape Town

David A. Martin
University of Virginia

V. Vijayakumar
National Law School of India University

Deborah Benedict
Student,
Michigan Law School

Jonathan Chudler
Student,
Michigan Law School

Anne Cusick
Student,
Michigan Law School

Michael Kagan
Student,
Michigan Law School

Sheila Minihane
Student,
Michigan Law School

Lakshmi Nayar
Student,
Michigan Law School

Frank Richter
Student,
Michigan Law School

Ali Saidi
Student,
Michigan Law School

Kathryn Socha
Student,
Michigan Law School

26. يجب على الدولة باحثة طلب اللجوء أن تخطر طالب اللجوء بوضوح إنها بصدد ــ أو تنظر في مسألة ــ تطبيق الحماية الداخلية، كما يجب عليها أيضاً إخطار طالب اللجوء بكافة المعلومات المطلوبة والمُتعلقة عند حدوث أي طعن أو خلاف حول الحماية الداخلية. والسبب في ذلك ضمان أن يكون تطبيق تحليل "الحماية الداخلية" متماشياً مع المعايير الدولية المحددة من قبل القانون الدولي للاجئين. ويجب على مُتخذ القرار في كافة الأحوال أن يكون مُنصفاً وأن يضمن إخبار طالب اللجوء بكافة المعلومات التي يتم الاستناد اليها لتطبيق الحماية الداخلية، وأن يضمن أن تتوافر لطالب اللجوء الفرصة الكافية للرد على والتعقيب على هذه المعلومات. ويقع على عاتق مُتخذ القرار أيضاً توفير الفرصة الكافية لطالب اللجوء لتقديم معلومات أخرى ذات صلة لدحض أو استكمال المعلومات محل البحث عند اتخاذ قرار منح صفة اللجوء أو تطبيق تحليل "الحماية الداخلية".

26. Чтобы обеспечить при оценке реальности «альтернативы внутренней защиты» соблюдение норм, установленных международным законодательством по правам беженцев, важно, чтобы государство потенциального убежища ясно информировало лицо, ищущее убежища, о том, что рассматривается вопрос об альтернативе внутренней защиты, а также предоставило информацию, на которую оно опирается в процессе такого рассмотрения. Лицо, принимающее решение, должно во всех случаях действовать справедливо и, в частности, добиваться того, чтобы не рассматривалась никакая информация в отношении наличия «альтернативы внутренней защиты», если у лица, ищущего убежища, нет возможности отреагировать на эту информацию и представить лицу, принимающему решение, другую, имеющую отношение к делу, информацию.

Efforts to promote the contemporary vitality of the Convention refugee definition have usually focused on refining our understanding of the circumstances in which an individual may be said to be at risk of "being persecuted," or on giving contemporary relevance to the content of the five grounds upon which risk must be based—race, religion, nationality, membership of a particular social group or political opinion. Comparatively little thought has been given to how best to conceive the causal linkage or nexus between the Convention ground and the risk of being persecuted. In what circumstances may the risk be said to be 'for reasons of' one of the five Convention grounds?

LES RECOMMANDATIONS DE MICHIGAN SUR LE LIEN DE CAUSALITÉ AVEC UN MOTIF CONVENTIONNEL

Les efforts pour adapter la définition conventionnelle du réfugié aux réalités contemporaines se sont généralement concentrés sur une interprétation évolutive soit des circonstances dans lesquelles un individu peut être considéré comme courant un risque de subir une persécution, soit des cinq motifs de persécution fondant ce risque – la race, la religion, la nationalité, l'appartenance à un certain groupe social ou l'opinion politique. À l'inverse, relativement peu de réflexions ont été consacrées à l'interprétation du lien de causalité, à la connexion entre les motifs de persécution et le risque de subir une persécution. Dans quelles circonstances peut-il être considéré que le risque existe « du fait de » l'un des motifs conventionnels de persécution?

LAS DIRECTRICES DE MICHIGAN SOBRE EL NEXO CON UN MOTIVO CONTEMPLADO EN LA CONVENCIÓN

Los esfuerzos para promover la vitalidad contemporánea de la definición de refugiado de la Convención generalmente se han centrado en refinar nuestra comprensión de las circunstancias en las que se puede decir que un individuo corre el riesgo de "ser perseguido", o en darle relevancia contemporánea al contenido de los cinco fundamentos en los que se basa el riesgo: raza, religión, nacionalidad, pertenencia a un determinado grupo social u opiniones políticas. En comparación, se ha reflexionado poco sobre la mejor forma de concebir el nexo o el vínculo causal entre el motivo contemplado en la Convención y el riesgo de ser perseguido. ¿En qué circunstancias se puede decir que el riesgo es "con motivo de" una de las cinco razones contempladas en la Convención?

The jurisprudence of many leading asylum states is simply silent on this issue, while decisions rendered in other states assume that causation in refugee law can be defined by uncritical analogy to standards in other branches of the law. Only rarely have senior courts sought carefully to conceive an understanding of causation of specific relevance to refugee law, including the critical questions of a standard of causation and the types of evidence which should inform the causation inquiry.

La jurisprudence de la plupart des principaux pays d'asile n'aborde pas cette question, tandis que des décisions rendues dans d'autres États présument que le lien de causalité en droit des réfugiés peut être interprété par analogie avec les standards développés dans d'autres branches du droit, sans prendre en considération les spécificités du droit des réfugiés. Ce n'est que dans de rares cas que des Cours suprêmes ont cherché à définir précisément le lien de causalité en droit des réfugiés, en ce compris en tranchant les questions délicates permettant de déterminer quel est le degré de causalité exigé et quels sont les éléments pertinents dans le cadre de l'analyse de causalité.

La jurisprudencia de muchos de los principales estados que brindan asilo simplemente no hace referencia a este tema, mientras que las decisiones tomadas en otros estados asumen que la causalidad en el derecho de los refugiados puede definirse por analogía falta de sentido crítico con las normas de otras ramas del derecho. Los tribunales superiores solo han intentado lograr comprender la causalidad de relevancia específica al derecho de refugiados en raras ocasiones, incluidas las cuestiones críticas de un estándar de causalidad y los tipos de pruebas que deberían informar la investigación de la causalidad.

دليل ميشيغان حول الارتباط السببي بالأسباب المنصوص عليها في الاتفاقية الدولية

لقد ارتكزت جهود المبذولة لربط تعريف اللاجئ كما توضحه الاتفاقية بالظروف الراهنة على إعادة تفسير الظروف التي يمكن بسببها القول أن شخص ما يتعرض " لخطر الاضطهاد"، أو على شرح مضمون الأسباب الخمسة ألا وهي العرق أو الدين أو الجنسية أو الانتماء لمجموعة اجتماعية معينه أو رأي سياسي والتي بسببها يمكن أن يتعرض الشخص لخطر الاضطهاد بشكل يتماشى مع الوقت المعاصر. ولكن إذا نظرنا للفقه المقارن، سوف نلاحظ أنه تم توجيه القليل من الجهود لشرح العلاقة بين أسباب الاضطهاد نفسه من جهة وبين وجود خطر الاضطهاد من جهة أخرى. أحد الأسئلة المهمة هنا هي: ففي أي الظروف يمكننا الجزم بأن خطر التعرض للاضطهاد مرتبط "بأحد" الأسباب الخمسة التي حددتها الاتفاقية الدولية؟

تخلو قوانين العديد من الدول الرائدة في مجال منح صفة اللجوء من تنظيم وشرح واضح لهذه الأسباب، وفي نفس الوقت تعتبر الكثير من الدول إنه يمكن استخدام تشريعات من أفرع قانونيه أخرى لتفسير العلاقة السببية في القانون الدولي للاجئين. وفي بعض الأحوال النادرة تحاول بعض المحاكم العليا الوصول لشرح أكثر دقة لمسألة السببية في الاتفاقية الدولية بالرجوع إلى قانون اللاجئين الدولي نفسه. وقد اشتملت هذه المحاولات على طرح بعض الأسئلة المحورية المتعلقة بالعلاقة السببية وأنواع الأدلة التي يمكن الاعتماد عليها عند التحقق من العلاقة السببية من الخوف من الاضطهاد والأسباب الواردة في الاتفاقية.

МИЧИГАНСКИЕ РЕКОММЕНДАЦИИ ОТНОСИТЕЛЬНО ПРИЧИННОЙ СВЯЗИ С ОСНОВАНИЯМИ КОНВЕНЦИИ

В современных условиях, меры по обеспечению жизнеспособности приводимого в Конвенции определения понятия "беженец", как правило, сосредоточены на совершенствовании нашего понимания обстоятельств, в которых индивидуума можно охарактерезовать как находящегося "под угрозой преследований", или на придании современного значения содержанию пяти признаков, на которых базируется понятие "риск преследования": раса, вероисповедание, граждан-ство, принадлежность к определенной социальной группе или политические убеждения. Сравнительно мало внимания уделялось тому, как лучше понять при-чинную связь (или нексус) между основанием Конвенции и угрозой стать жертвой преследований. При каких обстоятельствах можно сказать, что угроза возникла "по причинам" наличия одного из пяти признаков, указанных в Конвенции?

Судебная практика многих ведущих государств, предоставляющих убежище, попросту не освещает этот вопрос, тогда как решения, принимаемые в других странах, основываются на том, что причинность в области права, касающегося беженцев, может определяться посредством проведения некритичной аналогии со стандартами других областей права. Лишь изредка суды высокой инстанции добросовестно пытались прийти к пониманию причинности, как имеющей особое значение в законодательстве по правам беженцев, включая важнейшие вопросы о критерии причинности и видах доказательств, на которые должно опираться изучение причинности.

With a view to promoting a shared understanding of the basic requirements for the recognition of Convention refugee status, we have engaged in sustained collaborative study and reflection on the norms and state practice relevant to the causation inquiry. This research was debated and refined at the Second Colloquium on Challenges in International Refugee Law, convened in March 2001 by the University of Michigan's Program in Refugee and Asylum Law. These Guidelines are the product of that endeavor, and reflect the consensus of Colloquium participants on how the causal nexus to a Convention ground should be understood in international refugee law.

Afin de promouvoir une interprétation commune des conditions de reconnaissance du statut de réfugié au sens de la Convention, nous avons entrepris une étude et une réflexion approfondies et communes sur les normes et la pratique des États relatives à l'analyse du lien causalité. Les résultats de cette recherche ont été débattus et affinés à l'occasion du second colloque sur les défis du droit international des réfugiés, organisé en mars 2001 par le programme de droit d'asile et des réfugiés de l'université du Michigan. Ces recommandations sont le résultat de cette initiative et reflètent le consensus des participants au colloque sur l'interprétation du lien de causalité avec un motif conventionnel.

Con miras a promover una comprensión compartida de los requisitos básicos para reconocer la condición de refugiado en virtud de la Convención, hemos realizado un estudio y una reflexión sostenidos y colaborativos sobre las normas y la práctica estatal pertinentes para la investigación de la causalidad. Esta investigación se debatió y se perfeccionó en el Segundo Coloquio sobre Desafíos en el Derecho Internacional de los Refugiados, celebrado en marzo de 2001 por el Programa de Legislación en materia de Refugio y Asilo de la Universidad de Michigan. Estas directrices son el producto de dicho esfuerzo y reflejan el consenso de los participantes del Coloquio sobre cómo debe entenderse el nexo causal con un motivo contemplado en la Convención en el derecho internacional de los refugiados.

GENERAL CONSIDERATIONS

1 Not every person who is outside his or her own country and has a well-founded fear of being persecuted is a Convention refugee. The risk faced by the applicant must be causally linked to at least one of the five grounds enumerated in the Convention—race, religion, nationality, membership of a particular social group or political opinion.

CONSIDÉRATIONS GÉNÉRALES

1. Toute personne qui se trouve hors de son pays d'origine et qui éprouve une crainte fondée d'être persécutée n'est pas un réfugié au sens de la Convention. Le risque encouru doit résulter d'un lien de causalité avec au moins l'un des cinq motifs de persécution énumérés par la Convention – race, religion, nationalité, appartenance à un certain groupe social ou opinion politique.

CONSIDERACIONES GENERALES

1. No todas las personas que se encuentran fuera de su propio país y tienen un temor fundado de ser perseguidos son refugiados en virtud de la Convención. El riesgo que enfrenta el solicitante debe presentar una relación causal con al menos uno de los cinco motivos enumerados contemplados en la Convención: raza, religión, nacionalidad, pertenencia a un determinado grupo social u opiniones políticas.

2 In many states, the requisite causal linkage is explicitly addressed on the basis of the requirement that a refugee's well-founded fear of being persecuted be '. . . *for reasons of* race, religion, nationality, membership of a particular social group or political opinion . . .' In other states causation is not treated as a free-standing definitional requirement, but rather is subsumed within the analysis of other Convention requirements. Whether treated as an independent definitional factor or as part of a general understanding of refugee status, the existence of a nexus to a Convention ground must be assessed in the light of the text, context, objects and purposes of the Refugee Convention and Protocol.

2. Dans beaucoup d'États, le lien de causalité requis est interprété explicitement comme impliquant une crainte fondée de persécution dans le chef du demandeur « du fait de sa race, de sa religion, de sa nationalité, de son appartenance à un certain groupe social ou de ses opinions politiques ». Dans d'autres États, le lien de causalité n'est pas interprété comme une exigence distincte, mais est incorporé au sein de l'analyse des autres conditions de reconnaissance de la qualité de réfugié consacrées par la Convention. Qu'il soit analysé en tant que critère distinct ou relevant d'une appréciation générale des conditions de reconnaissance de la qualité de réfugié, le lien de causalité doit être interprété à la lumière du texte, du contexte, de l'objet et des objectifs de la Convention de Genève et de son protocole additionnel.

2. En muchos estados, el vínculo causal requerido se aborda explícitamente en base al requisito de que el temor fundado de un refugiado de ser perseguido sea *"por motivos de* raza, religión, nacionalidad, pertenencia a un determinado grupo social u opiniones políticas"*. En otros estados, la causalidad no se trata como un requisito de definición autónomo, sino que se incluye en el análisis de otros requisitos de la Convención. Ya sea que se trate como un factor de definición independiente o como parte de una comprensión general de la condición de refugiado, la existencia de un nexo con un motivo contemplado en la Convención debe evaluarse a la luz del texto, el contexto, los objetos y los propósitos de la Convención y el Protocolo de Refugiados.

ولتقديم فهم مشترك للمتطلبات الأساسية التي تشترطها الاتفاقية للاعتراف بصفة اللجوء، قمنا بعمل دراسة جماعية مستفيضة تبحث في المبادئ وممارسات الدول المرتبطة بالتحقق من العلاقات السببية. ولقد تم تخصيص الدورة الثانية من سلسلة ورش العمل لهذه الدراسة. وقد تم ذلك في شهر مارس 2001، حيث استضاف برنامج قانون اللاجئين والملاذ بجامعة ميشيغان هذه الورشة. ويمثل دليل ميشيغان نتيجة لهذا المجهود الجماعي، ويعبر عن توافق جماعي لكل المشاركين في ورش العمل، وخاصة حول كيفية فهم الأسباب المُبَّررة كأساس تطبيقي للاتفاقية الدولية، من خلال نظرة سياقية لهذه الأسباب كجزء من القانون الدولي للاجئين.

С целью обеспечить общее понимание основных требований к признанию статуса беженца в соответствии с Конвенцией, мы провели продолжительное совместное исследование и обсуждение норм и практики государств, представляющих ценный материал для изучения причинности. Результаты этого исследования обсуждались и уточнялись на Втором коллоквиуме по проблемам международного законодательства по правам беженцев, который состоялся в марте 2001 года в рамках Программы Мичиганского университета по законодательству о правах беженцев и предоставлении убежища. Данные *Рекоммендации* являются итогом этих усилий и отражают консенсус участников Коллоквиума по вопросу о том, как причинная связь с основанием Конвенции должна пониматься в международном законодательстве по правам беженцев.

اعتبارات عامة

1. لا يعتبر لاجئاً وفقاً للاتفاقية الدولية للاجئين أي شخص خارج أرض وطنه له ديه خوف معقول بتعرضه للاضطهاد أو الخطر بصفة عامة. لكن يجب أن يرتبط هذا الخطر أو الاضطهاد ارتباطاً سببياً بأحد الأسباب الخمسة التي حددتها الاتفاقية الدولية على سبيل الحصر وهي: العرق أو الدين أو الجنسية أو الانتماء لجماعة اجتماعية معينة أو تبنيه رأيا سياسيا معيناً.

ОБЩИЕ СООБРАЖЕНИЯ

1. Не каждый индивидуум, находящийся за пределами своей страны и имеющий вполне обоснованные опасения стать жертвой преследований, является, согласно Конвенции, беженцем. Риск, с которым сталкивается заявитель, должен иметь причинную связь, по меньшей мере, с одним из пяти признаков, перечисленных в Конвенции: раса, вероисповедание, гражданство, принадлежность к определенной социальной группе или политические убеждения.

---

2. تشترط بعض الدول أن يتم تعريف الارتباط السببي - بين الاضطهاد وبين أحد هذه الأسباب الخمسة السالفة الذكر - بطريقة واضحة ومستقلة بذاتها، كلما كان هناك طلب بأن هناك خوف معقول بحدوث الاضطهاد " بسبب العرق أو الدين أو الجنسية أو الانتماء لمجموعة اجتماعية معينة أو رأي سياسي. . . ". إلا أن دول أخرى لا ترى التحقق من توافر هذا الارتباط السببي مسألة مستقلة بذاتها بل يجب أن يأتي في السياق العام لاشتراطات الاتفاقية الدولية. وسواء تم التعامل مع الارتباط السببي بشكل مستقل كعامل تعريفي أو في السياق العام لمتطلبات الاتفاقية الدولية ككل، يجب أن يتم هذا التحقيق في ضوء نص وسياق وأهداف وغايات الاتفاقية الدولية للاجئين نفسها والبروتوكول المتعلق بها.

2. Во многих государствах требуемая причинная связь непосредственно рассматривается на основании того, что вполне обоснованные опасения беженца стать жертвой преследования должны возникнуть "... *по причине* расовой принадлежности, вероисповедания, гражданства, принадлежности к определенной социальной группе или политических взглядов . . .". В других странах причинность не рассматривается в качестве отдельного дефиниционного требования, но относится к какой-либо категории, анализируемой при рассмотрении других требований Конвенции. Независимо от того, рассматривается ли существование связи с конвенционным признаком как независимый определяющий фактор или как часть общего осмысления статуса беженца, оно должно оцениваться в свете текста, контекста, целей и задач Конвенции о беженцах и ее Протокола.

3. It is not the duty of the applicant accurately to identify the reason that he or she has a well-founded fear of being persecuted. The state assessing the claim to refugee status shall decide which, if any, Convention ground is relevant to the applicant's well-founded fear of being persecuted.

3. Il ne revient pas au demandeur d'identifier précisément le motif pour lequel il éprouve une crainte avec raison de persécution. L'autorité en charge de la détermination du statut de réfugié doit évaluer si un motif conventionnel constitue un facteur d'une quelconque pertinence dans la crainte avec raison du demandeur.

3. El solicitante no tiene la obligación de identificar con precisión la razón por la cual tiene un temor fundado a ser perseguido. El estado que evalúa la solicitud de reconocimiento de la condición de refugiado decidirá cuál de los fundamentos de la Convención, si los hay, es relevante en cuanto al temor fundado del solicitante a ser perseguido.

4. The risk of being persecuted may sometimes arise in circumstances where two or more Convention grounds combine in the same person, in which case the combination of such grounds defines the causal connection to the well-founded fear of being persecuted.

4. Le risque de subir une persécution peut résulter de circonstances où deux ou plusieurs motifs de persécution se mêlent, auquel cas l'évaluation du lien de causalité doit se réaliser en prenant en considération leur effet combiné.

4. El riesgo de ser perseguido a veces puede surgir en circunstancias en las que dos o más motivos de la Convención se combinen en la misma persona, en cuyo caso la combinación de tales motivos define la conexión causal con el temor fundado a ser perseguido.

5. An individual shall not be expected to deny his or her protected identity or beliefs in order to avoid coming to the attention of the State or non-governmental agent of persecution.

5. Il ne peut être exigé d'un individu qu'il abandonne une caractéristique individuelle protégée ou une croyance afin d'échapper à l'attention de l'État ou d'acteurs non étatiques de persécution.

5. No se debe esperar que un individuo niegue su identidad o creencias protegidas para evitar llamar la atención del Estado o del agente no gubernamental que lo persigue.

NATURE OF THE REQUIRED CAUSAL LINK

6. The causal connection required is between a Convention ground and the applicant's well-founded fear of 'being persecuted' (in French, '. . . d'être persécutée . . .') The focus on the applicant's predicament follows both from the passive voice employed in the official texts of the Convention and from the Convention's fundamental purpose of defining the circumstances in which surrogate international protection is warranted.

LA NATURE DU LIEN DE CAUSALITÉ

6. Le lien de causalité est requis entre un motif conventionnel et la crainte avec raison du demandeur d'« être persécuté » (en anglais, « of being persecuted »). L'usage de la forme passive dans la version officielle de la Convention, de même que son objectif principal, qui consiste à identifier les circonstances dans lesquelles une protection internationale, subsidiaire à la protection nationale, est nécessaire, impliquent que l'analyse doit se concentrer sur la situation personnelle du demandeur.

NATURALEZA DEL NEXO CAUSAL REQUERIDO

6. La conexión causal requerida es entre un motivo contemplado en la Convención y el temor fundado del solicitante a "ser perseguido" (en francés, "d'etre persécuté"). El foco en la difícil situación del solicitante se ve reflejado tanto en la utilización de la voz pasiva en los textos oficiales de la Convención como en el propósito fundamental de la Convención de definir las circunstancias en las que se justifica la protección internacional sustitutiva.

3. لا يتحمل مقدم طلب اللجوء مسؤولية تحديد السبب الذي على أساسه يتعرض لخطر الاضطهاد. لكن على الدولة التي تلقت طلب اللجوء إن تحقق من الارتباط السببي بين حاله هذا الشخص وأي من الأسباب الخمسة التي حددتها الاتفاقية من عدمها.

3. В обязанности заявителя не входит точное определение причины, по которой он или она испытывает вполне обоснованные опасения стать жертвой преследования. Государство, оценивающее ходатайство о предоставлении статуса беженца, должно решить, какое основание Конвенции, если таковое имеется, относится к вполне обоснованным опасениям заявителя стать жертвой преследований.

4. أحياناً يمكن إن يتعرض الشخص لخطر الاضطهاد إلى سببين أو أكثر م الأسباب المذكورة في الاتفاقية، في تلك الحالات، فأن البحث في الارتباط السببي يكون عن لمدى توافر العلاقة بين هذه الأسباب مجتمعة ووجود الاضطهاد أو خطر التعرض له بدلاً من البحث في مدى توافر كل سبب على حدة.

4. Угроза подвергнуться преследованию иногда возникает при таких обстоятельствах, когда в отношении одного и того же лица совмещаются два или более основания Конвенции, и в этом случае сочетание названных оснований определяет причинную связь с вполне обоснованными опасениями стать жертвой преследований.

5. يجب ألا يتوقع من الشخص إنكار هويته أو معتقداته ــ اللذين يخضعا للحماية ــ خشية أن يصل ذلك إلى علم الدولة أو الجماعة الأهلية اللذان يلاحقانه بالاضطهاد.

5. Не следует ожидать от индивидуума, что он или она откажется от возможности защитить свою личность или взгляды ради того, чтобы не попасть в сферу пристального внимания государства или негосударственного лица, от которых исходит угроза преследования.

طبيعة الارتباط السببي المطلوب توافره

6. إن الارتباط السببي الذي يشترط توافره يجب أن يتحقق بين وجود أساس معقول للخوف (الخوف المُبرر) لدى طالب اللجوء من جهة وبين أحد الأسس الخمسة التي يُبنى عليها الاضطهاد، كما وردت بالاتفاقية من جهة أخرى. وبالطبع، يُتوقع من صاحب الطلب التركيز على العقبات التي تواجهه والتي تبرر طلبه للجوء. ويمكن تقديم هذه العقبات من خلال تأويل نصوص الاتفاقية التي جاءت في معظمها في صيغة المبني للمجهول من ناحية والبحث في الغرض الأساسي للاتفاقية، والذي يرتبط بتعريف الظروف التي يمكن فيها استبدال الحماية الداخلية الضرورية أو المعقولة بأخرى خارجية من ناحية أخرى.

СУЩНОСТЬ ТРЕБУЕМОЙ ПРИЧИННОЙ СВЯЗИ

6. Требуемая причинная связь является связью между одним из пяти признаков, указанных в Конвенции и вполне обоснованными опасениями заявителя *"стать жертвой преследований"* (по-французски ". . . *d'etre persecute* . . ."). Сосредоточение внимания на затруднительном положении заявителя следует как из страдательного залога, используемого в официальных текстах Конвенции, так и из основного предназначения Конвенции, заключающегося в определении обстоятельств, при которых предоставление суррогатной международной защиты оправдано.

7. Because it is the applicant's predicament which must be causally linked to a Convention ground, the fact that his or her subjective fear is based on a Convention ground is insufficient to justify recognition of refugee status.

7. Puisque la situation personnelle du demandeur doit être en lien causal avec un motif conventionnel, la circonstance qu'il fonde subjectivement sa crainte sur pareil motif est insuffisante pour justifier la reconnaissance de la qualité de réfugié.

7. Debido a que la situación del solicitante debe presentar una relación causal con un motivo contemplado en la Convención, el hecho de que su temor subjetivo se base en un motivo contemplado en la Convención es insuficiente para justificar el reconocimiento de la condición de refugiado.

8. The causal link between the applicant's predicament and a Convention ground will be revealed by evidence of the reasons which led either to the infliction or threat of a relevant harm, or which cause the applicant's country of origin to withhold effective protection in the face of a privately inflicted risk. Attribution of the Convention ground to the applicant by the state or non-governmental agent of persecution is sufficient to establish the required causal connection.

8. Le lien de causalité entre la situation personnelle du demandeur et un motif conventionnel peut être identifié au travers d'une analyse des preuves établissant les motifs à l'origine de la menace ou de la souffrance invoquée, ou de l'absence de protection effective émanant des autorités du pays d'origine face à un risque émanant d'un acteur privé. L'attribution au demandeur d'un motif conventionnel par l'État ou un acteur non étatique de persécution suffit à établir le lien de causalité.

8. El nexo causal entre la situación del solicitante y un motivo de contemplado en la Convención se revelará mediante pruebas de los motivos que hayan conducido a la pronunciación de amenazas o provocación de daños relevantes, o que hagan que el país de origen del solicitante niegue la protección efectiva frente a un riesgo causado por particulares. El hecho de que el agente de persecución estatal o no gubernamental atribuya el motivo contemplado en la Convención al solicitante es suficiente para establecer la conexión causal requerida.

9. A causal link may be established whether or not there is evidence of particularized enmity, malignity or *animus* on the part of the person or group responsible for infliction or threat of a relevant harm, or on the part of a State which withholds its protection from persons at risk of relevant privately inflicted harm.

9. Un lien de causalité peut être établi sans qu'il y ait preuve d'une animosité, d'un dol ou d'un *animus* spécial dans le chef de la personne ou du groupe à l'origine d'une menace ou d'une souffrance, ou dans le chef de l'État qui n'octroie pas de protection face aux agissements d'un acteur privé.

9. Se puede establecer un vínculo causal ya sea que haya o no evidencia de enemistad, malignidad o *ánimo* particular por parte de la persona o el grupo responsable de la pronunciación de amenazas o provocación de daños relevantes, o por parte de un Estado que se niegue a brindar protección a personas que se encuentren en riesgo de sufrir daños relevantes causados por un particular.

10. The causal link may also be established in the absence of any evidence of intention to harm or to withhold protection, so long as it is established that the Convention ground contributes to the applicant's exposure to the risk of being persecuted.

10. Le lien de causalité peut également être établi en l'absence de toute preuve d'une intention de causer une souffrance ou de ne pas accorder de protection, pour autant qu'il soit établi que le motif conventionnel contribue à exposer le demandeur à un risque d'être persécuté.

10. El nexo causal también puede establecerse en ausencia de evidencia de intención de dañar o de negar protección, siempre y cuando se establezca que el motivo contemplado en la Convención contribuye a la exposición del solicitante al riesgo de ser perseguido.

7. أن المصاعب التي قد يواجها الشخص يجب إن تظهر علاقة شرطيه بالأسباب المذكورة في المعاهدة إلا أن هذا الارتباط في حد ذاته لا يمثل بالضرورة اعترافا بصفة اللاجئ لذلك الشخص.

7. Поскольку затруднительное положение, в котором находится заявитель, должно иметь причинную связь с одним из признаков, закрепленных Конвенцией, самого факта, что субъективные опасения заявителя связаны с Конвенцией, недостаточно для того, чтобы обосновать предоставление статуса беженца.

---

8. يمكن استنتاج وجود ارتباط بين العقبات التي تواجه طالب اللجوء وأحد الأسباب الخمسة المحددة بالاتفاقية من خلال التحقق من وجود أدلة على وجود أسباب أدت إلى الإيذاء الفعلي أو تهديد هذا الشخص بالإيذاء من حكومة الدولة التي ينتمي إليها طالب اللجوء، أو أن يكون هذا الإيذاء أو التهديد به قد وقع من قبل جماعة أهلية في الدولة، ولم تستطع حكومته أو توقفت عن توفير حماية فعالة له. ويكفي لصاحب الطلب أن يثبت إن حكومة أو جماعة أهلية في بلده الأصلي تقوم باضطهاده أو بتهديده بالاضطهاد وإن هذا الاضطهاد أو التهديد به يرجع لأحد الأسباب الخمسة المحددة في الاتفاقية لكي يتوافر الارتباط السببي الذي يشترط وجوده لمنح صفة اللجوء.

8. Причинная связь между затруднительным положением заявителя и одним из Конвенционных признаков выявляется через приведение свидетельств, которые привели либо к нанесению существенного вреда, либо к угрозе такового, или которые послужили поводом того, что страна происхождения заявителя вынуждена была отказаться от предоставления эффективной защиты перед лицом опасности, исходящей от частного лица. Отнесение признака Конвенции к заявителю, преследуемому государством или негосударственным лицом, является достаточным для установления требуемой причинной связи.

---

9. لا يُشترط لإثبات وجود ارتباط سببي بين الاضطهاد وأحد أسبابه الخمسة المحددة في الاتفاقية تقديم أدلة أو إثبات على وجود حاله عداء أو كراهية أو نقد شديد بين طالب اللجوء والجهة المسؤولة عن اضطهاده أو إيذائه، أو إثبات إن حالة العداء هذه تتوفر بين طالب اللجوء والمسؤولين في المكان أو القطاع أو الدولة الذي قرر منع أو توقيف الحماية الداخلية لهذا الشخص.

9. Причинная связь может быть установлена вне зависимости от наличия доказательств конкретной враждебности, злонамеренности или предвзятого отношения [animus] со стороны какого-либо лица или группы, ответственных за нанесение вреда или угрозу такового, или со стороны государства, отказавшегося от предоставления защиты лицам, которым угрожает существенная опасность, исходящая из неофициального источника.

---

10. لا يُشترط أيضاً لإثبات وجود ارتباط سببي بين الاضطهاد وأحد أسبابه الخمسة المحددة في الاتفاقية تقديم أدلة أو إثبات وجود قصد أو نية لإيذاء أو اضطهاد شخص طالب اللجوء. يكفي أن يتم التحقق من أن طالب اللجوء قد تم اضطهاده بالفعل أو أنه مُعرض للاضطهاد بسبب أحد الأسباب الخمسة المحددة في الاتفاقية.

10. Причинная связь может быть также установлена при отсутствии каких-либо доказательств намерений причинить ущерб или отказать в защите, если будет доказано, что основание Конвенции способствует пониманию того, что заявитель может стать жертвой преследования.

STANDARD OF CAUSATION

11. Standards of causation developed in other branches of international or domestic law ought not to be assumed to have relevance to the recognition of refugee status. Because refugee status determination is both protection-oriented and forward-looking, it is unlikely that pertinent guidance can be gleaned from standards of causation shaped by considerations relevant to the assessment of civil or criminal liability, or which are directed solely to the analysis of past events.

LE DEGRÉ DE CAUSALITÉ

11. Il ne peut être présumé que les divers degrés de causalité exigés par d'autres branches du droit international ou national sont pertinents pour aboutir à la reconnaissance du statut de réfugié. La procédure de détermination du statut de réfugié étant orientée vers la protection effective du demandeur et l'évaluation du risque futur, il est peu probable que des critères pertinents puissent se déduire des standards de causalité élaborés en fonction de considérations relatives à la responsabilité civile ou pénale, ou qui s'appliquent exclusivement à une évaluation d'événements passés.

ESTÁNDAR DE CAUSALIDAD

11. No se debe suponer que las normas de causalidad desarrolladas en otras ramas del derecho internacional o nacional tienen relevancia para el reconocimiento de la condición de refugiado. Dado que la determinación de la condición de refugiado está orientada a la protección y al futuro de la persona en cuestión, es poco probable que pueda obtenerse una orientación pertinente de las normas de causalidad determinadas por consideraciones relevantes para la evaluación de la responsabilidad civil o penal, o que estén dirigidas únicamente al análisis de acontecimientos pasados.

12. The standard of causation must also take account of the practical realities of refugee status determination, in particular the complex combinations of circumstances which may give rise to the risk of being persecuted, the prevalence of evidentiary gaps, and the difficulty of eliciting evidence across linguistic and cultural divides.

12. Le degré de causalité doit également prendre en considération les difficultés concrètes qui se posent dans le cadre de la procédure de détermination du statut de réfugié, en particulier la combinaison complexe de diverses circonstances qui engendrent un risque d'être persécuté, l'existence de circonstances ne pouvant être prouvées et la difficulté de collecter des preuves en raison d'obstacles linguistiques et culturels.

12. El estándar de causalidad también debe tener en cuenta las realidades prácticas de la determinación de la condición de refugiado. En particular, las complejas combinaciones de circunstancias que pueden dar lugar al riesgo de ser perseguido, la prevalencia de brechas probatorias y la dificultad de recoger evidencia debido a barreras de tipo lingüístico y cultural.

13. In view of the unique objects and purposes of refugee status determination, and taking account of the practical challenges of refugee status determination, the Convention ground need not be shown to be the sole, or even the dominant, cause of the risk of being persecuted. It need only be a contributing factor to the risk of being persecuted. If, however, the Convention ground is remote to the point of irrelevance, refugee status need not be recognized.

13. La particularité de l'objet et des objectifs de la procédure de détermination du statut de réfugié, de même que les difficultés pratiques qui se posent, impliquent que le motif conventionnel ne doit pas être le seul motif à l'origine du risque d'être persécuté, ni même le motif dominant. Il suffit qu'il soit un motif contribuant au risque d'être persécuté. S'il s'avère toutefois que la contribution du motif au risque d'être persécuté est à ce point accessoire que ce motif perd toute pertinence, le statut de réfugié ne doit pas être reconnu.

13. En vista de los objetos y propósitos únicos de la determinación de la condición de refugiado, y teniendo en cuenta los desafíos prácticos de la determinación de la condición de refugiado, no es necesario demostrar que el motivo contemplado en la Convención sea la única causa del riesgo de ser perseguido, ni siquiera la causa dominante. Solo necesita ser un factor que contribuya al riesgo de ser perseguido. Sin embargo, si el motivo contemplado en la Convención es remoto hasta el punto de la irrelevancia, no es necesario reconocer la condición de refugiado.

EVIDENCE OF CAUSATION

14. The requisite causal connection between the risk of being persecuted and a Convention ground may be established by either direct or circumstantial evidence.

LA PREUVE DU LIEN DE CAUSALITÉ

14. Le lien de causalité requis entre le risque d'être persécuté et un motif conventionnel peut être établi par des preuves directes ou circonstancielles.

EVIDENCIA DE CAUSALIDAD

14. La conexión causal requerida entre el riesgo de ser perseguido y un motivo contemplado en la Convención puede establecerse mediante pruebas directas o circunstanciales.

معيار الارتباط السببي

11. Критерии причинности, выработанные в других отраслях международного права или национального законодательства не должны приниматься во внимание при признании статуса беженца. Поскольку установление статуса беженца ориентировано как на предоставление защиты в настоящем, так и обращено к будущему, маловероятно, что соответствующее руководство можно извлечь из критериев причинности, выработанных соображениями, касающимися оценки гражданской и уголовной ответственности, или направленных исключительно на анализ событий прошлого.

11. يجب عدم الاسترشاد بالمعايير السببية المستخدمة في فروع القوانين الأخرى سواء المحلية أو الدولية عند البحث في مسألة منح صفة اللجوء. والسبب في ذلك هو أن قرارات تحديد ومنح صفة اللجوء هي قرارات تهدف للحماية وتسعى لخلق علاقات مستقبلية. كما أنه من غير المتوقع أن تكون معايير تحديد رابطة السببية في الأفرع المختلفة للقانون ذات فائدة إرشادية كبيرة، نظراً لأن مثل هذه المعايير تخضع لاعتبارات ضيقة محددة تتعلق بتحديد المسؤولية الجنائية أو المدنية، كما أن هذه المعايير معظمها مخصص لإقرار أمور تتعلق بمسؤوليات وقعت في الماضي.

12. Критерий причинности должен также учитывать практические реалии процедуры установления статуса беженца, в особенности сложные переплетения обстоятельств, являющихся потенциальной причиной угрозы преследований, распространенность пробелов в доказательной базе и сложность получения доказательств в силу языковых и культурных различий.

12. يجب أخذ الكثير من الأمور الهامة التي تتعلق بالوقائع والصعوبات العملية في الاعتبار عند البحث في وجود ارتباط سببي عند إقرار صفة اللجوء. ومن أمثلة هذه الوقائع والصعوبات: تلك الظروف المتشابكة والمعقدة التي تساهم في خلق خطر التعرض للاضطهاد، أو حالة ما إذا كانت هناك فجوات أو صعوبات في الحصول على أدلة، أو الصعوبات التي يمكن أن تعيق الاستنباط من أدلة معينة بسبب وجود بعض الصعوبات أو الحواجز اللغوية والثقافية.

13. Учитывая уникальные цели и задачи установления статуса беженца, и принимая во внимание практические трудности при установлении этого статуса, нет необходимости доказывать, что Конвенционные признаки являются единственной или даже доминирующей мотивировкой в определении угрозы оказаться жертвой преследований. Это должно быть лишь фактором, способствующим установлению наличия угрозы стать жертвой преследований. Однако, если признаки, закрепленные в Конвенции, настолько далеки от реальности, что становятся незначащими, нет необходимости в признании статуса беженца.

13. عند إقرار صفة اللجوء من عدمها، لا يجب النظر لأي من الأسباب الخمسة للاضطهاد أو خطر الاضطهاد ـ كما وردت بالاتفاقية ـ باعتبارها الأسباب الوحيدة أو الأغلب لوجود خطر الاضطهاد أو الاضطهاد الفعلي، حيث يجب أخذ الكثير من الأمور الأخرى الهامة في الاعتبار عند إقرار هذه الصفة. ومن أمثلة هذه الاعتبارات الأهداف والغايات الفريدة لقرار تحديد صفة اللجوء، وأيضاً كافة الصعوبات العملية المتعلقة بتحديد هذه الصفة. فيكفي عند تحديد صفة اللجوء وجود أحد هذه الأسباب الخمسة كأحد العوامل المُساهمة لخلق حالة الاضطهاد. لكن إذا ظهر بالطبع إن هذا السبب من الضعف لدرجة انعدام صلته تماماً بحدوث الاضطهاد، فأنه من المنطقي رفض إقرار صفة اللجوء في هذه الحالة.

الأدلة المعتبرة لإقرار الارتباط السببي

ДОКАЗАТЕЛЬСТВА ПРИЧИННОСТИ

14. Требуемая причинная связь между риском оказаться жертвой преследований и одним из оснований Конвенции может быть установлена посредством как прямых, так и косвенных доказательств.

14. يمكن الاعتماد على أدلة مباشرة أو أدلة ظرفية لإقرار وجود ارتباط سببي بين حدوث الاضطهاد وأحد الأسباب الواردة في الاتفاقية.

15. A fear of being persecuted is for reasons of a Convention ground whether it is experienced as an individual, or as part of a group. Thus, evidence that persons who share the applicant's race, religion, nationality, membership of a particular social group or political opinion are more at risk of being persecuted than others in the home country is a sufficient form of circumstantial evidence that a Convention ground was a contributing factor to the risk of being persecuted.

15. Il existe une crainte d'être persécuté en raison d'un motif conventionnel lorsque cette crainte est ressentie en tant qu'individu isolé ou en tant qu'individu membre d'un groupe. Il en résulte que des preuves selon lesquelles des individus qui partagent la race, la religion, la nationalité, l'appartenance à un certain groupe social ou les opinions politiques du demandeur subissent un risque plus élevé de subir une persécution dans le pays d'origine, sont des preuves circonstancielles suffisantes pour établir qu'un motif conventionnel a contribué à l'émergence du risque pour cet individu d'être persécuté.

15. El temor a ser perseguido se debe a motivos de la Convención, ya sea que se experimente como individuo o como parte de un grupo. Por lo tanto, la evidencia de que las personas que comparten la raza, religión, nacionalidad, pertenencia a un determinado grupo social u opiniones políticas del solicitante corren más riesgo de ser perseguidas que otras personas en el país de origen es evidencia suficiente de que un motivo contemplado en la Convención fue un factor que contribuyó al riesgo de ser perseguido.

16. There is, however, no requirement that an applicant for asylum be more at risk than other persons or groups in his or her country of origin. The relevant question is instead whether the Convention ground is causally connected to the applicant's predicament, irrespective of whether other individuals or groups also face a well-founded fear of being persecuted for the same or a different Convention ground.

16. Il n'y a, toutefois, pas d'exigence qu'un demandeur d'asile soit soumis à un risque d'être persécuté plus important que d'autres personnes ou groupes de son pays d'origine. Il s'agit plutôt de déterminer si le motif conventionnel est en lien causal avec la situation personnelle du demandeur, indépendamment de la question de savoir si d'autres individus ou groupes sont également confrontés à une crainte fondée d'être persécutés pour un motif conventionnel identique ou distinct.

16. Sin embargo, no existe un requisito en cuanto a que un solicitante de asilo corra más riesgo que otras personas o grupos en su país de origen. En cambio, la cuestión relevante es si el motivo contemplado en la Convención presenta una relación causal con la situación del solicitante, independientemente de si otras personas o grupos también enfrentan un temor fundado a ser perseguidos por el mismo motivo contemplado en la Convención o por uno diferente.

17. No special rule governs application of the causal nexus standard in the case of refugees who come from a country in which there is a risk of war or other large-scale violence or oppression. Applicants who come from such a country are not automatically Convention refugees. They are nonetheless entitled to be recognized as refugees if their race, religion, nationality, membership of a particular social group or political opinion is a contributing factor to their well-founded fear of being persecuted in such circumstances. For example, persons in flight from war may be Convention refugees where either the reason for the war or the way in which the war is conducted demonstrates a causal link between a Convention ground and the risk of being persecuted.

17. Il n'existe pas de règle particulière permettant de déterminer si le lien de causalité est rencontré dans l'hypothèse où des réfugiés viennent d'un pays où le risque résulte d'une guerre ou d'autres situations de violence de grande ampleur ou d'oppression. Les demandeurs qui fuient pareilles circonstances ne sont pas nécessairement des réfugiés au sens de la Convention. Ils sont toutefois en droit d'obtenir la reconnaissance du statut de réfugié s'il s'avère que leur race, leur religion, leur nationalité, l'appartenance à un certain groupe social ou leurs opinions politiques contribuent à leur crainte fondée d'être persécutés dans pareilles situations. Par exemple, les personnes qui fuient la guerre peuvent prétendre au statut de réfugié au sens de la Convention si les causes du conflit ou la manière dont il est mené démontrent un lien de causalité entre un motif conventionnel et le risque d'être persécuté.

17. No existe ninguna norma especial que regule la aplicación del estándar del nexo causal en el caso de los refugiados que provienen de un país en el que existe el riesgo de guerra u otra situación de violencia u opresión a gran escala. Los solicitantes que provienen de un país en dichas circunstancias no se convierten en refugiados en virtud de la Convención de manera automática. Sin embargo, tienen derecho a ser reconocidos como refugiados si su raza, religión, nacionalidad, pertenencia a un determinado grupo social u opiniones políticas son un factor que contribuye a su temor fundado de ser perseguidos en tales circunstancias. Por ejemplo, los individuos que huyen de la guerra pueden ser refugiados en virtud de la Convención cuando el motivo de la guerra o la forma en que se lleve a cabo la guerra demuestre un nexo causal entre un motivo contemplado en la Convención y el riesgo de ser perseguido.

يتحقق وجود الخوف من الاضطهاد ـ اعتمادا على أحد الأسباب الواردة في الاتفاقية ـ سواء كان الشخص المعرض للاضطهاد يختبر ذلك بطريقة فردية أو كجزء من جماعة. وبناء على ذلك، يكفي لإقرار وجود خطر الاضطهاد وجود دليل يثبت أن أشخاص ما، يشاركون طالب اللجوء الأصل العرقي أو الدين أو الجنسية أو الانتماء لجماعة اجتماعية معينة أو تبني رأيا سياسياً معيناً، يتعرضون للاضطهاد أكثر من غيرهم لهذا السبب في دولة طالب اللجوء. فيعتبر مثل الدليل دليلاً ظرفياً كاف لإقرار وجود خطر الاضطهاد لطالب اللجوء.

16. بالطبع لا يُشترط أن يكون طالب اللجوء مُعرض للاضطهاد أو خطر الاضطهاد أكثر من آخرين في بلده الأصلي لإقرار وجود صفة اللجوء بالنسبة له. السؤال الأهم الذي يستحق التحقيق ـ عند البحث في توافر هذه الصفة من عدمه ـ هو هل يوجد ارتباط سببي بين أحد الأسباب المحددة في الاتفاقية الدولية من جهة بين أن تعرض هذا الشخص للاضطهاد أو وجود صعوبات أو معوقات تشير إلى وجود خطر الاضطهاد من جهة أخرى. ونظراً لأن السؤال الأهم عند البحث هو مدى توافر أحد الأسباب المحددة الواردة في الاتفاقية الدولية كمبرر للاضطهاد ومدى توافر الخوف المعقول لدي مقدم طلب اللجوء، فإن البحث في مدى وجود خوف معقول لأشخاص آخرين يتعرضون للاضطهاد لذات السبب الذي يتعرض بسببه طالب اللجوء للاضطهاد يعتبر أمر غير ذو صلة.

17. لا توجد قاعدة خاصة تحكم التحقيق في وجود رابطة السببية لحالات اللاجئين الذين قدموا من دول تعاني من أخطار الحرب أو وجود عنف يمارس على نطاق واسع على أراضيها. فلا يعتبر طالبي اللجوء من هذه البلاد لاجئين بطريقة أوتوماتيكية. وبالرغم من ذلك، فأنه يحق لهؤلاء الأشخاص الحصول على صفة اللجوء إذا كان انتمائهم العرقي أو الديني أو لجنسية معينة أو انتمائهم لجماعة اجتماعية معينة أو تبنيهم رأيا سياسيا معيناً سبباً مساهماً لوجود خوف معقول بحدوث الاضطهاد في مثل هذه الحالات (أخطار الحرب أو وجود عنف يمارس على نطاق واسع على أراضي دول هؤلاء الأشخاص الأصلية.

15. Опасение стать жертвой преследований является одним из оснований Конвенции независимо от того, испытывает ли его заявитель как отдельное или же как член какой-либо группы. Следовательно, подтверждение того, что лица, обладающие той же, что и у заявителя, расовой, религиозной, гражданской принадлежностью, являющиеся членами той же социальной группы или имеющие те же политические убеждения, в большей степени находятся под угрозой преследования, нежели другие лица, являющиеся гражданами или постоянно проживающими в той же стране. Вышесказанное является достаточной формой косвенного доказательства того, что основания Конвенции являются одним из дополнительных факторов, способствующих установлению угрозы оказаться жертвой преследований.

16. Не существует, однако, такого требования, чтобы лицу, ходатайствующему о предоставлении убежища, угрожала бóльшая опасность, чем другим лицам или группам лиц в стране его происхождения. Напротив, важным является вопрос, имеет ли одно из оснований Конвенции причинную связь с затруднительным положением заявителя, независимо от того, испытывают ли другие лица или группы лиц вполне обоснованные опасения стать жертвами преследования по тому же самому или иному основанию Конвенции.

17. Не существует особых правил, регулирующих установление причинной связи в отношении беженцев, прибывших из страны, в которой имеются предпосылки для начала войны или других видов массового насилия или притеснений. Заявители, прибывающие из таких стран, не становятся автоматически беженцами в соответствии с Конвенцией. Тем не менее, они имеют право быть признанными беженцами в случае, если их расовая принадлежность, вероисповедание, гражданство, принадлежность к определенной социальной группе или политические убеждения являются фактором, способствующим при таких обстоятельствах наличию у них вполне обоснованных опасений стать жертвами преследований. Например, лица, спасающиеся бегством от военных действий, могут быть признаны беженцами в соответствии с Конвенцией в тех случаях, когда либо причины, либо способы ведения войны демонстрируют причинную связь между одним из признаков Конвенции и угрозой стать жертвой преследований.

18. Refugee status is not restricted to persons who are members of a political, religious or other minority group. While members of minority groups are in practice more commonly exposed to the risk of being persecuted than are persons who are part of majority populations, the only requirement for recognition of refugee status is demonstration that a Convention ground is a contributing factor to the risk of being persecuted.

18. Le statut de réfugié n'est pas réservé aux membres d'un mouvement politique, religieux ou de toute autre minorité. Bien qu'en pratique les membres d'un groupe minoritaire font face à un risque d'être persécuté plus élevé que les membres d'un groupe majoritaire, la seule exigence pour la reconnaissance du statut de réfugié est d'établir qu'un motif conventionnel a contribué au risque d'être persécuté.

18. La condición de refugiado no está restringida a personas que sean miembros de un grupo político, religioso u otro grupo minoritario. Si bien los miembros de grupos minoritarios en la práctica están más expuestos al riesgo de ser perseguidos que las personas que forman parte de grupos de población mayoritarios, el único requisito para el reconocimiento de la condición de refugiado es demostrar que un motivo contemplado en la Convención es un factor que contribuye al riesgo de ser perseguido.

These Guidelines reflect the consensus of all the participants at the Second Colloquium on Challenges in International Refugee Law, held at Ann Arbor, Michigan, USA, on March 23–25, 2001.

James C. Hathaway
Colloquium Convener
University of Michigan

Rodger P.G. Haines, Q.C.
Colloquium Chair
University of Auckland

Michael Kagan
Colloquium Rapporteur
Cairo Asylum and Refugee Aid Project

T. Alexander Aleinikoff
Georgetown University

Catherine Dauvergne
University of Sydney

Suzanne J. Egan
University College Dublin

Walter Kälin
University of Bern

Jens Vedsted-Hansen
Aarhus University

Vanessa Bedford
Student
Michigan Law School

Stephanie Browning
Student
Michigan Law School

Michelle Foster
Student
Michigan Law School

Nicole Green
Student
Michigan Law School

William Johnson
Student
Michigan Law School

Noah Leavitt
Student
Michigan Law School

Elizabeth Marsh
Student
Michigan Law School

Barbara Miltner
Student
Michigan Law School

Kate Semple-Barta
Student
Michigan Law School

The Colloquium deliberations benefited from the counsel of Mr. Volker Türk, Chief, Standards and Legal Advice Section United Nations High Commissioner for Refugees

18. لا يقتصر الحصول على صفة اللاجئين على الأشخاص الذين ينتمون إلى أقليات سياسية أو دينية أو أية أقليات أخرى. بينما يشهد الواقع العملي تعرض الأشخاص الذين ينتمون إلى أقليات للاضطهاد أكثر من غيرهم من المجموعات الأخرى التي تشكل أغلبية سكانية، إلا إن الشرط الأساسي لإقرار وجود صفة اللجوء هو التأكد من إن من أحد الأسباب الخمسة الواردة في الاتفاقية يشكل سبباً مساهماً يتعرض بسببه طالب اللجوء لخطر الاضطهاد.

18. Статус беженца не ограничивается представителями политических, религиозных или иных меньшинств. Хотя на практике представители меньшинств чаще подвергаются риску стать жертвами преследований, нежели представители большинства населения, единственное требование для признания статуса беженца заключается в демонстрации того, что основания Конвенции являются одним из дополнительных факторов, способствующих установлению угрозы стать жертвой преследований.

An individual qualifies as a Convention refugee only if he or she has a 'well-founded fear' of being persecuted. While it is generally agreed that the 'well-founded fear' requirement limits refugee status to persons who face an actual, forward-looking risk of being persecuted (the 'objective element'), linguistic ambiguity has resulted in a divergence of views regarding whether the test also involves assessment of the state of mind of the person seeking recognition of refugee status (the 'subjective element').

LES RECOMMANDATIONS DE MICHIGAN SUR LA CRAINTE AVEC RAISON

Seule la personne qui éprouve une « crainte avec raison » d'être persécutée peut se voir reconnaître la qualité de réfugié au sens de la Convention. Bien qu'il soit généralement admis que l'exigence d'une « crainte avec raison » implique que le statut de réfugié soit limité aux personnes confrontées à un risque réel et futur d'être persécuté (dit l'« élément objectif »), l'ambiguïté du texte de la Convention a conduit à une divergence d'interprétation quant à la question de déterminer si l'évaluation du caractère fondé de la crainte implique également d'évaluer l'état d'esprit de la personne qui demande la reconnaissance du statut de réfugié (dit l'« élément subjectif »).

LAS DIRECTRICES DE MICHIGAN SOBRE EL TEMOR FUNDADO

Un individuo califica como refugiado en virtud de la Convención solo si tiene un "temor fundado" a ser perseguido. Si bien en general se acepta que el requisito del "temor fundado" limita la condición de refugiado a las personas que corren un riesgo real de ser perseguidos en el futuro (el "elemento objetivo"), la ambigüedad lingüística ha provocado una divergencia de opiniones sobre si la prueba también implica la evaluación del estado mental de la persona que busca el reconocimiento de la condición de refugiado (el "elemento subjetivo").

The view that the assessment of well-founded fear includes consideration of the state of mind of the person seeking recognition of refugee status is usually implemented in one of three ways. The predominant approach defines a showing of 'fear' in the sense of trepidation as one of two essential elements of the well-founded fear test. In the result, refugee status may be denied to at-risk applicants who are not in fact subjectively fearful, or whose subjective fear is not identified as such by the decision-maker. A second view does not treat the existence of subjective fear as an essential element, but considers it instead to be a factor capable of overcoming an insufficiency of evidence of actual risk. Under this formulation, persons who are more timid or demonstrative, or who are simply able to articulate their trepidation in ways recognizable as such by the decision-maker, are advantaged relative to others who face the same level of actual risk, but who are more courageous, more reserved, or whose expressions of trepidation are not identified as such. A third understanding of a subjective element neither conditions refugee status on evidence of trepidation, nor advantages claims where such trepidation exists. The requirement to take account of 'fear' is instead treated as a general duty to give attention to an applicant's specific circumstances and personal vulnerabilities in the assessment of refugee status.

Le point de vue selon lequel l'évaluation du caractère fondé de la crainte implique de s'interroger sur l'état d'esprit de la personne qui demande la reconnaissance du statut de réfugié trouve généralement son expression au travers de trois approches distinctes. L'approche dominante considère que la démonstration d'une « crainte », au sens d'un sentiment de peur, relève de l'un des deux éléments constitutifs de la « crainte avec raison ». Il en résulte que le statut de réfugié peut être refusé à un demandeur risquant d'être persécuté lorsqu'il ne ressort pas de son attitude qu'il éprouve un sentiment de peur, ou lorsque ce sentiment n'est pas identifié comme tel par l'agent en charge de la détermination du statut de réfugié. Une seconde approche ne considère pas la crainte subjective comme un élément constitutif essentiel, mais l'analyse comme un facteur de nature à justifier la reconnaissance du statut de réfugié face à l'insuffisance de preuves d'un risque réel. Il en résulte que ceux qui sont moins timides et plus démonstratifs, ou simplement qui sont en mesure de formuler leurs sentiments de peur d'une manière identifiable par l'agent en charge de la détermination du statut de réfugié, disposent d'un avantage par rapport à d'autres confrontés à un risque de même intensité, mais qui sont plus téméraires, plus réservés, ou dont le sentiment de peur n'est pas identifié comme tel. Une troisième approche consiste à ne pas conditionner la reconnaissance du statut de réfugié à la démonstration d'un sentiment de peur et à ne pas accorder de traitement plus favorable lorsque pareil sentiment est exprimé. L'exigence de prendre en considération la « crainte » du demandeur est alors comprise comme l'expression d'une obligation plus générale de tenir compte des spécificités propres à la situation du demandeur et de ses vulnérabilités personnelles dans le cadre de l'examen de sa demande de reconnaissance de la qualité de réfugié.

La opinión de que la evaluación del temor fundado incluye la consideración del estado de ánimo de la persona que pretende que se le reconozca la condición de refugiado generalmente se aplica de una de tres maneras. El enfoque predominante define una demostración de "temor" en el sentido de pánico como uno de los dos elementos esenciales de la prueba de temor fundado. En consecuencia, se puede denegar la condición de refugiado a los solicitantes en riesgo que en realidad no sientan temor de manera subjetiva, o cuyo temor subjetivo no sea identificado como tal por el responsable de tomar decisiones. Un segundo punto de vista no trata la existencia del temor subjetivo como un elemento esencial, sino que lo considera un factor capaz de superar una insuficiencia de evidencia de riesgo real. Según esta formulación, las personas que son más tímidas o demostrativas, o que simplemente son capaces de articular su miedo de tal manera que el responsable de tomar decisiones puede reconocerlo, corren con ventaja frente a otras que enfrentan el mismo nivel de riesgo real, pero que son más valientes o más reservadas, o cuyas expresiones de miedo no se identifican como tales. Una tercera comprensión de un elemento subjetivo no condiciona la condición de refugiado en función de evidencia de miedo, ni planta que existan ventajas debido a manifestaciones del miedo. El requisito de tener en cuenta el "temor" se trata, en cambio, como un deber general de prestar atención a las circunstancias específicas y las vulnerabilidades personales del solicitante al evaluar el reconocimiento de la condición de refugiado.

دليل ميشيغان الإرشادي حول إذا ما كان طالب اللجوء يعاني من خوف له ما يبرره

يُعتبر شخص ما مؤهلاً للحصول على صفة اللاجئ وفقاً للاتفاقية الدولية الخاصة بتحديد صفة اللاجئين إذا كان هذا الشخص لديه "خوف له ما يبرره" من التعرض للاضطهاد بشكل مباشر أو خطر التعرض للاضطهاد بشكل مستقبل. وبالرغم من وجود اتفاق عام على إن اشتراط " خوف له ما يبرره" يُقيد من فرص الحصول على صفة اللجوء، بجعلها قاصرة على الأشخاص الواقعون تحت خطر حدوث اضطهاد مستقبلي (وهذا مثابة الركن المادي أو الشق الموضوعي)؛ بالرغم من ذلك الاتفاق العام، إلا انه لازال هناك جدلاً كبير وتعدداً في الآراء يظهر عند تطبيق الاتفاقية الدولية فيما يتعلق بالحالة الذهنية للشخص طالب اللجوء (الركن المعنوي أو الشق الشخصي). ولقد تسبب في هذا الجدل بعض اللبس اللغوي، مما استلزم بعض التوضيح أو الشرح المفصل للوضعية المعنوية للشخص طالب اللجوء.

МИЧИГАНСКИЕ РЕКОМЕНДАЦИИ ПО УСТАНОВЛЕНИЮ ВПОЛНЕ ОБОСНОВАННЫХ ОПАСЕНИЙ ПРЕСЛЕДОВАНИЯ

Согласно Конвенции о беженцах, лицо может быть признано беженцем только в том случае, если оно имеет "вполне обоснованные опасения" подвергнуться преследованиям. В то время как существует общепринятая точка зрения на то, что требование "вполне обоснованных опасений" ограничивает предоставление статуса беженца кругом лиц, находящихся под угрозой реально существующей или ожидаемой опасности подвергнуться преследованиям ("объективный элемент"), языковая амбивалентность приводит к расхождению во взглядах относительно того, должна ли проверка указанных лиц включать в себя также оценку душевного состояния лиц, претендующих на получение статуса беженца ("субъективный элемент").

ويشهد الواقع وجود 3 صور أو أراء مختلفة تؤخذ فيها الحالة الذهنية لطالب اللجوء في الاعتبار عند البحث في منحه صفة اللجوء. ويعتمد تعريف " الخوف" وفقاً للصورة السائدة من هذه الصور الثلاث على اشتراط أن هذا الخوف يجب أن يظهر في صورة قلق أو فزع لدى طالب اللجوء، وباعتبار أن ظهور هذا القلق أو الفزع يعتبر أحد عنصرين أساسيين مطلوبين يجب البحث عنهما والتحقق من وجودهما أثناء عملية التحقيق في مدى وجود الخوف من عدمه لدى طالب اللجوء. وكثيراً ما يترتب على تبني هذا الرأي رفض منح صفة اللجوء للأشخاص والذين على الرغم من تعرضهم لخطر الاضطهاد إلا إن حالتهم تتسم بأحد المظهرين التاليين: إما أن خطر الاضطهاد لا يمكن إثباته أو أن صانع القرار لم يعترف بوجود هذا الخطر. أما الأسلوب الثاني فلا ينظر إلى الحالة الذهنية كعنصر جوهري ولكن ينظر إليه باعتباره مجرد عامل من العوامل التي يمكن أن تعوض غياب بعض الأدلة على وجود خطر الاضطهاد. ويترتب على تبني هذا الاتجاه كأساس لتقييم حالة الخوف، منح صفة اللجوء للأشخاص القادرين على التعبير عن خوفهم، أو الذين ينجحون ببساطة في شرح حالة الخوف سواء بشكل واضح أو على خجل مقارنة بزملائهم الذين لم يستطيعوا شرح وجود خوفهم بشكل يقنع صانع القرار بوجوده هذا الخوف سواء عبروا عنه بشكل شجاع أو متحفظ طالما لم يستطيعوا شرح قضيتهم. أما الطريقة الثالثة للنظر للحالة الذهنية فلا تأسس قرار منح صفة اللجوء على عنصر خوف طالب اللجوء ولا تعطي أفضلية للطلبات التي يظهر فيها هذا الفزع أو الخوف. لكن يُنظر للخوف وفقاً لهذا الرأي على أنه أحد العوامل التي يجب النظر إليها لفهم ظروف مقدم الطلب ومواضع ضعفه عند تقييم حالته لمنح صفة اللاجئ.

Подход к оценке вполне обоснованных опасений включает в себя рассмотрение душевного состояния лица, претендующего на получение статуса беженца, и обычно осуществляется в одном из трех направлений. Преобладающий подход определяет признаки существования "опасений" в смысле наличия страха, как одного из двух основных элементов проверки вполне обоснованных опасений. В этом случае, может быть отказано в предоставлении статуса беженца тем заявителям, которые в действительности либо не испытывают субъективных опасений, либо тем, чьи субъективные опасения не являются таковыми с точки зрения лица, принимающего соответствующее решение. Вторая точка зрения не рассматривает наличие субъективных опасений в качестве основного компонента, однако учитывает его в качестве фактора, преодолевающего недостаточность доказательств наличия реальной угрозы. В соответствии с данной формулировкой, лица, которые в большей степени напуганы или выглядят таковыми, либо те, которые способны выразить свою тревогу так, что она будет признана таковой лицом, принимающим соответствующее решение, - имеют определенное преимущество перед теми, кто столкнулся с той же степенью опасности, но оказался храбрее, сдержаннее, либо чья демонстрация чувства страха не была признана таковой. Третье толкование элемента субъективности не является ни условием получения статуса беженца на основании наличия опасений, ни каким-либо преимуществом для тех заявлений, в которых наличествуют таковые опасения. Вместо этого, требование принять во внимание "опасения" трактуется как общепринятая обязанность обращать внимание на особые обстоятельства заявителя и его персональную уязвимость при установлении статуса беженца.

We have engaged in sustained collaborative study and reflection on the doctrinal and jurisprudential foundations of the well-founded fear standard, and have concluded that continued reference to distinct 'subjective' and 'objective' elements of the well-founded fear standard risks distortion of the process of refugee status determination. The existence of subjective fearfulness in the sense of trepidation should neither be a condition precedent to recognition of refugee status, nor advantage an applicant who faces an otherwise insufficiently well-established risk. An approach which recognizes a subjective element in order to take account of an applicant's circumstances and vulnerabilities does not pose protection risks of the kind associated with the first understanding of a subjective element, nor raise the unfairness concerns of the second approach. Reliance on a subjective element to particularize the inquiry into well-founded fear is, however, unnecessary, and may result in the devaluation of evidence of real value to the assessment of actual risk of being persecuted.

Nous avons entrepris une étude et une réflexion approfondie et commune sur les fondements doctrinaux et jurisprudentiels des critères permettant d'identifier une crainte avec raison, et en avons déduit qu'une référence systématique à la distinction entre les éléments « subjectifs » et « objectifs » de la crainte avec raison risque de fausser la procédure de détermination du statut de réfugié. L'existence d'une crainte subjective au sens d'un sentiment de peur ne devrait ni conditionner la reconnaissance du statut de réfugié ni avantager un demandeur pour lequel un degré suffisant de risque n'est par ailleurs pas établi. La troisième approche qui déduit de l'élément subjectif la nécessité de prendre en considération les circonstances et vulnérabilités propres au demandeur évite les risques en termes de protection impliqués par la première approche et les questionnements en termes de justice inhérents à la seconde approche. Toutefois, il n'est pas nécessaire de se référer à un élément subjectif pour individualiser l'analyse d'une demande de reconnaissance de la qualité de réfugié, car cela pourrait conduire à négliger l'importance à accorder aux éléments de preuve réellement pertinents pour évaluer le risque réel de persécution.

Hemos realizado un estudio y una reflexión colaborativos y sostenidos sobre los fundamentos doctrinales y jurisprudenciales del estándar del temor fundado, y hemos concluido que la referencia continua a elementos "subjetivos" y "objetivos" distintos del estándar de temor fundado arriesga la distorsión del proceso de determinación de la condición de refugiado. La existencia de temor subjetivo en el sentido de miedo no debe ser una condición previa al reconocimiento de la condición de refugiado, ni beneficiar a un solicitante que se enfrenta a un riesgo que, de no ser por esta característica, no estaría suficientemente establecido. Un enfoque que reconoce un elemento subjetivo para tener en cuenta las circunstancias y vulnerabilidades de un solicitante no presenta riesgos de protección del tipo asociado con la primera comprensión de un elemento subjetivo, ni plantea las preocupaciones de injusticia del segundo enfoque. Sin embargo, la dependencia de un elemento subjetivo para particularizar la investigación del temor fundado es innecesaria y puede dar como resultado la devaluación de la evidencia de valor real para evaluar el riesgo real de ser perseguido.

These Guidelines are intended to promote a shared understanding of a unified approach to the well-founded fear inquiry and related aspects of the Convention refugee definition that both avoids the protection risks increasingly associated with assertions of a 'subjective element,' and ensures that due regard is accorded all particularized risks faced by an applicant for recognition of refugee status.

Ces recommandations entendent promouvoir une approche commune de l'examen du caractère fondé de la crainte et des aspects de la définition conventionnelle du réfugié qui y sont liés, afin d'éviter les risques en termes de protection qui résultent de l'importance accrue accordée à l'« élément subjectif » et de garantir une prise en considération adéquate des éléments propres aux risques spécifiques auxquels un demandeur de la reconnaissance de la qualité de réfugié est confronté.

Estas directrices pretenden promover una comprensión compartida de un enfoque unificado para la investigación del temor fundado y aspectos relacionados de la definición de refugiado de la Convención. El mismo evita los riesgos de protección cada vez más asociados con las afirmaciones de un "elemento subjetivo" y garantiza que se tengan debidamente en cuenta todos los riesgos particulares a los que se enfrenta un solicitante de reconocimiento de la condición de refugiado.

ولقد قمنا بعمل مجهود جماعي لعمل دراسة نُقدم فيها تصورنا حول الأسس القانونية والفقهية لمعايير تقدير وجود الخوف المعقول أو المبرر. وفي إطار هذه الدورة من سلسلة ورش العمل قمنا أيضاً بعمل استنتاج أساسي يعتمد عليه شرحنا هذا. هذا الاستنتاج الأساسي هو إن محاولة الفصل بين العوامل الموضوعية والعوامل الشخصية لتقدير وجود الخوف ربما يترتب عليه تشويها للحقيقة ويؤدي إلى بعض التأثير السلبي على قرار منح صفة اللجوء. فلا يمكن مثلاً أن يكون الاعتماد على العوامل الشخصية فقط ـ بمعنى القلق أو الفزع الشخصين ـ شرطاً مسبقاً لمنح صفة اللجوء. ولا يجب من جهة أخرى أن يكون الاستناد إلى العوامل الشخصية بهذا المفهوم الضيق بمثابة ميزة إضافية لطالب اللجوء الذي لا يتعرض لخطر حقيقي وكاف. ونعتقد أن الطريقة السليمة التي بموجبها تقييم العوامل الشخصية لوجود الخوف هي تلك التي تتضمن أخذ الظروف العامة الشخصية وعوامل الضعف التي يعاني منها طالب اللجوء في الاعتبار. ونرى إن هذا المنظور يجب أن يتلافى عيوب التصورات الأولي والثانية التي طُرحت سابقاً. فيجب مثلاً أن يتلافى عيب تجاهل أو التضحية بطالبي اللجوء الذين يتعرضون لخطر حقيقي إذا لم يستطيعوا التعبير الشخصي عن وجود هذا الخطر بطريقة كافية، حيث يؤدي إلى تلك النتيجة تبني وجهة النظر الأولي. كما يجب أن يتلافى التصور المُقترح الطريقة غير المنصفة لوجهة النظر الثانية. ونحن نعتقد أن الاعتماد على العوامل الشخصية لوجود خوف له ما يبرره يعتبر غير كاف (وربما غير ضروري)، وخاصة لأن هذا الاعتماد أحياناً ما يتضمن التقليل من شأن بعض الأدلة الهامة على وجود خطر حقيقي بالاضطهاد.

Мы участвовали в длительном коллективном процессе изучения и дискуссий теоретических и правоведческих основ критерия наличия вполне обоснованных опасений, и пришли к заключению, что постоянное обращение к различию элементов "субъективности" и "объективности" в критерии наличия вполне обоснованных опасений, рискует исказить процесс предоставления статуса беженца. Существование субъективных опасений, учитывая испытываемый страх, не должно быть ни условием, предшествующим признанию статуса беженца, ни преимуществом заявителя, который, в противном случае, столкнется с недостаточной обоснованностью наличия опасности. Подход, который признает наличие элемента субъективности с тем, чтобы принять во внимание обстоятельства, в которых находится заявитель, равно как и его уязвимость, не угрожают отсутствием защиты, которая связана с первой из предложенных интерпретаций элемента субъективности, а также не вызывает опасений возможной несправедливости, описанных во второй интерпретации. Нет необходимости, однако, опираться на элемент субъективности с тем, чтобы детализировать исследование вполне обоснованных опасений, так как это может привести к девальвации свидетельств, обладающих реальной значимостью для оценки фактического риска преследования.

وتهدف هذا الدليل الإرشادي إلى تقديم منظور جماعي موحد للمساعدة عند التحقيق في أو البحث في مدى وجود خوف له ما يبرره وكافة الأمور المتصلة به لتحديد صفة اللجوء وفقاً للاتفاقية الدولية. ونعتقد أن هذا المنظور يتلافى الكثير من أوجه القصور التي تترتب على تبني وجهات النظر السائدة لتقدير العوامل الشخصية عند البحث في وجود الخوف لدى طالب اللجوء، مثل تلك التي تُغلب العوامل الشخصية وتؤدي إلى تجاهل منح الحماية وصفة اللجوء لبعض الأشخاص الذين يستحقون الحماية لكنهم لم يكونوا قادرين على التعبير عن وجود الخوف لديهم. كما إن هذا المنظور يضمن أخذ كافة الأخطار المحددة التي تواجه طالب اللجوء في الاعتبار عند أخذ قرار منح صفة اللجوء.

Данные Рекомендации призваны распространить принятое толкование единого подхода к установлению вполне обоснованных опасений и связанных с ним аспектов определения статуса беженца согласно Конвенции о беженцах. Это определение одновременно позволяет избегнуть риска лишиться защиты, все более связываемого с понятием "субъективного элемента", а также обеспечить должное внимание ко всем специфицированным видам риска, которым подвергается заявитель, претендующий на статус беженца.

UNABLE OR UNWILLING

1. An applicant's state of mind is relevant to determining whether he or she "is unable or, owing to such fear, is unwilling to avail himself [or herself]" of the protection of his or her country or countries of citizenship or, in the case of a stateless person, country or countries of former habitual residence. Specifically, a state party's duty of protection under the Convention is engaged through an expression by or on behalf of an applicant of inability or unwillingness to avail himself or herself of the protection of the relevant country or countries.

NE PEUT OU NE VEUT

1. L'état d'esprit d'un demandeur est pertinent pour déterminer s'il « ne peut ou, du fait de cette crainte, ne veut se réclamer de la protection » de son ou ses pays de nationalité ou, s'il est apatride, de son ou ses pays de résidence habituelle. Plus précisément, l'obligation de protection d'un État partie à la Convention est engagée par l'expression par un individu, ou par celui qui agit en son nom, de son incapacité (« ne peut ») ou de son refus (« ne veut ») de se réclamer de la protection de son ou de ses pays d'origine.

INCAPACIDAD O FALTA DE VOLUNTAD

1. El estado de ánimo del solicitante es relevante para determinar si "no puede o, debido a ese temor, no está dispuesto a acogerse" a la protección de su país o países de ciudadanía o, en el caso de una persona apátrida, de país o países de residencia habitual en el pasado. Específicamente, el deber de protección de un estado parte en virtud de la Convención se ejerce a través de una expresión por parte del solicitante, o en su nombre, de la incapacidad o falta de voluntad de acogerse a la protección del país o países pertinentes.

---

2. The required assertion of inability or unwillingness need not be made in any particular form. In substance, the applicant need only provide information or make claims which *may* engage the Refugee Convention obligations of the state.

2. L'affirmation par le demandeur de son incapacité ou de son refus de se réclamer de la protection de son ou de ses pays d'origine ne doit pas être réalisée suivant des formes particulières. Il suffit que le demandeur produise des informations ou formule une prétention qui *pourrait* engager les obligations que la Convention de Genève fait peser sur l'État.

2. La afirmación de incapacidad o falta de voluntad requerida no necesita realizarse de ninguna forma en particular. En esencia, el solicitante solo necesita proporcionar información o hacer reclamos que *puedan* comprometer las obligaciones de la Convención de Refugiados del estado.

WELL-FOUNDED FEAR

3. In contrast to the question of whether an applicant is unable or unwilling to avail himself or herself of the country of origin's protection, the assessment of well-founded fear does not comprise any evaluation of an applicant's state of mind.

CRAINTE AVEC RAISON

3. Contrairement à la question de déterminer si un demandeur ne peut ou ne veut se réclamer de la protection de son pays d'origine, l'évaluation du caractère fondé de la crainte n'implique aucun examen de l'état d'esprit du demandeur.

TEMOR FUNDADO

3. A diferencia de la cuestión de si un solicitante no puede o no quiere acogerse a la protección del país de origen, la evaluación del temor fundado no comprende ninguna evaluación del estado de ánimo del solicitante.

---

4. Most critically, the protection of the Refugee Convention is not predicated on the existence of 'fear' in the sense of trepidation. It requires instead the demonstration of 'fear' understood as a forward-looking expectation of risk. Once fear so conceived is voiced by the act of seeking protection, it falls to the state party assessing refugee status to determine whether that expectation is borne out by the actual circumstances of the case. If it is, then the applicant's fear (that is, his or her expectation of being persecuted) should be adjudged well-founded.

4. Il est important de souligner que la protection accordée par la Convention de Genève n'est pas conditionnée à l'existence d'une « crainte », au sens d'un sentiment de peur. Elle exige la preuve d'une « crainte », au sens de la démonstration de l'existence d'un risque futur. Dès que pareille crainte est exprimée au travers de l'introduction d'une demande de protection, il revient à l'État de déterminer si cette prévision d'un risque futur est justifiée par les circonstances concrètes de l'espèce. Si cela s'avère le cas, la crainte du demandeur (au sens de la prévision d'un risque futur) d'être persécuté devrait être considérée comme étant fondée.

4. Lo más importante es que la protección de la Convención de Refugiados no se basa en la existencia de "temor" en el sentido de miedo. En su lugar, requiere la demostración de "temor" entendido como una expectativa de riesgo a futuro. Una vez que el temor así concebido se manifiesta mediante el acto de buscar protección, le corresponde al estado parte que evalúa la condición de refugiado determinar si esa expectativa se confirma por las circunstancias reales del caso. De ser así, el temor del solicitante (es decir, su expectativa) de ser perseguido debe considerarse fundado.

НЕСПОСОБНОСТЬ ИЛИ НЕЖЕЛАНИЕ.

1. Душевное состояние заявителя является существенным для определения его или ее "неспособности или, вследствие такового опасения, его (или ее) нежелания воспользоваться" защитой страны или стран, гражданином или гражданкой которой он или она являются, либо, в том случае лиц без гражданства, страны или стран бывшего постоянного места жительства. В частности, обязанность страны предоставить защиту согласно Конвенции заключается в выражении самим заявителем либо от лица заявителя, его или ее неспособности или нежелания воспользоваться защитой соответствующей страны или стран.

2. Требуемое утверждение таковой неспособности или нежелания не нуждается в какой-либо особой форме выражения. По существу, заявитель должен лишь предоставить информацию либо сделать заявление, которое *может* отражать обязательства данной страны в соответствии с Конвенцией о статусе беженцев.

ВПОЛНЕ ОБОСНОВАННЫЕ ОПАСЕНИЯ

3. В отличие от вопроса о неспособности или нежелании заявителя воспользоваться защитой страны происхождения, определение вполне обоснованных опасений не включает в себя какой-либо оценки душевного состояния заявителя.

4. Что является наиболее важным, защита, предоставляемая Конвенцией о беженцах, не основывается на существовании "опасений" в значении тревоги. Вместо того, требуется продемострировать "опасения", понимаемые как ожидание предполагаемой опасности. В случае, когда таковые опасения выражены посредством акта поиска защиты, обязанностью страны, устанавливающей статус беженца, является определение того, вызвано ли упомянутое ожидание действительными обстоятельствами рассматриваемого дела. Если дело обстоит именно так, то опасения заявителя (то есть его или ее ожидание предполагаемой опасности преследований) должно быть признано вполне обоснованным.

غير قادر أو غير راغب

1. تُعتبر الحالة الذهنية لطالب اللجوء أمراً ذو صلة يؤخذ في الاعتبار عند تحديد ما إذا كان طالب اللجوء " غير قادر بسبب حالة الخوف لديه أو غير راغب في تسليم نفسه" لحماية دولة أو دول التي يحمل جنسيتها، أو في حالة الأشخاص بدون جنسية لدولة أو دول الإقامة المُعتادة، يرتبط دور أي دولة طرف في اتفاقية تحديد وضع اللاجئين بتقديم الحماية وفقاً للاتفاقية بناء على رغبة طالب اللجوء أو من ينوب عنه عند عدم قدرته أو عدم رغبته في تسليم نفسه لحماية الدولة أو الدول المعنية.

2. لا يُشترط أن يأخذ التعبير عن عدم القدرة أو عدم الرغبة المُشار إليهما بصورة محددة. فمن حيث الجوهر، يكفي أن يقدم طالب اللجوء بعض المعلومات الأساسية أو يوضح عند تقديم طلب رغبته في اللجوء، حيث تبدأ التزامات الدولة التي تفحص الطلب المبنية على الاتفاقية الدولية مجرد تقديم هذه المعلومات أو تقديم هذا الطلب.

خوف له ما يبرره

3. على العكس من تقييم أذا ما كان مقدم طلب اللجوء غير قادر أو غير راغب في تسليم نفسه لحماية الدولة صاحبة الشأن فإن تقييم ما كان طالب اللجوء يعاني من وجود خوف له ما يبرره لا يأخذ حالة طالب اللجوء المعنوية في الاعتبار.

4. وبصفة أساسية، لا يتوقف تقديم الحماية وفقاً للاتفاقية الدولية على وجود "الخوف" بمعنى وجود هلع أو فزع لكن يكفي في هذا الشأن أن يظهر وجود خوف من ما من خطر منظور ومتوقع. ويعتبر تقديم طلب اللجوء والحماية بمثابة تعبير عن وجود هذا الخوف. ومجرد تقديم هذا الطلب يقع على عاتق الدولة التي تفحص هذا الطلب تحديد مدى حقيقية هذا الخطر المنظور في ضوء كافة الظروف الواقعية للحالة موضع البحث. فإذا أظهرت هذه الظروف المُختلفة أن هناك خطراً منظوراً ومتوقعاً بوجود الاضطهاد،* فأنه يمكن من ثم الجزم بوجود خوف له ما يبرره بالاضطهاد لدى طالب اللجوء.

* وباختصار شديد، فأن هذا التوضيح من قبل دليل ميشيغان ينصرف إلى أهمية البحث في وجود الركن الموضوعي أو المادي (أي توافر خطر الاضطهاد نفسه) بدلاً من البحث في الركن المعنوي (توافر الخوف) لدى طالب اللجوء. ويعرف المتخصصون القانونيون بصفة عامة انه يسهل البحث في الركن المادي بدلاً من الركن المعنوي، في القانون الجنائي مثلاً. وربما يعتبر هذا المنهج في التفكير من قبل دليلي ميشيغان تسهيلاً على المحقق، لكنه قبل كل شيء يهدف إلى تلافي عيوب التركيز على الشق الشخصي أو المعنوي، التي تم الإشارة إليها سابقا، كما انه يستهدف توفير قدر أكبر من الحماية لطالبي اللجوء الذين لا يستطيعون التعبير عن وجود الخوف لديهم (توضيح من المترجم إلى اللغة العربية).

5. An understanding of "fear" as forward-looking expectation of risk is fully justified by one of the plain meanings of the English text, and is confirmed by dominant interpretations of the equally authoritative French language text (*"craignant avec raison"*), which do not canvass subjective trepidation. This construction avoids the enormous practical risks inherent in attempting objectively to assess the feelings and emotions of an applicant. It is moreover consistent with the internal structure of the Convention, for example with the principle that refugee status ceases when the actual risk of being persecuted comes to an end, though not on the basis of an absence of trepidation (Art. 1(C)5–6), and with the fact that the core duty of *non-refoulement* applies where there is a genuine risk of being persecuted, with no account taken of whether a refugee stands in trepidation of that risk (Art. 33). More generally, the human rights context of the Convention requires that protection be equally open to all on the basis of evidence of an actual and relevant form of risk.

5. Interpréter la « crainte avec raison » au sens de la prévision d'un risque futur est entièrement justifié par la version française de la Convention et l'une des significations littérales du terme employé en anglais (« *fear* »), qui n'exigent pas un sentiment de peur. Pareille interprétation évite les difficultés pratiques inhérentes à toute tentative d'évaluer les sentiments et les émotions d'un demandeur. Elle est en outre cohérente avec la logique de la Convention, qui prévoit par exemple la cessation du statut de réfugié lorsque le risque de persécution a disparu, sans que la cessation ne puisse résulter de la disparition d'un sentiment de peur (art. 1, C, §§5 et 6), et avec le principe cardinal de non-refoulement dont le respect s'impose en cas de risque réel de subir une persécution, sans qu'il ne soit exigé que le réfugié éprouve un sentiment de peur (art. 33). Plus généralement, le contexte de la Convention, qui a été établie afin de participer à garantir les droits de l'homme, implique que la protection qu'elle consacre soit également ouverte à tous face à la preuve d'un risque réel et pertinent.

5. La comprensión del "temor" como una expectativa de riesgo a futuro está totalmente justificada por uno de los significados claros del texto en inglés, y confirmada por las interpretaciones dominantes del texto en francés igualmente autorizado (*"craignant avec raison"*), que no exploran la inquietud subjetiva. Esta construcción evita los enormes riesgos prácticos inherentes al intento de evaluar objetivamente los sentimientos y las emociones de un solicitante. Además, es coherente con la estructura interna de la Convención. Por ejemplo, con el principio de que la condición de refugiado termina cuando el riesgo real de persecución llega a su fin, aunque no sobre la base de una ausencia de miedo (artículo 1 (C)5-6), y con el hecho de que el deber central de no devolución se aplica cuando existe un riesgo real de ser perseguido, sin tener en cuenta si un refugiado muestra miedo frente a ese riesgo (artículo 33). De manera más general, el contexto de derechos humanos de la Convención exige que la protección esté disponible para todos por igual en base a evidencia de una forma de riesgo real y relevante.

6. The determination of whether an applicant's "fear"—in the sense of forward-looking expectation of risk—is, or is not, "well-founded" is thus purely evidentiary in nature. It requires the state party assessing refugee status to determine whether there is a significant risk that the applicant may be persecuted. While the mere chance or remote possibility of being persecuted is insufficient to establish a well-founded fear, the applicant need not show that there is a clear probability that he or she will be persecuted.

6. Déterminer si le demandeur « craint » – dans le sens de prévoir un risque futur – « avec raison » est une question de preuve. Cela implique que l'État qui examine la demande de reconnaissance du statut de réfugié doit évaluer s'il existe un risque significatif que le demandeur soit persécuté. Si une probabilité simple ou éloignée ne suffit pas pour établir le caractère fondé de la crainte, le demandeur n'a pas l'obligation de démontrer qu'il existe une probabilité certaine qu'il sera persécuté.

6. Por lo tanto, la determinación de si el "temor" de un solicitante —en el sentido de una expectativa de riesgo a future— es "fundado" o no, es de naturaleza puramente probatoria. Requiere que el estado parte que evalúa la condición de refugiado determine si existe un riesgo significativo de que el solicitante sea perseguido. Si bien la simple posibilidad o remota posibilidad de ser perseguido es insuficiente para establecer un temor fundado, el solicitante no necesita demostrar que existe una clara probabilidad de que sea perseguido.

ESTABLISHING WELL-FOUNDED FEAR

7. To determine whether an applicant faces a significant risk of being persecuted, all material evidence from whatever source must be considered with care, and in context. Equivalent attention must be given to all forms of material evidence, with a decision on the relative weight to be assigned to different forms of evidence made on the basis of the relative veracity and cogency of the evidence adduced.

L'ÉTABLISSEMENT DE LA CRAINTE AVEC RAISON

7. Afin de déterminer si un demandeur est confronté à un risque significatif de subir une persécution, toutes les preuves matérielles doivent être examinées avec rigueur et compte tenu du contexte, quelle que soit leur source. Une attention égale doit être accordée à toutes les formes de preuve matérielle, la décision d'accorder un poids distinct aux preuves produites ne pouvant être fondée que sur des considérations liées à leur force probante respective.

DETERMINACIÓN DE LA EXISTENCIA DE TEMOR FUNDADO

7. Para determinar si un solicitante enfrenta un riesgo significativo de ser perseguido, todas las pruebas materiales de cualquier fuente deben analizarse con cuidado y en un contexto. Se debe prestar la misma atención a todas las formas de evidencia material, y decidir sobre el peso relativo que debe asignarse a las diferentes formas de evidencia basadas en la veracidad relativa y la contundencia de la evidencia presentada.

5. Понимание "опасений" как ожидания предполагаемой опасности полностью оправдывается одним из прямых значений текста на английском языке и подтверждается основными толкованиями столь же авторитетного текста на французском языке ("*craignant avec raison*"), которое не рассматривает понятие субъективного страха. Данное толкование стремится избежать значительной практической опасности, которая присуща попыткам объективно оценить чувства и эмоции заявителя. Это тем более соответствует внутренней структуре Конвенции, в частности, принципу, в соответствии с которым статус беженца аннулируется в случае исчезновения действительного риска преследования, но не на основании отсутствия боязни преследования (Ст. 1(C) 5–6), а также в силу того, что суть принципа *невысылки* (*non-refoulement*) применима тогда, когда наличествует подлинный риск преследования, независимо от рассмотрения того, испытывает ли беженец страх по этому поводу (Ст. 33). В общем и целом, контекст Конвенции в части соблюдения прав человека требует обеспечения защиты, равно доступной всем на основе свидетельства о наличии действительной и существенной формы риска.

٥. يعتبر فهم "الخوف" ــ بوصفه متعلقاً بخطر منظور ومتوقع ــ كافياً بالرجوع للمعنى اللغوي المباشر السائد في المراجع اللغوية الإنجليزية والفرنسية، حيث يُفهم الخوف على انه قلق أو فزع، ذلك المعنى الذي لا يتضمن وجود الفزع أو القلق اللذان يتحددان بناءً على الظروف الشخصية فقط. ويتجنب هذا المفهوم للخوف العديد من المشاكل العملية التي تترتب على محاولة فهم وتقييم مشاعر وعواطف طالب اللجوء بطريقة موضوعية صرفة. كما يُعتبر هذا المنظور للخوف مُتسقاً أيضا مع النصوص الواضحة للاتفاقية الدولية، وذلك على سبيل المثال حين أكدت الاتفاقية الدولية على إيقاف وضع اللجوء عندما يزول الخطر الحالي بالاضطهاد المُعرض له اللجئ. ووفقاً لنص المادة 1 في فقرتها الثالثة أرقام 5 و6 من الاتفاقية فأن صفة اللجوء تنتهي بنهاية خطر الاضطهاد وليس على نهاية الشعور بالخوف بوصفه غياب لحالة الفزع الشخصية. كما أن هذا المفهوم يعتبر مُتسقاً أيضا مع مادتها رقم 33، والتي ربطت واجب عدم إعادة أو إبعاد اللجوء بوجود اضطهاد حقيقي بغض النظر عن شعور هذا اللاجئ وإدراكه بوجود هذا الخطر. وبصفة عامة، فإن هذا المفهوم يتماشى مع سياق حقوق الإنسان والذي يعتبر الغرض الأساسي الأول للاتفاقية الدولية والذي يتطلب أن تُقدم الحماية بطريقة متساوية اعتماداً فقط على وجود أدلة على وجود خطر حقيقي بالاضطهاد.

6. Таким образом, установление факта "вполне обоснованных опасений" заявителя – понимаемых как ожидание предполагаемой опасности – по своей природе основано исключительно на их доказательности. От страны, устанавливающей статус беженца, требуется определить наличие существенного риска для заявителя подвергнуться преследованиям. В то время как наличие всего лишь возможности или отдаленной вероятности подвергнуться преследованиям является недостаточным для установления наличия вполне обоснованных опасений, заявителю не нужно демонстрировать существование очевидной вероятности того, что он или она будет подвергаться преследованиям.

٦. يتوقف تحديد ما إذا كان "خوف" طالب اللجوء ــ بناء على ارتباطه بخطر منظور ومتوقع ــ معقولاً أو مبرراً من عدمه بصفة أساسية على وجود أدلة. والمقصود بأن تحديد الخوف المعقول والمبرر يتوقف بطريقة أساسية على الأدلة التي تبحث عليها الدولة باحثة الطلب أن الدولة باحثة الطلب أن تحقق بصفة رئيسية في مدى وجود خطر بالاضطهاد عند بحثها في منح صفة اللجوء. ويشهد الواقع العملي بعض الحالات القليلة التي لا يمكن الاستدلال منها على وجود خوف معقول أو مبرر بناء على وجود خطر الاضطهاد. وبالرغم من ذلك، فأنه لا يشترط على طالب اللجوء أن يُثبت أو يقدم ما يُفيد بأن خطر الاضطهاد الذي يتعرض له هو أمر محتمل بطريقة كبيرة أو واضحة وقطعية.

УСТАНОВЛЕНИЕ ВПОЛНЕ ОБОСНОВАННЫХ ОПАСЕНИЙ

7. Для того, чтобы установить, подвергнется ли заявитель серьезной опасности преследования, все существенные доказательства, полученные из каких-либо источников, должны быть рассмотрены тщательно и в надлежащем контексте. Равное внимание должно быть уделено всем формам материальных доказательств, с учетом относительного преобладания различных форм доказательств, основанного на относительной достоверности и убедительности приведенных доказательств.

تأسيس وجود خوف له ما يبرره

٧. عند البحث في مسألة مدى تعرض طالب اللجوء لخطر الاضطهاد من عدمه يجب أخذ كافة الأدلة المادية المتوافرة ومن أي مصدر كان في الاعتبار، ويجب أن تُبحث هذه الأدلة بعناية وأن تُقيم في ضوء السياق والظروف المُحيطة بها. كما يجب أن تُبحث كافة الأدلة بقدر متناسب من الاهتمام، بالرغم من انه يمكن منح بعض الأدلة وقتاً أكثر من البحث بناء على الوزن النسبي لها الذي يتوقف على قوة الحجة في هذه الأدلة أو مدى قطعيتها وتماسكها.

8. Evidence unique to the applicant, including evidence of personalized and relevant past persecution, is directly relevant to the determination of well-founded fear, but is not a prerequisite. An applicant who, prior to departure from his or her country of origin, was not subject to persecution, nor directly threatened with persecution, can establish by other evidence a well-founded fear of being persecuted in the foreseeable future.

8. Une preuve propre au demandeur, en ce compris une preuve d'une persécution passée, est directement pertinente pour établir la crainte fondée, mais n'est pas nécessairement requise. Un demandeur qui, avant de quitter son pays d'origine, n'a pas été soumis à une persécution, ni à une menace directe de persécution, peut user d'autres moyens de preuve pour établir une crainte avec raison de subir une persécution dans un futur proche.

8. Las pruebas exclusivas del solicitante, incluida la evidencia de persecuciones pasadas personalizadas y relevantes, son directamente relevantes para la determinación del temor fundado, pero no son un requisito previo. Un solicitante que antes de partir de su país de origen no haya sido objeto de persecución ni amenazado directamente con ser perseguido, puede establecer un temor fundado de ser perseguido en el futuro previsible a través de otras pruebas.

9. The assessment of well-founded fear may be based largely, or even primarily, on the applicant's own credible testimony. While the applicant's testimony is not necessarily the best evidence of forward-looking risk, it may well constitute the best evidence of risk, depending on the circumstances of the case.

9. L'évaluation du caractère fondé de la crainte de subir une persécution peut-être largement, voire même essentiellement, fondée sur le témoignage personnel crédible du demandeur. Bien que le témoignage du demandeur ne soit pas nécessairement la meilleure preuve d'un risque futur, il se peut qu'il soit la meilleure preuve de ce risque, compte tenu des circonstances propres à l'espèce.

9. La evaluación del temor fundado puede basarse en gran medida, o incluso principalmente, en el testimonio creíble del propio solicitante. Si bien el testimonio del solicitante no necesariamente es la mejor evidencia del riesgo prospectivo, puede constituir la mejor evidencia de riesgo, dependiendo de las circunstancias del caso.

10. In light of the shared duty of fact-finding, an applicant must make best efforts to provide the state party assessing refugee status with corroboration of his or her testimony. However, where such corroboration cannot reasonably be secured, an applicant's credible and unrefuted testimony standing alone is sufficient to establish a well-founded fear of being persecuted.

10. En raison du partage de la charge d'établir les faits, un demandeur a l'obligation d'entreprendre tous les efforts nécessaires pour apporter à l'État en charge de la détermination du statut de réfugié les éléments qui viennent au soutien de son témoignage. S'il s'avère, toutefois, qu'il n'est raisonnablement pas possible de fournir pareille preuve, le seul témoignage du demandeur, crédible et non contredit par d'autres éléments de preuve, suffit à établir une crainte avec raison de subir la persécution.

10. A la luz del deber compartido de investigación, el solicitante debe hacer todo lo posible para proporcionar evidencia que corrobore su testimonio al estado parte que evalúa el reconocimiento de la condición de refugiado. Sin embargo, cuando dicha corroboración no se puede asegurar de manera razonable, el testimonio creíble y no refutado del solicitante es suficiente para establecer un temor fundado de ser perseguido.

11. An applicant's testimony may only be deemed not credible on the basis of a specific, cogent concern about its veracity on a significant and substantively relevant point.

11. Le témoignage d'un demandeur ne peut être considéré comme non crédible que lorsqu'un doute précis et sérieux existe quant à la véracité d'un élément du récit d'asile qui soit significatif et pertinent.

11. El testimonio de un solicitante solo puede considerarse no creíble en base a una preocupación específica y contundente acerca de su veracidad en un punto significativo y sustancialmente relevante.

8. تعتبر كافة الأدلة المرتبطة شخصياً بطالب اللجوء، مثل تلك التي تدل على وجود اضطهاد سابق ضده، هي أدلة ذات صلة يجب أخذها في الاعتبار عند التحقيق في وجود خوف له ما يبرره من عدمه. وكون هذه الأدلة ذات صلة ليس معناه اعتبارها شرطاً ضرورياً لإثبات وجود الخوف المعقول أو المبرر لدى طالب اللجوء. وعلى ذلك، فإنه يمكن التحقُّق من وجود خوف له ما يبرره بوجود اضطهاد منظور ومتوقع في المستقبل ضد شخص ما، بالرغم من إن هذا الشخص لم يتعرض للاضطهاد أو هدد بالاضطهاد قبل مغادرته لدولته الأصلية.

8. Доказательства, являющиеся уникальными для данного заявителя, включая доказательства фактов личного и существенно важного преследования в прошлом, имеют прямую значимость для установления вполне обоснованных опасений, однако не являются необходимым условием. Заявитель, который до отъезда из своей страны происхождения не подвергался преследованиям, равно как и не подвергался прямой опасности преследований, может предоставить другие доказательства наличия вполне обоснованных опасений подвергнуться преследованиям в обозримом будущем.

9. يمكن الاستناد إلى شهادة طالب اللجوء المتأكدة بشكل جزئي أو حتى بصفة رئيسية عند التحقيق من وجود خوف له ما يبرره من عدمه. وبالرغم من أنه لا يمكن الاعتماد على شهادة طالب اللجوء وحدها بوصفها أفضل الأدلة على وجود خطر منظور ومتوقع، إلا انه يمكن أن تعتبر هذه الشهادة من أفضل الأدلة بناء على الظروف المختلفة في كل حالة من الحالات.

9. Оценка вполне обоснованных опасений может основываться в значительной степени или даже главным образом на заслуживающем доверия свидетельстве самого заявителя. В то время как свидетельство заявителя не является непременно лучшим доказательством ожидаемой опасности, оно все же может, в зависимости от обстоятельств дела, быть лучшим свидетельством наличия опасности.

10. وفي ضوء ما جاء من واجب مُشترك في تقصي الحقائق بين طالب اللجوء والدولة باحثة الطلب، يجب على طالب اللجوء أن يبذل أقصى ما في وسعه لتقديم أدلة تعزز الشهادة التي أدلى بها وأن يتعاون في شهادته مع الدولة باحثة الطلب عند بحث منح صفة اللجوء. وفي حالة عدم إمكانية تأمين وجود هذه الأدلة أو هذا التعاون الحقيقي بين طالب اللجوء والدولة باحثة الطلب، يمكن الاكتفاء بوجود شهادة طالب اللجوء المؤكدة باعتبارها أساساً لإثبات وجود خوف له ما يبرره بوجود الاضطهاد.

10. В свете того, что получение соответствующих сведений является общей обязанностью, заявитель должен приложить максимум усилий для того, чтобы предоставить подтверждение его или ее показаний стороне, устанавливающей статус беженца. Однако, в тех случаях, когда таковое подтверждение, в силу объективных причин, не может быть предоставлено, неопровержимые и заслуживающие доверия показания заявителя сами по себе являются достаточными для установления вполне обоснованных опасений преследования.

11. لا يمكن وضع شهادة طالب اللجوء محل تشكيك إلا في حالة وجود بعض الثغرات أو التناقض حول اتساقها وفيما يتعلق بأحد الأمور الجوهرية المحددة ذات الصلة فقط.

11. Показания заявителя могут быть признаны не заслуживающими доверия только на основе конкретных, обоснованных опасений относительно их достоверности касательно важного и существенно значимого вопроса.

12. Even where there is a finding that an applicant's testimony is not credible, in whole or in part, the decision-maker must nonetheless assess the actual risk faced by an applicant on the basis of other material evidence. In particular, the existence of a well-founded fear may be grounded in evidence that the applicant is a member of a relevant, at-risk group of persons shown by credible country data or the credible testimony of other persons to face a significant risk of being persecuted.

12. Même lorsque le témoignage du demandeur est considéré comme non crédible, en tout ou en partie, l'autorité en charge de la détermination du statut de réfugié doit évaluer le risque réel auquel le demandeur est confronté, sur le fondement d'autres preuves matérielles. En particulier, l'existence d'une crainte avec raison de subir une persécution peut être établie au motif que le demandeur relève d'un groupe à risque, dont les membres sont confrontés à un risque significatif de persécution tel que démontré par des informations objectives relatives à la situation dans le pays d'origine, ou les témoignages crédibles d'autres individus.

12. Incluso cuando si se determina que el testimonio de un solicitante no es creíble, ya sea en parte o en su totalidad, el responsable de tomar decisiones de todas formas debe evaluar el riesgo real que corre un solicitante sobre la base de otras pruebas materiales. En particular, la existencia de un temor fundado puede basarse en la evidencia de que el solicitante es miembro de un grupo de personas relevante que se encuentra en riesgo considerable de ser perseguido, lo cual se puede demostrar mediante datos creíbles del país o testimonios creíbles de otras personas.

BEING PERSECUTED

13. The particular circumstances of a person seeking recognition of refugee status are not relevant simply to the question of whether he or she can be said to have a well-founded fear. The determination of whether the risk faced is appropriately adjudged to amount to a risk of "being persecuted" also requires careful consideration of matters which may be unique to the individual concerned.

ÊTRE PERSÉCUTÉ
13. Les circonstances propres à l'individu qui sollicite la reconnaissance du statut de réfugié ne sont pas uniquement pertinentes pour déterminer si ce dernier éprouve une crainte avec raison. Déterminer correctement si le risque existant peut être considéré comme un risque « d'être persécuté » suppose également un examen attentif des circonstances qui peuvent être propres à l'individu concerné.

SER PERSEGUIDO
13. Las circunstancias particulares de un individuo que pretende que se le reconozca la condición de refugiado no son relevantes simplemente a la pregunta de si puede decirse que tiene un temor fundado. La determinación de si el riesgo enfrentado efectivamente se considera un riesgo de "ser perseguido" también requiere una consideración cuidadosa de asuntos que pueden ser exclusivos del individuo en cuestión.

14. As a general rule, the determination of whether a given risk amounts to a risk of 'being persecuted' must enquire into the personal circumstances and characteristics of each applicant, recognizing that by virtue of such circumstances and characteristics some persons will experience different degrees of harm as the result of a common threat or action.

14. En principe, déterminer si un risque donné peut être considéré comme un risque « d'être persécuté » implique d'opérer une évaluation des circonstances et caractéristiques propres à chaque demandeur, dans la mesure où pareilles circonstances et caractéristiques personnelles peuvent influer sur le degré de souffrance résultant d'un acte ou d'une menace identique.

14. Como regla general, la determinación de si un riesgo dado equivale a un riesgo de "ser perseguido" debe investigar las circunstancias personales y las características de cada solicitante reconociendo que, en virtud de tales circunstancias y características, algunas personas sufrirán daños de diferentes grados como resultado de una amenaza o acción común.

15. Thus, for example, the psychological vulnerabilities of a specific applicant may be such that the risk of harms which would be insufficiently grave to justify recognition of refugee status for most persons will nonetheless amount to torture, cruel, inhuman or degrading treatment for him or her. Where this is so, the forward-looking risk of such psychological harms may appropriately be regarded as a risk of 'being persecuted.'

15. Il en résulte, par exemple, que les vulnérabilités psychologiques d'un demandeur peuvent être telles qu'en ce qui le concerne, le risque de subir certaines souffrances qui seraient insuffisamment graves pour justifier la reconnaissance du statut de réfugié à la plupart des individus, pourrait toutefois être considéré comme de la torture ou des traitements inhumains ou dégradants. En pareil cas, le risque futur de subir de telles souffrances psychologiques peut être considéré comme un risque « d'être persécuté ».

15. Así, por ejemplo, las vulnerabilidades psicológicas de un solicitante específico pueden ser tales que un riesgo de sufrir daños que no sería lo suficientemente grave como para justificar el reconocimiento de la condición de refugiado de todas formas equivaldrá, para la mayoría de las personas, a una situación de tortura, trato cruel, inhumano o degradante. En casos de este tipo, el riesgo prospectivo de sufrir tales daños psicológicos se puede considerar apropiadamente como un riesgo de "ser perseguido".

12. حتى في حالة ما إذا تم الوصول إلى قرار بعدم مصداقية شهادة طالب اللجوء بشكل كلي أو جزئي، يجب على باحث طالب اللجوء ومتخذ القرار ألا يتجاهل أي أدلة أخرى متوافرة تدل على وجود خطر حقيقي بالاضطهاد يواجه طالب اللجوء. فيمكن مثلاً إثبات وجود خوف معقول أو مبرر بناء على أدلة أخرى مثل قواعد البيانات ذات المصداقية التي تدل على عضوية طالب اللجوء في جماعة تتعرض لخطر الاضطهاد وشهادة أشخاص آخرين تدل على تعرضهم وتعرض طالب اللجوء لخطر الاضطهاد.

12. Даже в тех случаях, когда имеются сведения, что показания заявителя не заслуживают доверия в целом или частично, лицо, принимающее соответствующее решение, должно, тем не менее, оценить опасность, действительно существующую для заявителя, на основе других реально существующих доказательств. В частности, наличие вполне обоснованных опасений может основываться на доказательствах того, что заявитель является представителем соответствующей группы лиц, подвергающихся риску, что подтверждается достоверной информацией о стране происхождения, или достоверными свидетельствами других лиц, подвергающимися существенному риску преследования.

التعرض للاضطهاد

13. عند التحقيق من وجود خوف له ما يبرره لا ينبغي التوقف عند الظروف المحددة المتعلقة بشخص طالب اللجوء وحدها. ويُشترط للتحقيق من التعرض لخطر الاضطهاد والبحث في درجة التعرض لهذا الخطر القيام بعمل بحثاً متأنياً والأخذ في الاعتبار الظروف الفريدة المتعلقة بظروف كل شخص على حده.

СТАТЬ ЖЕРТВОЙ ПРЕСЛЕДОВАНИЙ

13. Особые обстоятельства лица, претендующего на получение статуса беженца, не могут быть приняты во внимание только при решении вопроса о вполне обоснованных опасениях. Установление того, является ли опасность, которой подвергается данное лицо, равной опасности "подвергнуться преследованиям", также требует тщательного рассмотрения обстоятельств, касающихся исключительно данного индивидуума.

---

14. وكقاعدة عامة، يجب أن يأخذ التحقيق إذا ما كان الخطر الذي يتعرض له الشخص يصل لمرحلة الاضطهاد بعين الاعتبار كافة الظروف والسمات الشخصية لطالب اللجوء. حيث أن درجة التعرض للإيذاء تختلف وفقاً لظروف كل شخص على حدي بدون تعميم.

14. Как правило, установление того, является ли опасность, которой подвергается данное лицо, соответствующей опасности "подвергнуться преследованиям", должно быть исследовано с учетом индивидуальных обстоятельств и специфических условий каждого заявителя, принимая во внимание тот факт, что в силу индивидуальных обстоятельств и специфических условий, некоторые лица, в результате общей для всех угрозы или иных действий, могут в разной степени подвергаться опасности.

---

15. فعلى سبيل المثال، يمكن النظر إلى أن حالة الضعف النفسية للأحد طالبي اللجوء على إنها غير كافية لمنحه صفة اللجوء إلا إنها في معظم الأحوال يمكن تظهر خطر التعرض للتعذيب، أو المعاملة اللاإنسانية لطالب اللجوء. وفي هذه الحالة فإن الخطر المتوقع من هذا الأذى النفسي يعد كافياً بما يتحقق معه إثبات خطر وجود التعرض الحقيقي للاضطهاد.

15. Так, например, психологическая уязвимость конкретного заявителя может быть таковой, что опасность ущерба, недостаточно тяжкого для оправдания предоставления статуса беженца в большинстве случаев, тем не менее, подвергнет данное лицо пыткам, жестокому, негуманному или унизительному обращению. В тех случаях, когда дело обстоит именно так, ожидаемая опасность нанесения такового психологического ущерба может соответствующим образом рассматриваться как опасность "преследования".

These Guidelines reflect the consensus of all participants at the Third Colloquium on Challenges in International Refugee Law, held at the University of Michigan Law School, Ann Arbor, Michigan, USA, on March 26–28, 2004.

James C. Hathaway
Colloquium Convener
University of Michigan

Roger P.G. Haines, Q.C.
Colloquium Chair
University of Auckland

Michelle Foster
Colloquium Rapporteur
SJD Candidate
University of Michigan

Jenny Bedlington
JennGen Consulting

Ryan Goodman
Harvard University

Kay Hailbronner
University of Konstanz

Stephen Legomsky
Washington University

Penelope Mathew
Australian National University

Gregor Noll
Lund University

Catherine Phuong
University of Newcastle

Lisa Bagley
Student
University of Michigan

Umbreen Bhatti
Student
University of Michigan

Bill Hicks
Student
University of Michigan

Carsten Hoppe
Student
University of Michigan

Wonda Joseph
Student
University of Michigan

Wondwossen Kassa
Student
University of Michigan

Niketa Kulkarni
Student
University of Michigan

Louise Moor
Student
University of Michigan

Matt Pryor
Student
University of Michigan

Azadeh Shahshahani
Student
University of Michigan

Larissa Wakim
Student
University of Michigan

Dawson Williams
Student
University of Michigan

The Colloquium deliberations benefited from the counsel of Mr. Christoph Bierwirth, Senior Liaison Officer, United Nations High Commissioner for Refugees, Geneva

Refugees increasingly encounter laws and policies which provide that their protection needs will be considered or addressed somewhere other than in the territory of the state where they have sought, or intend to seek, protection.

LES RECOMMANDATIONS DE MICHIGAN SUR LA PROTECTION AILLEURS

Les réfugiés sont de plus en plus confrontés aux législations et politiques qui prévoient que leurs besoins de protection seront pris en charge ailleurs que dans l'État où ils ont sollicité l'asile, ou entendent le faire.

LAS DIRECTRICES DE MICHIGAN SOBRE PROTECCIÓN EN OTRO LUGAR

Los refugiados encuentran cada vez más leyes y políticas que estipulan que sus necesidades de protección serán consideradas o abordadas en un sitio ajeno al territorio del estado en el que han buscado, o pretenden buscar, protección.

Such policies-including 'country of first arrival,' 'safe third country,' and extraterritorial processing rules and practices-raise both opportunities and challenges for international refugee law. They have the potential to respond to the Refugee Convention's concern 'that the grant of asylum may place unduly heavy burdens on certain countries' by more fairly allocating protection responsibilities among states. But insistence that protection be provided elsewhere may also result in the denial to refugees of their rights under the Refugee Convention and international law more generally. The challenge is to identify the ways in which the protection regime may be made more flexible without compromising the entitlements of refugees.

Ces politiques – qui reposent notamment sur l'usage des concepts de « premier pays d'arrivée », de « pays tiers sûr » et sur les règles et pratiques d'examen extraterritorial des demandes d'asile – représentent à la fois des défis et des opportunités pour le droit international des réfugiés. Elles pourraient offrir une réponse à l'une des préoccupations soulevées par la Convention de Genève, qui indique dans son préambule qu'« il peut résulter de l'octroi du droit d'asile des charges exceptionnellement lourdes pour certains pays », en permettant de distribuer plus équitablement entre les États la responsabilité d'accorder une protection. Toutefois, placer l'accent sur la possibilité d'obtenir une protection ailleurs peut également avoir pour conséquence de dénier aux réfugiés les droits qui leurs sont conférés par la Convention de Genève et plus généralement par le droit international. Le défi consiste à identifier des moyens de rendre le régime de protection internationale plus flexible, sans compromettre les droits des réfugiés.

Dichas políticas que incluyen el "país de primera llegada", el "tercer país seguro" y las normas y prácticas de procesamiento extraterritoriales plantean oportunidades y desafíos para el derecho internacional de los refugiados. Tienen el potencial de responder a la inquietud de la Convención de Refugiados "de que la concesión de asilo puede imponer cargas excesivas a ciertos países" al asignar las responsabilidades de protección entre los estados de manera más justa. Pero la insistencia en que la protección se proporcione en otro lugar también puede hacer que a los refugiados se les nieguen sus derechos en virtud de la Convención de Refugiados y el derecho internacional en general. El desafío es identificar las formas en que el régimen de protección puede ser más flexible sin poner en riesgo los derechos de los refugiados.

توصيات دليل ميشيغان الإرشادي
توفير الحماية في موقع بديل
مقدمة

МИЧИГАНСКИЕ РЕКОМЕНДАЦИИ ПО ПРЕДОСТАВЛЕНИЮ ЗАЩИТЫ В ДРУГОМ МЕСТЕ

Беженцы все чаще сталкиваются с законами и правилами, в соответствии с которыми потребность в защите будет рассматриваться или будет удовлетворена где-либо за пределами территории государства, где они искали или намеревались искать защиты.

يخضع اللاجئين بصفة متزايدة لعدد كبير من القوانين والسياسات. وأحياناً كثيرة يؤدي إتباع هذه السياسات والقوانين أن يتم البحث في تقديم الحماية للاجئين على أراضي دول أخرى غير الدولة التي تم طلب الحماية أو التي يخطط لطلب الحماية على أراضيها.

ومن أمثلة هذه السياسات "سياسة دولة الوصول الأولى" و "سياسة الدولة الثالثة الآمنة" وأيضاً كافة الإجراءات والممارسات الأخرى التي تشمل تدخل أكثر من دولة. وتخلق هذه السياسات الكثير من الفرص والتحديات أثناء تطبيق القانون الدولي للاجئين. فتقدم هذه السياسات بعض الحلول الممتازة لمواجهة التخوف من أن "مجرد منح صفة اللجوء سوف يمثل عبئاً ثقيلاً لا يمكن تحمله من قبل بعض الدول" وذلك لأن هذه السياسات تسمح وتضمن أن تتشارك الدول المختلفة في توزيع مسؤولية تقديم الحماية للاجئين. ولكن يجب الأخذ في الاعتبار أن الإصرار على أن الحماية سيتم منحها في موقع بديل، يمكن أن يؤدى إلى حرمان اللاجئين من الحقوق المخولة لهم بموجب معاهدة اللاجئين والقانون الدولي. أما من ناحية التحديات التي تواجه هذه السياسات عند التطبيق فتتمثل في كيفية ضمان أن تكون سياسات ونظم الحماية مرنة دون المساس بالحقوق الأساسية المخولة للاجئين بموجب القوانين الدولية.

Подобные правила – включая "страну первоначального прибытия", "третью безопасную страну", а также нормы и практика экстратерриториального рассмотрения ходатайств – создают для международного законодательства о беженцах как дополнительные возможности, так и трудности. В них заключен потенциал урегулирования высказываемого Конвенцией о статусе беженцев опасения "что предоставление убежища может налагать несоразмерно тяжкое бремя на некоторые страны", путем более справедливого распределения ответственности среди государств. Но настойчивое требование предоставления защиты в другом месте также может привести к отказу беженцам в правах, предусмотренных Конвенцией о статусе беженцев и международным правом. Задача заключается в том, чтобы найти способы сделать режим предоставления защиты более гибким, не ущемляя при этом прав беженцев.

To this end, we have engaged in sustained collaborative study and reflection on the legal basis of protection elsewhere policies. Research conducted by the University of Melbourne's Research Programme in International Refugee Law was debated and refined at the Fourth Colloquium on Challenges in International Refugee Law, convened in November 2006 by the University of Michigan's Program in Refugee and Asylum Law. These Guidelines are the product of that endeavor. They reflect the consensus of Colloquium participants on the minimum international legal requirements for valid protection elsewhere policies, as well as our views on the procedures by which international legal obligations may reliably be fulfilled in the implementation of such policies.

Afin de relever ce défi, nous avons entrepris une étude et une réflexion approfondie et commune relativement aux fondements légaux des politiques exigeant des réfugiés qu'ils sollicitent une protection ailleurs (dite plus simplement en anglais, « politique de protection ailleurs », soit « protection elsewhere politics »). Les résultats de l'étude menée par le programme de recherche en droit international des réfugiés de l'université de Melbourne ont été discutés et affinés à l'occasion du quatrième colloque sur les défis du droit international des réfugiés, organisé en novembre 2006 par le programme de droit d'asile et des réfugiés de l'université du Michigan. Les présentes recommandations sont le résultat de cette initiative. Elles reflètent le consensus des participants au colloque relativement aux standards minimaux de droit international des réfugiés s'appliquant aux politiques exigeant des réfugiés qu'ils sollicitent une protection ailleurs, ainsi qu'aux procédures qui devraient permettre de respecter les obligations de droit international dans le cadre de la mise en œuvre de pareilles politiques.

Con este fin, hemos realizado un estudio y una reflexión colaborativos y sostenidos sobre la base legal de las políticas de protección en otro lugar. La investigación realizada por el Programa de Investigación de la Universidad de Melbourne en Derecho Internacional de Refugiados fue debatida y refinada en el Cuarto Coloquio sobre Desafíos en el Derecho Internacional de los Refugiados, celebrado en noviembre de 2006 por el Programa en Derecho de Refugiados y Asilo de la Universidad de Michigan. Estas directrices son el producto de dicho esfuerzo. Reflejan el consenso de los participantes del Coloquio sobre los requisitos legales internacionales mínimos para las políticas válidas de protección en otro lugar, así como nuestras opiniones sobre los procedimientos por los cuales las obligaciones legales internacionales pueden cumplirse de manera confiable al aplicar dichas políticas.

WHEN STATES MAY IMPLEMENT PROTECTION ELSEWHERE POLICIES

1. The 1951 Convention and 1967 Protocol relating to the Status of Refugees ("Convention") neither expressly authorize nor prohibit reliance on protection elsewhere policies. As such, protection elsewhere policies are compatible with the Convention so long as they ensure that refugees defined by Art. 1 enjoy the rights set by Arts. 2-34 of the Convention.

LES CIRCONSTANCES DANS LESQUELLES LES ÉTATS PEUVENT METTRE EN ŒUVRE DES POLITIQUES DE PROTECTION AILLEURS

1. La Convention de 1951 et le Protocole de 1967 relatifs au statut des réfugiés (« la Convention ») ne consacrent aucune autorisation ni interdiction expresse d'exiger des réfugiés qu'ils sollicitent une protection ailleurs. Pareille exigence n'est, en tant que telle, pas contraire à la Convention, pour autant que les réfugiés tels que définis à l'article 1 bénéficient des droits consacrés aux articles 2 à 34.

CUÁNDO LOS ESTADOS PUEDEN IMPLEMENTAR POLÍTICAS DE PROTECCIÓN EN OTRO LUGAR

1. La Convención de 1951 y el Protocolo de 1967 sobre la Condición de Refugiados ("Convención") no autorizan ni prohíben expresamente la dependencia de las políticas de protección en otro lugar. Por lo tanto, las políticas de protección en otro lugar son compatibles con la Convención siempre y cuando garanticen que los refugiados reconocidos por el artículo 1 gozan de los derechos establecidos por los artículos 2 a 34 de la Convención.

2. Because the Convention does not contemplate the devolution of protection responsibilities to a non-state entity, any sharing-out of protection responsibility must take place between and among states. While it is preferable that the state to which protection is assigned ('receiving state') be a party to the Convention, such status is not a requirement for implementation of a protection elsewhere policy which respects international law.

2. Étant donné que la Convention n'envisage pas de délégation de la responsabilité de reconnaître une protection à une entité non étatique, tout partage de cette responsabilité doit se réaliser entre États. Bien qu'il soit préférable que l'État auquel est assigné la responsabilité de reconnaître une protection (« l'État d'accueil ») soit partie à la Convention, il ne s'agit pas là d'une exigence conditionnant la conformité aux droits fondamentaux de la mise en œuvre de l'exigence de solliciter une protection ailleurs.

2. Debido a que la Convención no contempla la delegación de responsabilidades de protección a una entidad no estatal, cualquier responsabilidad de compartir la protección debe compartirse entre los estados. Si bien es preferible que el estado al cual se le asigna la protección ("estado receptor") sea parte de la Convención, tal condición no es un requisito para la aplicación de una política de protección en otro lugar que respete el derecho internacional.

وفي هذا السياق، قمنا بعمل دراسة جماعية مستفيضة حول الأسس القانونية لتطبيق سياسات توفير الحماية في موقع بديل. وقد تم تنظيم سلسلة من ورش العمل بجامعة ميتشغان والتي نظمها "برنامج دراسة قانون اللاجئين والملاذ" بكلية القانون بالجامعة. وتجدر الإشارة إلى أنه قد تم تخصيص الدورة الرابعة من هذه الورش ـ والتي نُظمت في نوفمبر 2006 ـ لمناقشة ودراسة مستفيضة للبحث الذي بدأه برنامج القانون الدولي للاجئين بجامعة ملبورن بأستراليا. وقد كان الدليل الحالي هو محصلة لهذا العمل الجماعي. ويعكس هذا الدليل رأياً توافقياً لجميع المشاركين في سلسلة ورش العمل على الحد الأدنى القانوني الدولي لتوفير الحماية الفعالة في موقع بديل، كما يعكس الدليل أيضاً الرأي التوافقي للمشاركين حول الإجراءات التي يمكن بواسطتها التأكد من الوفاء بالالتزامات القانونية الدولية المترتبة على تطبيق مثل هذه السياسات.

Для этого мы провели длительное совместное исследование и обсуждение правовой основы принципов защиты, предоставляемой в другом месте. Результаты исследований, проведенных Исследовательской программой Университета Мельбурна по международному законодательству по правам беженцев, обсуждались и были уточнены на Четвертом коллоквиуме по проблемам международного законодательства о беженцах, который был проведен в ноябре 2006 года Программой Мичиганского университета по законодательству о правах беженцев и предоставлению убежища. Результатом этой работы и стали настоящие Рекомендации. Они отражают консенсус участников Коллоквиума по вопросу о минимальных международных правовых требованиях к ныне действующим принципам защиты в другом месте, а также наши взгляды на методику, посредством которой международные правовые обязательства могут надежно выполняться при реализации таких принципов.

متى يمكن أن تطبق الدول سياسات "البحث عن توفير الحماية في موقع بديل"

1. معاهدة 1951 والبروتوكول الصادر عام 1967 الخاصين بتحديد صفة اللاجئين لم يسمحا أو يمنعا بشكل واضح الاعتماد على سياسات توفير الحماية في موقع بديل. وعلى هذا النحو، فإن سياسات توفير الحماية في موقع بديل تتماشى مع معاهدة اللاجئين طالما أن هذه السياسات تضمن أن يتمتع اللاجئين وفقاً للتعريف الخاص بهم في المادة 1 من الاتفاقية، بكافة الحقوق الممنوحة لهم بموجب المواد من 2 إلى 34 من الاتفاقية الدولية.

СЛУЧАИ, В КОТОРЫХ ГОСУДАРСТВА МОГУТ ОСУЩЕСТВЛЯТЬ ПОЛИТИКУ ЗАЩИТЫ В ДРУГОМ МЕСТЕ

1. Конвенция 1951 года о статусе беженцев и Протокол 1967 года (далее - "Конвенция") категорически не санкционируют и не запрещают использование принципов защиты в другом месте. Как таковые, принципы защиты в другом месте совместимы с Конвенцией до тех пор, пока они обеспечивают такое положение, при котором беженцы, определение понятия которых дано в Статье 1, пользуются правами, определенными в Статьях 2-34 Конвенции.

---

2. تقع مسؤولية حماية اللاجئين والمساهمة فيها على عاتق الدول والمشاركة فيما بينهم، حيث أن الاتفاقية الدولية لم تتحدث عن إمكانية تحويل مسؤولية حماية اللاجئين إلى كيانات أو هيئات أخرى. وبالرغم من أنه يُفضل أن تكون الدولة التي أصبحت مسؤولة عن توفير الحماية للاجئ (الدولة المُسْتَقبِلة) طرفاً في الاتفاقية الدولية، إلا أن توافر صفة الدولة الطرف لا يعد شرطاً لتطبيق سياسات توفير الحماية في موقع بديل، وذلك لأن هذه السياسات تخضع وتحتم قواعد القانون الدولي.

2. Поскольку Конвенция не рассматривает передачу обязанностей по защите негосударственному субъекту, всякое разделение ответственности должно осуществляться только между государствами. Хотя и предпочтительно, чтобы государство, за которым закрепляются обязанности по предоставлению защиты (далее - "принимающее государство") было участником Конвенции, такой статус не является обязательным для осуществления принципов защиты в другом месте, проводимых с соблюдением норм международного права.

3. Reliance on a protection elsewhere policy must be preceded by a good faith empirical assessment by the state which proposes to effect the transfer ('sending state') that refugees defined by Art. 1 will in practice enjoy the rights set by Arts. 2-34 of the Convention in the receiving state. Formal agreements and assurances are relevant to this inquiry, but do not amount to a sufficient basis for a lawful transfer under a protection elsewhere policy. A sending state must rather inform itself of all facts and decisions relevant to the availability of protection in the receiving state.

3. L'application d'une politique de protection ailleurs doit être précédée par un examen, mené de bonne foi et sur le fondement d'éléments objectifs, par l'État qui entend effectuer le transfert du réfugié (« l'État d'envoi »), afin de s'assurer que les réfugiés tels que définis par l'article 1 bénéficieront effectivement des droits consacrés par les articles 2 à 34 au sein de l'État d'accueil. Dans le cadre de cet examen, les accords et assurances formelles doivent être pris en considération, mais ils ne suffisent pas à garantir la légalité du transfert réalisé au motif que le réfugié doit solliciter une protection ailleurs. L'État d'envoi doit plutôt s'informer de l'ensemble des faits et circonstances pertinents pour déterminer si une protection sera accessible au sein de l'État d'accueil.

3. La dependencia de una política de protección en otro lugar debe estar precedida por una evaluación empírica de buena fe por parte del estado que propone efectuar la transferencia ("estado remitente") que demuestre que los refugiados reconocidos por el artículo 1 gozarán en la práctica de los derechos establecidos por los artículos 2 a 34 de la Convención en el estado receptor. Los acuerdos formales y las garantías son relevantes para esta investigación, pero no constituyen una base suficiente para una transferencia legal bajo una política de protección en otro lugar. Un estado remitente debe informarse sobre todos los hechos y decisiones relevantes para la disponibilidad de protección en el estado receptor.

4. Unless the receiving state acknowledges the refugee status of the person to be transferred or will in fact ensure that all rights set by Arts. 2-34 of the Convention are granted to him or her without need for recognition of refugee status, every transfer of protection responsibility must be predicated on a commitment by the receiving state to afford the person transferred a meaningful legal and factual opportunity to make his or her claim to protection. The sending state must in particular satisfy itself that the receiving state interprets refugee status in a manner that respects the true and autonomous meaning of the refugee definition set by Art. 1 of the Convention.

4. À moins que l'État d'accueil ne reconnaisse que la personne à transférer bénéficie du statut de réfugié, ou qu'il garantisse qu'en pratique tous les droits consacrés par les articles 2 à 34 de la Convention lui seront reconnus sans qu'il soit nécessaire de lui reconnaître ce statut, tout transfert de la responsabilité d'accorder une protection suppose l'engagement de l'État d'accueil d'accorder à la personne transférée la possibilité effective, en droit comme en fait, d'introduire une demande de protection. L'État d'envoi doit, en particulier, s'assurer que l'État d'accueil interprète le statut de réfugié en conformité avec la définition autonome du réfugié tel que consacrée par l'article 1 de la Convention.

4. A menos que el estado receptor reconozca la condición de refugiado del individuo que se trasladará o asegurará de que todos los derechos establecidos por los artículos 2 a 34 de la Convención se le concedan sin necesidad de reconocimiento de la condición de refugiado, cada transferencia de responsabilidad de protección debe basarse en el compromiso del estado receptor de permitir que la persona que se traslade disponga de una oportunidad legal y factual significativa de solicitar protección. En particular, el estado remitente debe asegurarse de que el estado receptor interprete la condición de refugiado de manera tal que se respete el significado verdadero y autónomo de la definición de refugiado establecida por el artículo 1 de la Convención.

5. Absent individuated evidence of risk based on national security or public order grounds, Art. 32 of the Convention prohibits the expulsion of a lawfully present refugee to any other state, even if there is no risk of being persecuted there. A transfer of protection responsibility which respects the requirements of international law may therefore be made only before the refugee concerned is 'lawfully present' in the sending state. Lawful presence must be defined by the sending state in good faith and in accordance with the requirements of international law. Lawful presence is in any event established not later than such time as a decision is reached on the admissibility of the protection claim.

5. En l'absence d'éléments de preuve indiquant qu'il présente personnellement un risque pour la sécurité nationale ou l'ordre public, le réfugié se trouvant régulièrement sur le territoire d'un État ne peut être expulsé vers tout autre État, quand bien même il n'y risque pas une persécution. Un transfert de la responsabilité d'accorder une protection ne peut donc être réalisé en conformité avec le droit international que s'il se réalise avant que le réfugié ne « se trouve régulièrement » sur le territoire de l'État d'envoi. La présence régulière doit être définie de bonne foi par l'État d'envoi et en conformité avec les exigences du droit international. Dans tous les cas, la présence régulière est établie au plus tard lorsque la demande d'asile est déclarée recevable.

5. Ante la falta de pruebas individuales de riesgo basado en razones de seguridad nacional u orden público, el artículo 32 de la Convención prohíbe la expulsión de un refugiado que esté presente en el territorio de manera legal a cualquier otro estado, incluso si no hay riesgo de que sea perseguido allí. Por lo tanto, una transferencia de la responsabilidad de protección que respete los requisitos del derecho internacional solo puede hacerse antes de que el refugiado en cuestión esté "presente de manera legal" en el estado remitente. La presencia legal debe ser definida por el estado remitente de buena fe y de acuerdo con los requisitos del derecho internacional. En cualquier caso, la presencia legal se establece a más tardar en el momento en que se llega a una decisión sobre la admisibilidad del reclamo de protección.

3. يجب أن يسبق الاعتماد على سياسات توفير الحماية في موقع بديل عمل دراسة حالة على أسس علمية تُجرى بحسن نية وبنزاهة من قبل الدولة التي تقترح نقل اللاجئ (الدولة المُرسلة) إلى دولة أخرى. ويجب أن ترتكز هذه الدراسة على أن اللاجئ المعرف عليه في المادة 1 في الاتفاقية سوف يتمتع بجميع الحقوق المنصوص عليها في المواد من 2 إلى 34 في الاتفاقية الدولية بعد نقله إلى الدولة المُستَقبِلة. وبالرغم من إنه يمكن الأخذ في الاعتبار كافة التعهدات أو الاتفاقات الرسمية والدبلوماسية أثناء إجراء دراسة الحالة المشار إليها، باعتبار إن تلك التعهدات والاتفاقات هي أمور ذات صلة، لكن يجب الأخذ في الاعتبار أيضاً أن كافة هذه التعهدات والاتفاقات لا تكفي في حد ذاتها للجزم بتوافر شروط نقل أو تحويل اللاجئين وفقاً لسياسات توفير الحماية في موقع بديل. ولكي يكون هذا النقل قانونياً، يجب أن تقوم الدولة المُرسلة بجمع وتوفير كافة الحقائق والقرارات التي تشير إلى إمكانية توافر الحماية فعلاً في الدولة المُستَقبِلة.

3. Применению принципа защиты в другом месте должна предшествовать добросовестная эмпирическая оценка государством, планирующим провести передачу (далее - "отправляющее государство") того, что в принимающем государстве беженцы, как то определено Статьей 1, на практике будут пользоваться правами, установленными Статьями 2-34 Конвенции. В ходе этой оценки могут иметь место официальные соглашения и гарантии, однако они не приравниваются к достаточным основаниям для передачи прав в соответствии с принципом защиты в другом месте. Отправляющее государство должно само получить сведения обо всех фактах и решениях, имеющих отношение к возможности получения защиты в принимающем государстве.

4. في حالة ما إذا لم تقم الدولة المُستَقبِلة فعلياً بمنح صفة اللجوء إلى الشخص المنقول، أو التعهد بتوفير كافة الحقوق الممنوحة له وفقاً للمواد من 2 إلى 34 من الاتفاقية مباشرة دون الحاجة إلى الاعتراف به كلاجئ، يجب أن يكون كل تحويل ونقل لمسؤولية الحماية مصحوباً بالتزام صريح من قبل الدولة المُستَقبِلة تتعهد فيه بأن توفر للشخص المنقول فرصته القانونية الحقيقية والواقعية في طلبه ومساعيه للحصول على هذه الحماية. ويجب على الدولة المُرسلة على وجه التحديد أن تقوم بالاطمئنان إلى أن الدولة المُستَقبِلة ــ عندما تتولى البحث في منح صفة اللجوء من عدمه ــ سوف تقوم بتفسير مدى توافر صفة اللجوء على وجه يحترم ويضمن المعنى الحقيقي والمتميز لتعريف صفة اللاجئ وفقاً لنص المادة 1 من الاتفاقية الدولية.

4. В случае, если принимающее государство не признает статус беженца лица, переданного ему, или не обеспечивает этому лицу всех прав, закрепленных Статьями 2-34 Конвенции, без предоставления статуса беженца, любая передача ответственности по защите должна основываться на обязательстве принимающего государства предоставить перемещаемому лицу реальную правовую и фактическую возможность обратиться с ходатайством о защите. Отправляющее государство должно, в частности, удостовериться в том, что принимающее государство истолковывает понятие "статус беженца" таким образом, который обеспечивает соблюдение истинного и независимого значения понятия "беженец", содержащегося в Статье 1 Конвенции.

5. لقد أكدت المادة 32 من الاتفاقية الدولية أنه في حالة غياب دليل على وجود خطر يهدد الأمن القومي أو النظام العام في الدولة المعنية، تحظر الاتفاقية الدولية إبعاد أي لاجئ ــ كان قد حصل على هذه الصفة بطريقة قانونية ــ إلى دولة أخرى، حتى ولو لم يكن هناك أي خطر بإمكانية وقوع اضطهاد لهذا اللاجئ في هذه الدولة الأخرى (الدولة التي أبعد إليها هذا اللاجئ). وعلى ذلك، ولكي تكون عملية نقل ومسؤولية حماية اللاجئ من دولة إلى أخرى عملية قانونية معترف بها وفقاً للقانون الدولي، يجب أن يحدث هذا النقل أثناء وبدون الشخص المنقول وجوداً شرعياً على إقليم الدولة المرسلة، وبالطبع فإن الوجود القانوني والشرعي يجب أن يتم بحثه وتوضيحه بنزاهة من قبل الدولة المرسلة وطبقاً لمتطلبات القانون الدولي. ومن البديهي أنه يجب التحقق من وجود هذا الشخص بطريقة قانونية على أراضي الدولة المُرسلة عند قبول طلب الحماية نفسه.

5. При отсутствии индивидуализированных доказательств риска на основании соображений национальной безопасности или общественного порядка Статья 32 Конвенции запрещает высылку в любое другое государство находящегося в стране на законных основаниях беженца, даже при отсутствии в этом последнем государстве риска преследования. Поэтому передача ответственности за защиту беженца в соответствии с требованиями международного права, может быть осуществлена только до того, как этот беженец будет "находиться на законных основаниях" на территории отправляющего государства. Нахождение на законных основаниях должно быть определено отправляющим государством добросовестно и в соответствии с требованиями международного права. Нахождение на законных основаниях должно быть в любом случае установлено не позднее того времени, когда будет принято решение о приемлемости ходатайства о предоставлении защиты.

RESPECT FOR REFUGEE RIGHTS

6. The most fundamental constraint on implementation of a protection elsewhere policy is the duty of *non-refoulement,* set by Art. 33 of the Convention. Because the duty is to avoid acts which result in a refugee's expulsion or return to the frontiers of a territory where life or freedom would be threatened 'in any manner whatsoever,' Art. 33 prohibits indirect *refoulement* of the kind that occurs when a refugee is sent to a state in which there is a foreseeable risk of subsequent *refoulement.* For the same reason, actions which amount to aiding, abetting, or otherwise assisting another state to breach Art. 33 are themselves in breach of the duty of *non-refoulement.*

LE RESPECT DES DROITS DU RÉFUGIÉ

6. Le respect du principe de non-refoulement, tel que consacré par l'article 33 de la Convention, constitue la plus importante condition à respecter pour mettre en œuvre une politique de protection ailleurs. Étant donné que l'article 33 prohibe tout acte conduisant à l'expulsion ou au refoulement « de quelque manière que ce soit » d'un réfugié sur les frontières des terri-toires où sa vie ou sa liberté serait menacée, le refoulement indirect, qui résulte du renvoi d'un réfugié vers un État où il risque d'être ensuite expulsé ou refoulé vers pareilles menaces, est interdit. Pour ce même motif, tout acte qui revient à aider, assister ou encourager de quelque autre manière un autre État à violer l'article 33 est en soi constitutif d'une violation de l'obli-gation de non-refoulement.

RESPETO POR LOS DERECHOS DE LOS REFUGIADOS

6. La restricción más fundamental para aplicar una política de protección en otro lugar es el deber de no devolución, estable-cido por el artículo 33 de la Convención. Dado que el deber es evitar actos que deriven en la expulsión de un refugiado o el regreso a las fronteras de un territorio donde la vida o la liber-tad estarían amenazadas "de cualquier manera", el artículo 33 prohíbe la devolución indirecta, del tipo que ocurre cuando un refugiado es enviado a un estado en el que existe un riesgo pre-visible de devolución posterior. Por la misma razón, las acciones que equivalen a ayudar, incitar o apoyar a otro estado a violar el artículo 33 constituyen una violación del deber de no devolución *(non-refoulement).*

---

7. A state is in violation of Art. 33 where a prohibited return or expulsion is attributable to that state under international law. An attribution of responsibility follows *inter alia* where the return or expulsion is effected by a state official, even if he or she is acting in excess of authority or in contravention of instructions; by a private person or entity acting on the instructions of, or under the direction or control of, the state; or by officials or organs of another state placed at the disposal of the state.

7. Un État viole l'article 33 dès qu'une expulsion ou un refoule-ment prohibé par cette disposition lui est imputable en vertu du droit international. L'attribution de responsabilité peut résulter entre autres des circonstances que l'expulsion ou le refoulement a été réalisé par un agent de l'État, quand bien même ce der-nier a commis un excès de pouvoir ou a agi contrairement aux instructions, ou par un particulier ou une entité non étatique agissant suivant les instructions de l'État ou sous sa direction ou son contrôle, ou encore par les agents ou organes d'un autre État mis à sa disposition.

7. Un estado viola el artículo 33 cuando un regreso o expul-sión prohibido es atribuible a ese estado en virtud del derecho internacional. Una atribución de responsabilidad continúa, entre otros, cuando el regreso o la expulsión es efectuada por un fun-cionario del estado, incluso si actúa cometiendo un exceso de autoridad o en contravención de instrucciones recibidas; en el caso de una persona o entidad privada que actúa bajo las instruc-ciones del estado, o bajo la dirección o el control del mismo; o en el caso de funcionarios u órganos de otro estado puestos a disposición del estado.

---

8. A refugee is entitled not simply to protection against *refoulement,* but more generally to benefit from the civil and socioeco-nomic rights set by Arts. 2-34 of the Convention. As such, any refugee transferred must benefit in the receiving state from all Convention rights to which he or she is entitled at the time of transfer. He or she must also acquire in the receiving state such additional rights as are mandated by the requirements of the Convention.

8. Un réfugié ne bénéficie pas uniquement d'une protection contre le refoulement, mais plus généralement des droits civils et socio-économiques consacrés par les articles 2 à 34 de la Convention. En conséquence, du seul fait de sa qualité, tout réfugié transféré vers un autre État doit bénéficier, au sein de cet État d'accueil, de l'ensemble des droits de la Convention aux-quels il pouvait prétendre au sein de l'État d'envoi au moment de son transfert. Il doit également bénéficier, au sein de l'État d'accueil, des droits supplémentaires auxquels il a droit confor-mément à la Convention.

8. Un refugiado tiene derecho no simplemente a recibir protec-ción frente a la devolución, sino que en términos más generales tiene derecho a beneficiarse de los derechos civiles y socioeco-nómicos establecidos por los artículos 2 a 34 de la Convención. Como tal, en el estado receptor cualquier refugiado trasladado debe beneficiarse de todos los derechos de la Convención a los que tiene derecho en el momento del traslado. El refugiado tam-bién debe adquirir en el estado receptor los derechos adicionales que sean ordenados por los requisitos de la Convención.

СОБЛЮДЕНИЕ ПРАВ БЕЖЕНЦЕВ

6. Наиболее фундаментальным ограничением для осуществления политики защиты в другом месте является обязательство по *невысылке* [*non-refoulement*], содержащееся в Статье 33 Конвенции. Поскольку это обязательство заключается в том, что государства "не будут никоим образом" высылать или возвращать беженцев на границу страны, где их жизни или свободе будет угрожать опасность. Статья 33 запрещает косвенную *высылку* [*refoulement*], предполагающую отправку беженца в государство, в котором существует предсказуемый риск последующей *высылки* [*refoulement*]. По этой же причине действия, которые приравниваются к пособничеству, соучастию или оказанию иного содействия другому государству в нарушении Статьи 33, сами по себе являются нарушением обязательства *невысылки* [*non-refoulement*].

7. Государство считается нарушившим Статью 33, когда, в соответствии с международным правом, нарушение запрета на возвращение или высылку беженца, может быть приписано этому государству. Установление ответственности имеет место, помимо прочего [*inter alia*], в том случае, когда возвращение или высылка осуществляются государственным чиновником, даже если он или она превышают свои полномочия или нарушают инструкции; частным лицом или субъектом, действующим в соответствии с указаниями или под руководством или контролем государства; или официальными лицами или органами другого государства, предоставленными в распоряжение данного государства.

8. Беженец имеет право не только на защиту от высылки [*refoulement*], но и, в более общем плане, на пользование гражданскими и социально-экономическими правами, определенными в Статьях 2-34 Конвенции. По существу, каждый перемещаемый беженец должен пользоваться в принимающем государстве всеми правами, предусмотренными Конвенцией, которые положены ему или ей на момент перемещения. Он или она должны также приобрести в принимающем государстве те дополнительные права, которые оговорены требованиями Конвенции.

9. The assessment of respect for refugee rights shall take account of the fact that most such rights are neither immediately owed nor absolute in character. In particular, the rights owed to a refugee increase as the level of attachment to the protecting state increases over time. Some rights inhere as soon as a refugee comes under a state's control or authority (e.g. *non-refoulement*); others once the refugee is physically present in a state's territory (e.g. right to identity documents); additional rights are owed once lawful presence is established (e.g. self-employment); lawful stay gives rise to a more inclusive set of rights (e.g. access to public housing and welfare systems); and a small number of rights are owed only once durable residence is established (e.g. exemption from legislative reciprocity).

9. L'évaluation du respect des droits du réfugié doit prendre en considération la circonstance que la plupart de ces droits ne sont pas immédiatement dus et n'ont pas un caractère absolu. Les droits du réfugié augmentent avec le passage du temps, simultanément à l'accroissement du degré d'attachement de ce réfugié à l'État qui lui offre une protection. Certains droits se matérialisent dès que le réfugié relève du contrôle ou de l'autorité de l'État (l'interdiction de refoulement, par exemple), d'autres dès que le réfugié est physiquement présent sur le territoire de l'État (le droit de se voir délivrer des documents d'identité, par exemple). Le fait de se trouver régulièrement sur le territoire de l'État implique le bénéfice de droits supplémentaires (le droit d'exercer une profession non salariée, par exemple), de même que le fait d'y résider régulièrement engendre l'accès à divers droits à l'intégration (l'accès à un logement public et aux systèmes d'assistance publique, par exemple). Quelques droits supposent que le réfugié réside durablement sur le territoire de l'État (la dispense de réciprocité législative, par exemple).

9. La evaluación del respeto de los derechos de los refugiados deberá tener en cuenta el hecho de que la mayoría de dichos derechos no se les debe ni de forma inmediata ni tienen carácter absoluto. En particular, los derechos que se le deben a un refugiado aumentan a medida que el nivel de apego al estado de protección aumenta con el tiempo. Algunos derechos son inherentes apenas un refugiadoqueda bajo el control o la autoridad del estado (p. ej., no devolución); otros, una vez que el refugiado se encuentra fisicamente presente en el territorio de un estado (p. ej., derecho a documentos de identidad); corresponden derechos adicionales una vez que se establece la presencia legal (p. ej., autoempleo); la permanencia legal da lugar a un conjunto de derechos más amplio (p. ej., acceso a vivienda pública y sistemas de bienestar); y se debe conceder una pequeña cantidad de derechos solo una vez que se establezca la residencia duradera (p. ej., exención de la reciprocidad legislativa).

10. The assessment of respect for refugee rights shall also take account of the fact that satisfaction of Convention rights is in most cases not conceived in absolute terms, but is rather defined by reference to the rights enjoyed by others in the receiving state. For example, refugees are entitled to the same rights to elementary education as citizens; the same right to engage in employment as most favored non-citizens; and the same right to freedom of movement as aliens generally.

10. L'évaluation du respect des droits des réfugiés devra également prendre en considération la circonstance que les droits de la Convention ne sont généralement pas définis en termes absolus, mais plutôt en référence aux droits dont d'autres bénéficient au sein de l'État d'accueil. Par exemple, les réfugiés ont le même droit que les nationaux d'accéder à l'enseignement primaire. Ils ont également le même droit d'exercer une activité professionnelle salariée que les ressortissants étrangers bénéficiant du traitement le plus favorable à cet égard, et la même liberté de circulation que celle des étrangers en général.

10. La evaluación del respeto de los derechos de los refugiados también tendrá en cuenta que la satisfacción de los derechos del Convenio en la mayoría de los casos no se concibe en términos absolutos, sino que se define en referencia a los derechos de los otros individuos en el estado receptor. Por ejemplo, los refugiados tienen derecho a los mismos derechos a la educación primaria que los ciudadanos; el mismo derecho a dedicarse al empleo que los no ciudadanos más favorecidos; y el mismo derecho a la libertad de circulación que los extranjeros en general.

11. Beyond ensuring that any refugee transferred to the receiving state will in practice enjoy rights in line with the requirements of Arts. 2-34 of the Convention, the sending state also must give effect to its obligations under international human rights law and international humanitarian law. The duty not to return anyone to the risk of torture is a clear example of a constraint arising outside the Refugee Convention which limits reliance on an otherwise lawful protection elsewhere policy.

11. L'État d'envoi ne doit pas uniquement s'assurer que tout réfugié transféré vers l'État d'accueil bénéficiera en pratique des droits consacrés par les articles 2 à 34 de la Convention, mais il doit également respecter ses obligations de droit international des droits de l'homme et de droit international humanitaire. L'interdiction de renvoyer un individu vers un pays où il risque la torture constitue un exemple d'obligation ne résultant pas de la Convention, mais contraignant la mise en œuvre d'une politique de protection ailleurs, à supposer même que cette dernière soit conforme à la Convention.

11. Además de garantizar que cualquier refugiado trasladado al estado receptor disfrute en la práctica de los derechos de acuerdo con los requisitos de los artículos 2 a 34 de la Convención, el estado remitente debe cumplir con sus obligaciones en virtud del derecho internacional sobre derechos humanos y el derecho internacional humanitario. El deber de no hacer que nadie vuelva a estar en riesgo de ser torturado es un claro ejemplo de una restricción que surge al margen de la Convención de Refugiados, que limita la dependencia de una política de protección en otro lugar que de otro modo sería legal.

9. عند تقييم مدى احترام حقوق اللاجئين تؤخذ الحقيقة الواقعية الآتية في الاعتبار، وهي أن غالبية هذه الحقوق ليست ذات طابع مطلق أو فوري، كما أن تحقيقها رما يتطلب بعض الوقت. وعلى وجه الخصوص يشهد الواقع أن الحقوق التي يمكن أن يتمتع بأحد اللاجئين تتزايد عبر الوقت كلما تزايدت درجة اندماج هذا اللاجئ بالدولة التي تُقدم له الحماية. وعلى سبيل المثال، هناك بعض الحقوق اللصيقة التي يحصل عليها اللاجئ مجرد دخوله تحت سلطة وحماية دولة الملاذ، مثل الحق في عدم الإبعاد أو الإعادة القسرين ((non-refoulment))، كما أن هناك حقوق أخرى مرتبطة بالوجود الفعلي لهذا اللاجئ في إقليم هذه الدولة، مثل الحق في الحصول على أوراق إثبات شخصية أو هوية. وهناك نوع آخر من الحقوق الذي يتطلب الإقامة المشروعة في إقليم هذه الدولة مثل حق التوظيف الذاتي (أن تدير عملاً حراً). كما إن استمرارية الإقامة المشروعة في إقليم دولة طلب الحماية تؤدي إلى منح اللاجئ مزيداً من الحقوق الأكثر شمول من الحقوق الأخرى مثل الحق في الحصول على سكن وحق الاستفادة من نظم الرعاية الاجتماعية. وهناك بعض الحقوق الأخرى القليلة التي لا تتطلب فحسب مجرد استمرار الإقامة القانونية، لكنها تتطلب وجودها بصفة دائمة وراسخة، مثل الحق في الإعفاء من نظام المعاملة بالمثل قانونيا.

9. При оценке соблюдения прав беженцев необходимо учитывать тот факт, что большинство подобных прав не предоставляются сразу и не являются по своему характеру абсолютными. В частности, права, принадлежащие беженцу, расширяются с течением времени по мере роста уровня связи с государством, предоставившим ему защиту. Некоторые права беженец получает сразу же, как только он подпадает под контроль или юрисдикцию данного государства (например, запрет высылки [*non-refoulement!*]); другие права вступают в действие в тот момент, когда беженец физически оказывается на территории данного государства (например, право на получение документов, удостоверяющих личность); дополнительные права беженец получает тогда, когда устанавливается его законное нахождение на территории страны (например, право заниматься самостоятельной предпринимательской деятельностью); законное пребывание влечет более обширный комплекс прав (например, доступ к государственному жилью и системе социального обеспечения); небольшое количество прав беженец получает только после долговременного проживания (например, освобождение от принципа взаимности в законодательстве).

10. عند تقييم مدى احترام حقوق اللاجئين، يجب إن يؤخذ في الاعتبار أيضاً إن احترام هذه الحقوق كما وردت في الاتفاقية الدولية، لا يجب أن يُفهم على أسس مُطلقة، بل ينبغي أن يتم تعريف هذه الحقوق بطريقة نسبية، وخاصة بالمقارنة مع كيفية ممارسة هذه الحقوق من قبل وتجاه كافة الأشخاص الذين يعيشون في الدولة المُستقبلة نفسها. وعلى سبيل المثال، فإن للاجئين الحق في أن يتمتعوا بالحق في الحصول على التعليم الأساسي مثل كافة مواطني الدولة المُستقبلة، ويتمتع للاجئين أيضا بالحق في العمل مثلما يتم التعامل مع الأجانب الأكثر تفضيلا الموجودين على إقليم الدولة المستقبلة. ولهم أن يتمتعوا بالحق في حرية التنقل، مثلهم مثل الآخرين من غير المواطنين، أي من المُقيمين أو المهاجرين الذين يعيشون في الدولة المُستقبلة بصفة عامة.

10. При оценке соблюдения прав беженцев следует также принимать во внимание тот факт, что соблюдение прав, предусмотренных Конвенцией, в большинстве случаев определено не в абсолютных терминах, а путем ссылки на права других лиц принимающего государства. Например, беженцы имеют те же права на начальное образование, что и граждане; то же право на трудоустройство, что и неграждане, пользующиеся наибольшим благоприятствованием; и то же право на свободу передвижения, что и иностранцы в целом.

11. بالإضافة إلى ضرورة التأكد من أن جميع اللاجئين المنقولين إلى الدولة المُستقبلة لهم حق في التمتع بكافة الحقوق الممنوحة لهم وفقاً لاشتراطات المواد من 2 إلى 34 من الاتفاقية الدولية، فإن ذلك لا ينفي أن الدولة المُرسلة عليها أيضاً الوفاء بكافة الالتزامات التي يُحملها إياها القانون الدولي لحقوق الإنسان والقانون الإنساني الدولي بصفة عامة. ويُعتبر الالتزام الواقع على جميع دول العالم بعدم إعادة أي شخص، بما في ذلك اللاجئين، إلى دولة ما يتوقع فيها تعذيبه مثالاً لهذه الالتزامات الدولية المُترتبة على الاتفاقيات الدولية الأخرى بخلاف الاتفاقية الدولية للاجئين. مثل هذا الالتزام الدولي يعتبر قيداً والتزاماً قانونياً ينبغي مراعاته عند التطبيق القانوني لسياسة توفير الحماية في موقع بديل.

11. Кроме обеспечения гарантий того, что любой беженец, перемещаемый в принимающее государство, на практике будет пользоваться правами в соответствии с требованиями Статей 2-34 Конвенции, отправляющее государство также должно выполнять свои обязательства в соответствии с международным законодательством в области прав человека и международным гуманитарным правом. Обязанность не возвращать кого-либо в условия, в которых ему или ей могут угрожать пытки, является наглядным примером ограничения, возникающего за пределами Конвенции о беженцах, которая устанавливает рамки в остальном законного применения принципа защиты в другом месте.

SAFEGUARDS

12. Any person to be transferred to another state under a protection elsewhere policy must be able to contest the legality of the proposed transfer before it is effected. The sending state shall notify any person to be transferred of this entitlement, and shall consider in good faith any challenge to the legality of transfer under a procedure that meets international standards of procedural fairness. Such procedure must in particular afford an effective remedy bearing in mind the nature of the rights alleged to be at risk in the receiving state.

GARANTIES

12. Toute personne transférée vers un autre État au motif qu'elle doit solliciter une protection ailleurs doit être en mesure de contester la légalité de son transfert avant qu'il ne soit effectué. L'État d'envoi doit notifier cette possibilité à toute personne qui sera transférée et doit examiner de bonne foi toute contestation de la légalité du transfert, suivant une procédure respectant les exigences d'équité procédurale consacrées par le droit international. En particulier, pareille procédure doit garantir un recours effectif, compte tenu de la nature des droits dont la violation au sein de l'État d'accueil est alléguée.

GARANTÍAS

12. Cualquier persona que deba ser trasladada a otro estado bajo una política de protección en otro lugar debe ser capaz de impugnar la legalidad del traslado propuesto antes de que se efectúe. El estado remitente informará acerca de este derecho a cualquier persona que se traslade, y considerará de buena fe cualquier impugnación a la legalidad del traslado conforme a un procedimiento que cumpla con los estándares internacionales de equidad procesal. Tal procedimiento debe, en particular, proporcionar un recurso efectivo teniendo en cuenta la naturaleza de los derechos que supuestamente estarán en riesgo en el estado receptor.

---

13. In line with the requirements of Art. 31(2) of the Convention, any refugee whose removal is contemplated under a protection elsewhere policy shall first be granted 'a reasonable period and all the necessary facilities to obtain admission into another country' of his or her choosing.

13. Conformément aux exigences de l'article 31, §2, de la Convention, tout réfugié dont le renvoi est envisagé en raison de l'exigence de solliciter une protection ailleurs doit d'abord bénéficier d'un « délai raisonnable ainsi que toutes facilités nécessaires » pour réussir à se faire admettre dans un autre pays de son choix.

13. De acuerdo con los requisitos del artículo 31 (2) de la Convención, cualquier refugiado cuya remoción de un territorio esté contemplada bajo una política de protección en otro lugar recibirá primero "un período razonable y todas las facilidades necesarias para ser admitido en otro país" de su elección.

---

14. If a receiving state fails to ensure that a transferred person who meets the requirements of Art. 1 of the Convention receives the benefit of Arts. 2-34 of the Convention, the sending state's original obligations to that refugee are no longer satisfied by reliance on the transfer of protection responsibility. The sending state in such circumstances should facilitate the return and readmission of the refugee in question to its territory, and ensure respect for his or her rights there in line with the requirements of the Convention.

14. Si un État d'accueil manque à son obligation de garantir à la personne transférée, qui relève de l'article 1 de la Convention, le bénéfice des droits consacrés par les articles 2 à 34 de la Convention, l'État d'envoi ne respecte plus ses obligations à l'encontre de ce réfugié en transférant sa responsabilité originelle de lui assurer une protection à un autre État. En pareilles circonstances, l'État d'envoi doit faciliter le retour et la réadmission de ce réfugié sur son territoire, et garantir le respect de ses droits en conformité avec les exigences de la Convention.

14. Si un estado receptor no se asegura de que una persona trasladada que cumple con los requisitos del artículo 1 de la Convención reciba el beneficio de los artículos 2 a 34 de la Convención, las obligaciones originales del estado remitente con ese refugiado ya no se cumplirán por confiar en la transferencia de la responsabilidad de protección. En dichas circunstancias, el estado remitente debe facilitar el regreso y la readmisión del refugiado en cuestión a su territorio, y garantizar el respeto de sus derechos allí de acuerdo con los requisitos de la Convención.

---

15. A sending state whose officials or decision-makers have actual or constructive knowledge of breach by a receiving state of the latter state's duty to respect the requirements of Arts. 1-34 of the Convention will ordinarily be unable to assert that Convention obligations are respected in the receiving state. It is thus disentitled from effecting any further transfers to that state under a protection elsewhere policy until and unless there is clear evidence that the breach has ceased.

15. L'État d'envoi dont tout agent ou autorité de décision prend connaissance de la violation, réelle ou présumée, par l'État d'accueil de ses obligations imposées par les articles 1 à 34 de la Convention, n'a généralement pas la possibilité effective d'imposer à l'État d'accueil de respecter les exigences conventionnelles. En conséquence, tant qu'il n'y pas d'indication claire que ces violations ont cessé, les réfugiés ne peuvent plus y être transférés au motif qu'ils doivent solliciter une protection ailleurs.

15. Un estado emisor cuyos funcionarios o responsables de tomar decisiones tengan conocimiento real o constructivo de que un estado receptor esté violando su deber de respetar los requisitos de los artículos 1 a 34 de la Convención, ordinariamente no podrán afirmar que el estado receptor cumple con las obligaciones de la Convención. Por lo tanto, no tiene derecho a efectuar ningún otro traslado a ese estado bajo una política de protección en otro lugar hasta que exista evidencia clara de que la violación de las obligaciones haya cesado.

12. Любое лицо, перемещаемое в другое государство в соответствии с принципом защиты в другом месте, должно иметь возможность оспорить законность предлагаемого перемещения до того, как это перемещение будет осуществлено. Отправляющее государство должно уведомить перемещаемое лицо об этом праве, и должно добросовестно рассмотреть любое обвинение касательно законности перемещения в рамках процедуры, соответствующей международным нормам справедливости таковой процедуры. Эта процедура, в частности, должна предоставлять эффективное средство судебно-правовой защиты с учетом природы этих прав, имея в виду предполагаемое существование таковых прав в принимающем государстве.

13. В соответствии с требованиями Статьи 31 (2) Конвенции, любой беженец, чья высылка будет осуществляться в соответствии с принципом защиты в другом месте, сначала должен получить "достаточный срок и все необходимые условия для получения права на въезд в другую страну" по своему выбору.

14. Если принимающее государство не обеспечивает того, чтобы перемещаемое лицо, соответствующее требованиям Статьи 1 Конвенции, пользовалось правами, определенными в Статьях 2-34 Конвенции, то изначальные обязательства отправляющего государства по отношению к этому беженцу более не считаются соответствующими передаче обязательства по защите. В этих обстоятельствах отправляющее государство должно содействовать возвращению и повторному приему данного беженца на своей территории, и обеспечить соблюдение там его или ее прав в соответствии с требованиями Конвенции.

15. Отправляющее государство, чьи руководители или лица, принимающие решения, располагают фактическими или умозрительными сведениями о нарушении принимающим государством своих обязанностей по соблюдению требований Статей 1-34 Конвенции, обычно не имеют возможности с уверенностью утверждать, что обязательства Конвенции соблюдаются в принимающем государстве. Таким образом, отправляющее государство лишается права в дальнейшем осуществлять передачу лиц в принимающее государство в соответствии с принципом защиты в другом месте до тех пор, пока не появятся убедительные доказательства того, что это нарушение более не имеет места.

16. Transfer under a protection elsewhere policy should ideally take place only under the auspices of a written agreement between the states in question. At a minimum, such an agreement should stipulate the duty of the receiving state to respect the refugee status of persons defined by Art. 1 of the Convention; to provide transferred refugees the rights set by Arts. 2-34 of the Convention; to ensure the right and ability of transferred refugees to notify the United Nations High Commissioner for Refugees (UNHCR) of any alleged breach of the responsibilities of the receiving state; to grant UNHCR the right to be present in the receiving state and to enjoy unhindered access to transferred refugees in order to monitor compliance with the receiving state's responsibilities towards them; and to abide by a procedure (whether established by the agreement or otherwise) for the settlement of any disagreement arising out of interpretation or implementation of the agreement.

16. Le transfert au motif que le réfugié doit solliciter une protection ailleurs devrait idéalement se réaliser en application d'un accord écrit entre les États concernés. Pareil accord devrait, au minimum, mentionner explicitement l'obligation de l'État d'accueil de respecter le statut de réfugié des personnes relevant de l'article 1er de la Convention, de conférer aux réfugiés transférés les droits consacrés par les articles 2 à 34 de la Convention, de garantir le droit et la possibilité aux réfugiés transférés de faire valoir auprès du Haut-commissariat aux réfugiés des Nations unies (« l'UNHCR ») toute allégation de violation de leurs droits par l'État d'accueil, d'accorder à l'UNHCR le droit d'être présent sur le territoire de l'État d'accueil et de bénéficier d'un accès illimité aux réfugiés transférés afin de s'assurer que leurs droits sont respectés, de se conformer à une procédure (établie par l'accord ou dans un autre texte) permettant de résoudre tout désaccord relativement à l'interprétation et à la mise en œuvre de l'accord.

16. El traslado bajo una política de protección en otro lugar idealmente debería tener lugar solo con el amparo de un acuerdo por escrito entre los estados en cuestión. Como mínimo, dicho acuerdo debe estipular el deber del estado receptor de respetar la condición de refugiado de las personas en virtud del artículo 1 de la Convención; proporcionar a los refugiados trasladados los derechos establecidos por los artículos 2 a 34 de la Convención; garantizar el derecho y la capacidad de los refugiados trasladados de informar al Alto Comisionado de las Naciones Unidas para los Refugiados (ACNUR) sobre cualquier supuesto incumplimiento de las responsabilidades del estado receptor; conceder al ACNUR el derecho a estar presente en el estado receptor y a disponer de libre acceso a los refugiados trasladados a fin de supervisar el cumplimiento de las responsabilidades del estado receptor para con ellos; y cumplir un procedimiento (ya sea establecido por el acuerdo o no) para solucionar cualquier desacuerdo que surja de la interpretación o aplicación de las disposiciones del acuerdo.

These Guidelines reflect the consensus of all participants at the Fourth Colloquium on Challenges in International Refugee Law, held at the University of Michigan Law School, Ann Arbor, Michigan, USA, on November 10-12, 2006.

James C. Hathaway
Colloquium Convener
University of Michigan

Rodger P.G. Haines
Colloquium Chair
University of Auckland

Michelle Foster
Colloquium Rapporteur
University of Melbourne

Mariano-Florentino Cuellar
Stanford University

Maryellen Fullerton
Brooklyn Law School

Justice A.M. North
Federal Court of Australia
President, Intl. Association of
    Refugee Law Judges

Mary Ellen O'Connell
University of Notre Dame

Guglielmo Verdirame
Cambridge University

Marjoleine Zieck
University of Amsterdam

Hedy Chang
Student
University of Michigan

Martin Jones
Research Scholar
University of Michigan

Alla Karagodin
Student
University of Michigan

Sarah Karniski
Student
University of Michigan

Allison Kent
Student
University of Michigan

Alicia Kinsey
Student
University of Michigan

Abby Rubinson
Student
University of Michigan

Lindsey Schatzberg
Student
University of Michigan

Rachel Simmons
Student
University of Michigan

Aref Wardak
Student
University of Michigan

The Colloquium benefited from the counsel of Ms Judith Kumin, Regional Representative for the Benelux and the European Institutions, United Nations High Commissioner for Refugees

16. إن أفضل صور تطبيق سياسات توفير الحماية في موقع بديل هي تلك الحالة التي تشهد وجود اتفاق مكتوب بين الدولتين محل البحث. وكحد أدنى يجب أن يشتمل هذا الاتفاق المكتوب على تعهداً من الدولة المُستقبلة تقر فيه بالآتي: الالتزام بأن تحديد صفة اللاجئ وفقاً للمادة 1 من الاتفاقية الدولية؛ احترام كافة حقوق اللاجئين ـ المنقولين إليها ـ الواردة في المواد من 2 إلى 34 من الاتفاقية الدولية؛ احترام حق هؤلاء اللاجئين في إخطار مفوضية الأمم المتحدة السامية لشؤون اللاجئين بأي خرق تقوم به الدولة المُستقبلة ذاتها؛ منح مفوضية الأمم المتحدة السامية لشؤون اللاجئين الحق في الوجود على أراضيها وبأن يكون للمفوضية الحق في الاتصال الفوري وبدون عوائق باللاجئين المنقولين إلى هذه الدولة وذلك لكي تتمكن المفوضية الدولية من مراقبة مدى التزام هذه الدولة باحترام تعهداتها وواجباتها القانونية تجاه هؤلاء الأشخاص المنقولين إليها؛ وأخيراً تلتزم الدولة المُستقبلة أيضاً بتوفير كافة الإجراءات (سواء تلك التي نص عليها اتفاق النقل مع الدولة المُرسلة صراحة أو كافة الإجراءات التي نص عليها القانون) الكافية التي موجبها يحق للأشخاص المنقولين الطعن في أي خلافات أو نزاعات تتعلق بتفسير أو تطبيق الاتفاق بين الدولتين المُرسلة و المُستقبلة، والذي تم موجبه نقل اللاجئ إلى الدولة الأخيرة.

16. В идеале передача в соответствии с принципом защиты в другом месте должна происходить только при наличии письменного соглашения между данными государствами. Как минимум, такое соглашение должно устанавливать обязанность принимающего государства по соблюдению статуса беженца лиц, определенную в Статье 1 Конвенции; предоставлять передаваемым беженцам права, определенные в Статьях 2-34 Конвенции; обеспечивать право и возможность передаваемым беженцам сообщать Управлению Верховного комиссара ООН по делам беженцев (УВКБ ООН) о любых предполагаемых нарушениях принимающим государством своих обязательств; предоставлять УВКБ ООН право присутствовать в принимающем государстве и пользоваться беспрепятственным доступом к передаваемым беженцам в целях наблюдения за выполнением принимающим государством своих обязанностей в отношении беженцев; а также подчиняться процедуре (как установленной соглашением, так и иной) урегулирования любых разногласий, вызванных толкованием или выполнением соглашения.

THE MICHIGAN GUIDELINES ON THE RIGHT TO WORK (2009)

(Abridged Version: full text available at (2010) 31 Mich. J. Int'l. L. 293)

The right to work is fundamental to human dignity. It is central to survival and development of the human personality . . . Work is interrelated, interdependent with, and indivisible from the rights to life, equality, the highest attainable standard of physical and mental health, an adequate standard of living, the right to social security and/or social assistance, freedom of movement, freedom of association, and the rights to privacy and family life, among others.

LES RECOMMANDATIONS DE MICHIGAN SUR LE DROIT AU TRAVAIL

(Version courte. La version longue peut être consultée dans le Michigan Journal of International Law, vol. 31, p. 293)

Le droit au travail est une composante fondamentale de la dignité humaine. Il est essentiel à la survie et au développement personnel de tout être humain. Le travail est intimement lié, interdépendant et indivisible avec, notamment, le droit à la vie, l'égalité, le niveau le plus élevé de santé physique et mentale, un niveau de vie adéquat, le droit à la sécurité sociale et/ou à une assistance sociale, la liberté de circulation, la liberté d'association et le droit à la vie privée et familiale.

LAS NORMAS DE MICHIGAN SOBRE EL DERECHO AL TRABAJO

Versión abreviada: *Texto complete disponible en (2010) 31 Mich. Int'l. L. 293)*

El derecho al trabajo es fundamental para la dignidad humana. Es fundamental para la supervivencia y el desarrollo humano. El trabajo está interrelacionado con, y es interdependiente e indivisible del, derecho a la vida, la igualdad, el más alto nivel posible de salud física y mental, un nivel de vida adecuado, el derecho a un seguro social y/o asistencia social, la libertad de circulación, la libertad de asociación y los derechos a la privacidad y la vida familiar, entre otros.

Numerous international and regional human rights instruments, as well as many national constitutions, protect the right to work . . . Several regional instruments also recognize the right to work . . . In addition, rights at work are protected by international labor standards, particularly the eight 'fundamental' ILO conventions and the four 'priority' ILO conventions. . . .

De nombreux instruments internationaux et régionaux de protection des droits de l'homme, de même que de nombreuses constitutions nationales, protègent le droit au travail. Le droit au travail est également consacré par divers instruments régionaux. En outre, les droits au travail sont protégés par les standards du droit international du travail, en particulier les huit Conventions de l'O.I.T. dites « fondamentales » et les quatre Conventions de l'O.I.T. dites « prioritaires » ou « de gouvernance ».

Numerosos instrumentos internacionales y regionales de derechos humanos, así como muchas constituciones nacionales, protegen el derecho al trabajo. Varios instrumentos regionales también reconocen el derecho al trabajo. Además, los derechos del trabajo están protegidos por las normas internacionales del trabajo, particular en por los ocho convenios "fundamentales" de la OIT y los cuatro convenios "prioritarios" de la OIT.

At the core of the right to work is freedom to gain a living by work freely chosen or accepted. This right entails access to the labor market, as well as the ability to participate in self-employment and the liberal professions. In most human rights instruments, this freedom is expressed as a universal entitlement, and is protected on a non-discriminatory basis.

La liberté de gagner sa vie par un travail librement choisi ou accepté constitue le cœur du droit au travail. Cette liberté implique de pouvoir accéder au marché du travail, de même que de pouvoir exercer une activité de travailleur indépendant ou une profession libérale. Dans la majorité des instruments de protection des droits fondamentaux, cette liberté est consacrée de manière universelle et est garantie à l'aide du principe de non-discrimination.

En el núcleo del derecho al trabajo está la libertad de ganarse la vida mediante un trabajo elegido o aceptado libremente. Este derecho implica el acceso al mercado laboral, así como la capacidad de participar en el empleo independiente y profesiones independientes. En la mayoría de los instrumentos de derechos humanos, esta libertad se expresa como un derecho universal y se protege de forma no discriminatoria.

دليل ميشيغان الإرشادي حول الحق في العمل*

الحق في العمل أساسي لكرامة الإنسان ولبقائه وتنمية شخصيته . . . فطبقا لمنظمة العمل الدولية فإن العمل اللائق "تلخيص لتطلعات الناس في العمل ولتطلعاتهم في الحصول على فرص العمل والأجور العادلة والتمتع بكل الحقوق والامتيازات، وحرية التعبير. . . ." لأن الحق في العمل مرتبط ومتكامل وغير قابل للتجزئة من حقوق الإنسان في الحياة والمساواة وتحقيق أعلى مستوى ممكن بلوغه من الصحة البدنية والعقلية والمستوى المعيشي اللائق والحق في الضمان الاجتماعي و/ أو المساعدة الاجتماعية وحرية التنقل وحرية التنظيم والحق في الخصوصية والحياة الأسرية، من ضمن أمور أخرى.

* نسخة مختصره ممكن الاطلاع على النص الكامل في (العدد رقم 31 لعام 2010 من مجلة ميشيغان للقانون الدولي ص. 293).

МИЧИГАНСКИЕ РУКОВОДЯЩИЕ ПРИНЦИПЫ: ПРАВО НА ТРУД

Сокращенная версия: полный текст доступен (2010) 31 Mich. J. Int'l. L. 293

Право на труд имеет основополагающее значение для человеческого достоинства. Оно имеет решающее значение для выживания и развития человеческой личности . . . Труд тесно взаимосвязан и неотделим, среди прочего, от права на жизнь, равенства, хорошего физического и психического здоровья, достаточного жизненного уровня, права на социальное обеспечение и/или социальную помощь, свободы передвижения, свободы ассоциации, а также права на неприкосновенность частной и семейной жизни.

تحمي العديد من الصكوك الدولية والإقليمية لحقوق الإنسان، فضلا عن العديد من الدساتير الوطنية، الحق في العمل . . . كما تعترف العديد من الصكوك الإقليمية بالحق في العمل . . . وبالإضافة إلى ذلك، فإن الحق في العمل محمي بموجب معايير العمل الدولية، وخاصة اتفاقيات منظمة العمل الدولية الثمانية «الأساسية» واتفاقيات منظمة العمل الدولية الأربعة «ذات الأولوية». . . .

Многочисленные международные и региональные нормы по правам человека, а также многие национальные конституции защищают право на труд . . . Некоторые региональные документы также признают право на труд . . . Кроме того, право на труд защищено международными трудовыми стандартами, в частности восемью «фундаментальными» конвенциями Международной организации труда (МОТ) и четырьмя «приоритетными» конвенциями МОТ . . .

ويكمن في جوهر الحق في العمل حرية كسب الرزق من خلال عمل يختاره الشخص ويقبله بحرية. وينطوي هذا الحق على الدخول إلى سوق العمل، فضلا عن القدرة على المشاركة في الأعمال والمهن الحرة. وفي معظم صكوك حقوق الإنسان، يُعبر عن هذه الحرية بوصفها استحقاق عالمي، محمي للجميع بدون تمييز.

В основе права на труд лежит свобода зарабатывать на жизнь с помощью работы, которую человек свободно выбрал или согласился с ней. Это право подразумевает доступ к рынку труда, а также возможность вести самостоятельную трудовую деятельность в свободных профессиях. В большинстве международных норм в области по правам человека эта свобода признается универсальной, и защищена на основе принципа недискриминации.

Freedom to work is a right that is fundamental to the protection of refugees and others seeking protection which must not be confused with the reasons for their flight. Unable to return to their country of origin or nationality, and being without the protection of their own country, refugees must have rights to work in the country of refuge. As stated by one of the framers of the Refugee Convention, 'without the right to work, all other rights were meaningless.' It is also in the interest of countries of refuge that refugees are allowed to work. The ability to engage in decent work empowers refugees, enabling self-reliance and contribution to the economy and society . . .

La liberté de travailler est un droit essentiel à la protection des réfugiés et des autres personnes sollicitant une protection, qui ne doit toutefois pas être confondue avec les motifs de leur fuite. C'est parce qu'il ne leur est pas possible de retourner dans leur pays d'origine ou de nationalité, et qu'ils ne peuvent pas bénéficier de la protection de leur propre pays, que les réfugiés doivent avoir le droit de travailler dans le pays d'asile. Comme cela a été souligné par l'un des concepteurs de la Convention relative au statut des réfugiés (« la Convention »), « sans le droit au travail, tous les autres droits deviennent dénués de sens ». Il est également dans l'intérêt des pays d'asile d'autoriser les réfugiés à travailler. La capacité de réaliser un travail décent donne aux réfugiés les moyens d'être autonomes et de contribuer à l'économie et à la vie de la société d'accueil.

La libertad de trabajo es un derecho fundamental para la protección de los refugiados y otras personas que buscan protección, lo cual no debe confundirse con los motivos de su huida. Incapaces de regresar a su país de origen o nacionalidad, y sin la protección de su propio país, los refugiados deben tener derecho a trabajar en el país de acogida. Como afirmó uno de los artífices de la Convención sobre el Estatuto de los Refugiados: "Sin el derecho al trabajo, todos los demás derechos carecían de sentido". También es de interés para los países de acogida que los refugiados puedan trabajar. La capacidad de realizar un trabajo decente empodera a los refugiados, lo que permite la autosuficiencia y la contribución a la economía y a la sociedad.

In order to uphold the right to work for refugees and others seeking protection, we have engaged in sustained collaborative study and reflection on the international legal norms and state practice relevant to refugees' right to work. This research was debated and refined at the Fifth Colloquium on Challenges in International Refugee Law, convened between November 13 and 15, 2009 by the University of Michigan Law School's Program in Refugee and Asylum Law. These Guidelines are the product of that endeavor, and reflect the consensus of Colloquium participants.

Afin d'assurer le respect du droit au travail des réfugiés et des autres personnes sollicitant une protection, nous nous sommes engagés dans une étude et réflexion systématique sur les normes de droit international et la pratique des États relatives au droit au travail. Les résultats de cette recherche ont été débattus et affinés à l'occasion du cinquième colloque sur les défis du droit international des réfugiés, qui s'est tenu du 13 et 15 novembre 2009 à l'initiative du programme en droit de l'asile et des réfugiés de la faculté de droit de l'université du Michigan. Les recommandations sont le fruit de ce travail collectif et reflètent le consensus des participants au colloque.

Con el fin de defender el derecho al trabajo de los refugiados y otras personas que buscan protección, hemos realizado un estudio y una reflexión colaborativos y sostenidos sobre las normas jurídicas internacionales y la práctica estatal relevante para el derecho al trabajo de los refugiados. Esta investigación fue debatida y definida en el Quinto Coloquio sobre Desafíos en el Derecho Internacional de los Refugiados, llevado a cabo entre el 13 y el 15 de noviembre de 2009 por el Programa de Legislación en materia de Refugio y Asilo de la Facultad de Derecho de la Universidad de Michigan. Estas directrices son el producto de ese esfuerzo y reflejan el consenso de los participantes del coloquio.

والحرية في العمل حق أساسي لحماية اللاجئين وغيرهم من طالبي الحماية ولا يجب الخلط بينها وبين أسباب هروبهم. حيث انهم لا يستطيعون العودة إلى بلدهم الأم أو البلد التي يحملون جنسيتها، ومن دون حماية بلدهم، فإنه يجب أن يكون للاجئين الحق في العمل في بلد اللجوء. كما ذكر أحد واضعي اتفاقية اللاجئين، «من دون الحق في العمل، فإن جميع الحقوق الأخرى لا معنى لها». كما أنه من مصلحة بلدان اللجوء السماح للاجئين بالعمل. حيث أن القدرة على الانخراط في العمل اللائق تُمكن اللاجئين وتزودهم بالقدرة على الاعتماد الذاتي والمساهمة في الاقتصاد والمجتمع . . .

Свобода труда — это право, которое имеет основополагающее значение для защиты беженцев и других лиц, ищущих защиты, которое не следует путать с причинами их бегства. Не имея возможности вернуться в родную страну или страну своего гражданства, находясь без защиты своей собственной страны, беженцы должны иметь право на труд в стране убежища. Как заявил один из создателей Конвенции о статусе беженцев: «Без права на труд все другие права были бы бессмысленными». Кроме того, предоставить беженцам право на труд — в интересах страны, предоставившей убежище. Способность найти достойную работу дает беженцам больше возможностей, позволяет обрести экономическую самодостаточность и внести свой вклад в экономическую ситуацию и развитие общества.

ومن أجل دعم الحق في العمل للاجئين وغيرهم ممن يلتمسون الحماية، شاركنا في دراسة تعاونية مستمرة والتفكير في المعابر القانونية الدولية وممارسات الدول ذات الصلة بحق اللاجئين في العمل. تمت مناقشة هذا البحث وتنقيحه في الندوة الخامسة حول التحديات في قانون اللاجئين الدولي، والتي عقدت من 13 إلى 15 نوفمبر 2009 في برنامج كلية الحقوق في جامعة ميشيغان حول قانون اللاجئين واللجوء. وهذه المبادئ التوجيهية هي نتاج هذا المسعى، وتعكس توافق آراء المشاركين في الندوة.

В целях обеспечения права на труд для беженцев и других лиц, ищущих защиты, мы проводили последовательное совместное изучение и сопоставление международных правовых норм и практики государств в сфере права беженцев на труд. Эти исследования обсуждались и уточнялись на пятом коллоквиуме по проблемам международных прав беженцев, который проходил 13–15 ноября 2009 года в рамках Программы юридического факультета Университета штата Мичиган относительно законодательства о беженцах и убежище. Данные Руководящие принципы являются результатом указанных усилий и отражают единое мнение участников коллоквиума.

FREEDOM TO WORK—A FUNDAMENTAL RIGHT FOR REFUGEES

1. . . . Refugees who are unable to work may be compelled by sheer economic desperation to return to a place of persecution, resulting in a violation of the obligation of *non-refoulement*. Failure to permit access to the labor market may render refugees destitute. It may also result in the unauthorized work of refugees in dangerous and degrading conditions, and can expose them to physical, sexual, and gender-based violence . . . States are legally obliged to prevent and protect persons from such exploitation under, *inter alia*, the prohibition on inhuman and degrading treatment; the prohibition on slavery and forced labor; treaties for the suppression of human trafficking and people smuggling; and numerous treaties concerning nondiscrimination. In particular, the rights of asylum-seeking and refugee women must be respected, protected, and fulfilled under CEDAW and other guarantees of equality.

LA LIBERTÉ DE TRAVAILLER, UN DROIT FONDAMENTAL DES RÉFUGIÉS

1. Les réfugiés qui ne peuvent pas travailler peuvent se trouver dans un état de privation tel qu'ils sont contraints de retourner là où ils risquent la persécution, en violation du principe de non-refoulement. Ne pas autoriser les réfugiés à accéder au marché du travail peut avoir pour conséquence de les plonger dans un état de pauvreté extrême. Cela les incite également à travailler illégalement, dans des conditions dangereuses et dégradantes, et les expose à des abus physiques, sexuels ainsi qu'à des violences liées au genre. Les États ont l'obligation légale de prévenir et de protéger les individus contre ces formes d'exploitation en vertu, notamment, de l'interdiction des traitements inhumains et dégradants, de l'interdiction de l'esclavage et du travail forcé, des traités visant à éliminer la traite et le trafic d'êtres humains et des nombreux traités interdisant les discriminations. En particulier, les droits des demandeuses d'asile et des réfugiées doivent être respectés, protégés et mis en œuvre conformément à la Convention sur l'élimination de toutes les formes de discrimination à l'égard des femmes et les autres instruments consacrant le principe d'égalité.

LIBERTAD PARA TRABAJAR: UN DERECHO FUNDAMENTAL PARA LOS REFUGIADOS

1. Los refugiados que no pueden trabajar pueden verse obligados por pura desesperación económica a regresar a un lugar de persecución, lo cual resulta en un incumplimiento de la obligación de no devolución (*non-refoulement*). Si no se les permite acceder al mercado laboral, los refugiados pueden volverse indigentes. Esto también puede dar lugar al trabajo no autorizado de los refugiados en condiciones peligrosas y degradantes, y puede exponerlos a violencia física, sexual y por motivos de género. Las naciones están legalmente obligadas a evitar dicha explotación y proteger a estas personas en virtud de, entre otros, la prohibición del trato inhumano y degradante; la prohibición de la esclavitud y el trabajo forzado; los tratados para la represión de la trata de personas y el tráfico de personas; y numerosos tratados sobre la no discriminación. En particular, se deben respetar, proteger y cumplir los derechos de las mujeres refugiadas y solicitantes de asilo en virtud de la CEDAW y otras garantías de igualdad.

---

2. Permitting refugees' access to the labor market enables them to contribute to the economy and to become self-reliant, benefiting themselves and the local population . . . By contrast, the enforced unemployment of refugees prevents the acquisition of new skills and leads to loss of existing skills, dependency, lack of confidence, and diminished financial resources . . . As stated by the Executive Committee of the Programme of the United Nations High Commissioner for Refugees, 'the enhancement of basic economic and social rights, including gainful employment, is essential to the achievement of self-sufficiency and family security for refugees and is vital to the process of re-establishing the dignity of the human person and of realizing durable solutions to refugee problems.'

2. Autoriser les réfugiés à accéder au marché de l'emploi leur permet de bénéficier des moyens de contribuer à l'économie et de devenir auto-suffisant, ce qui bénéficie également à la population locale. À l'inverse, l'absence de travail empêche les réfugiés d'acquérir de nouvelles compétences et mène à la détérioration des compétences acquises, à la dépendance, à un manque de confiance et à un amoindrissement des ressources financières. Comme noté par le Comité exécutif du programme du Haut commissaire des Nations unies pour les réfugiés, « l'accroissement des droits économiques et sociaux fondamentaux, y compris à un emploi rémunéré, est essentiel à la réalisation de l'autosuffisance et de la sécurité familiale pour les réfugiés et est indispensable à la restauration de la dignité de la personne humaine et à la mise en œuvre de solutions durables aux problèmes des réfugiés ».

2. Permitir que los refugiados accedan al mercado laboral significa permitirles contribuir a la economía y ser autosuficientes, beneficiándose a sí mismos y a la población local. En cambio, el desempleo forzoso de refugiados impide la adquisición de nuevas habilidades y conduce a la pérdida de las habilidades existentes, a la dependencia, a la falta de confianza y a la disminución de recursos financieros. Tal como lo afirmó el Comité Ejecutivo del Programa del Alto Comisionado de las Naciones Unidas para los Refugiados (ACNUR): "La mejora de los derechos económicos y sociales básicos, incluido el empleo remunerado, es esencial para el logro de la autosuficiencia y seguridad familiar para los refugiados, y es vital para el proceso de restablecimiento de la dignidad de la persona humana y de la materialización de soluciones duraderas para los problemas de los refugiados".

الحرية في العمل - حق أساسي للاجئين

1.... قد يضطر اللاجئون غير القادرين على العمل بسبب اليأس الاقتصادي الهائل إلى العودة إلى مكان الاضطهاد، مما يؤدي إلى انتهاك الالتزام بعدم الإعادة القسرية. قد يؤدي عدم السماح للاجئين بدخول سوق العمل بأن يصبحوا معوزين. وقد يؤدي ذلك أيضًا إلى عمل اللاجئين بشكل غير مرخص في ظروف خطيرة ومهينة، مما قد يعرضهم إلى العنف الجسدي والجنسي والعنف القائم على النوع الاجتماعي ... ومن هذا المنطلق فإن الدول ملزمة قانونًا بمنع وحماية الأشخاص من هذا الاستغلال، من بين أمور أخرى، بموجب منع المعاملة اللاإنسانية والمهينة وحظر الرق والعمل الجبري والاتجار بالبشر وتهريب الأشخاص والعديد من المعاهدات المتعلقة بعدم التمييز. وعلى وجه الخصوص، يجب احترام وحماية وتحقيق حقوق طالبي اللجوء واللاجئين من النساء بموجب اتفاقية القضاء على جميع أشكال التمييز ضد المرأة وغيرها من الضمانات التي تكفل المساواة.

СВОБОДА ТРУДА ЯВЛЯЕТСЯ ФУНДАМЕНТАЛЬНЫМ ПРАВОМ БЕЖЕНЦЕВ

1. Отчаянное экономическое состояние из-за невозможности трудиться может заставить беженцев вернуться туда, где они подвергались преследованию, что приведет к нарушению обязательств, связанных с *принципом невысылки*. Отсутствие доступа к рынку труда может привести беженцев к обнищанию. Это также может привести к несанкционированному трудоустройству в опасных и унижающих достоинство условиях, а также подвергнуть их физическому, сексуальному и гендерному насилию. Государство юридически обязано предотвращать и защищать людей от такой эксплуатации, *в частности*, наложить запрет на бесчеловечное и унижающее достоинство обращение; рабство и принудительный труд; обеспечить функционирование договоров по борьбе с торговлей и контрабандой людьми и многочисленных договоров о недопущении дискриминации. В частности, права женщин, ищущих убежища, и женщин-беженцев должны соблюдаться, защищаться и выполняться в соответствии с решениями Комитета по ликвидации дискриминации в отношении женщин (КЛДЖ) и другими гарантиями равенства.

2. السماح للاجئين بالدخول إلى سوق العمل يمكنهم من المساهمة في الاقتصاد وتحقيق الاعتماد الذاتي مما يكفل لهم الاستفادة وكذلك السكان المحليين ... وفي المقابل، فإن البطالة المفروضة على اللاجئين تحول دون اكتساب مهارات جديدة وتؤدي إلى فقدان المهارات الموجودة والتبعية وانعدام الثقة وتقلص الموارد المالية ... كما ذكرت اللجنة التنفيذية لبرنامج مفوض الأمم المتحدة السامي لشؤون اللاجئين، «إن تعزيز الحقوق الأساسية الاقتصادية والاجتماعية، بما في ذلك العمل بأجر، أمر ضروري لتحقيق الاكتفاء الذاتي والأمن العائلي للاجئين، فضلًا عن أنه أمر حيوي لعملية استعادة كرامة الإنسان والعثور على حلول دائمة لمشاكل اللاجئين».

2. Доступ беженцев на рынок труда позволяет им вносить свой вклад в экономическую жизнь страны и становиться самодостаточными, принося выгоду себе и местному населению. Напротив, вынужденная безработица препятствует приобретению новых навыков и ведет к потере имеющихся навыков, а также приводит к зависимости, недоверию и сокращению финансовых ресурсов. По мнению Исполнительного комитета Программы Верховного комиссара ООН по делам беженцев, «укрепление основных экономических и социальных прав, включая оплачиваемую работу, играет важную роль для самообеспечения и безопасности семей беженцев, а также для процесса восстановления достоинства человеческой личности и реализации долговременных решений проблем беженцев».

A DYNAMIC AND LIBERAL INTERPRETATION OF THE RIGHT TO WORK IS REQUIRED

3. The Refugee Convention refers to the Universal Declaration of Human Rights in its preamble. Therefore the Refugee Convention may be said to have anticipated the development of the core United Nations human rights treaties and, since that development, the Refugee Convention is no longer the sole framework of reference for the interpretation of its provisions. The Refugee Convention must now be viewed as part of the corpus of international human rights law, and read together with other human rights treaties. Every state is party to one or more of these instruments, ensuring a significant congruence of states parties. They are complementary and mutually reinforcing instruments that share the object and purpose of protecting human rights and fundamental freedoms.

LA NÉCESSITÉ D'UNE INTERPRÉTATION ÉVOLUTIVE DU DROIT AU TRAVAIL, ORIENTÉE VERS SA PROTECTION EFFECTIVE

3. Le préambule de la Convention se réfère à la Déclaration universelle des droits de l'homme. La Convention a donc anticipé, en quelque sorte, le développement des principaux traités des Nations unies protégeant les droits fondamentaux et n'est donc plus aujourd'hui le seul cadre de référence pour interpréter le contenu de ses dispositions. La Convention doit aujourd'hui se lire comme une composante du corpus du droit international des droits de l'homme, et s'interpréter à la lumière des autres traités de protection des droits fondamentaux. Tout État est partie au moins à l'un de ces instruments, voire davantage, ce qui démontre l'existence d'un certain consensus entre les États parties à la Convention. Il s'agit d'instruments complémentaires, qui se renforcent mutuellement et partagent un même objet et objectif, à savoir la protection des droits de l'homme et des libertés fondamentales.

SE REQUIERE UNA INTERPRETACIÓN DINÁMICA Y LIBERAL DEL DERECHO AL TRABAJO

3. La Convención sobre el Estatuto de los Refugiados se refiere a la Declaración Universal de los Derechos Humanos en su preámbulo. Por lo tanto, puede afirmarse que la Convención sobre el Estatuto de los Refugiados anticipó el desarrollo de los principales tratados de derechos humanos de las Naciones Unidas y, desde ese momento, dicha Convención ya no es el único marco de referencia para la interpretación de sus disposiciones. La Convención sobre el Estatuto de los Refugiados ahora debe considerarse como parte del corpus de las normas internacionales de derechos humanos e interpretarse junto con otros tratados de derechos humanos. Cada nación es parte de uno o más de estos instrumentos, lo cual garantiza una congruencia significativa de los estados partes. Son instrumentos complementarios y que se refuerzan mutuamente, los cuales comparten el objeto y el propósito de proteger los derechos humanos y las libertades fundamentales.

---

4. Human rights treaties require a dynamic interpretation in light of changing circumstances, and a liberal interpretation that best protects the individual rights-bearer. Such an interpretation is reinforced by 'savings clauses,' such as Article 5 of the Refugee Convention, which provides: 'Nothing in this Convention shall be deemed to impair any rights and benefits granted by a Contracting State to refugees apart from this Convention.' In cases where states are party to more than one relevant treaty and the treaties contain different obligations, refugees benefit from the most generous provisions. Similarly, any limitations on human rights must be construed narrowly. The burden rests on the state to justify any limitations in accordance with the usual requirements of necessity, legality, and proportionality. Where states assert a legitimate objective in restricting the right to work, the means taken to achieve that objective must be the least restrictive.

4. Les traités de protection des droits fondamentaux doivent faire l'objet d'une interprétation évolutive, à la lumière des évolutions des sociétés, et orientée vers l'effectivité de la protection, afin de protéger au mieux les droits de leurs bénéficiaires. Pareille interprétation évolutive est soutenue par les clauses dites de « sauvegarde », comme l'article 5 de la Convention selon lequel « Aucune disposition de cette Convention ne porte atteinte aux autres droits et avantages accordés, indépendamment de cette Convention, aux réfugiés ». Dans l'hypothèse où un État est partie à plusieurs traités qui consacrent des obligations de degrés divers, les réfugiés doivent bénéficier de la protection la plus généreuse. De même, toute limitation à un droit fondamental est d'interprétation restrictive. Il revient aux États de justifier toute limitation aux droits fondamentaux eu égard aux principes de nécessité, de légalité et de proportionnalité. Lorsque les États invoquent un objectif légitime pour restreindre le droit au travail, les moyens employés à cette fin doivent être les moins attentatoires possible.

4. Los tratados de derechos humanos requieren una interpretación dinámica en vista de las circunstancias cambiantes y una interpretación liberal que proteja mejor al titular individual de los derechos. Tal interpretación se ve reforzada por "cláusulas de salvedad", como el artículo 5 de la Convención sobre el Estatuto de los Refugiados, que establece lo siguiente: "Ninguna disposición de esta Convención podrá interpretarse en menoscabo de cualesquiera otros derechos y beneficios independientemente de esta Convención otorgados por los Estados Contratantes a los refugiados". En los casos en que las naciones sean parte de más de un tratado pertinente y los tratados contengan obligaciones diferentes, los refugiados se beneficiarán de las disposiciones más favorecedoras. Del mismo modo, cualquier limitación de los derechos humanos deberá interpretarse de manera restringida. La carga recae sobre la nación para justificar cualquier limitación de acuerdo con los requisitos habituales de necesidad, legalidad y proporcionalidad. Cuando las naciones afirmen un objetivo legítimo para restringir el derecho al trabajo, los medios que se adopten para alcanzar ese objetivo deberán ser los menos restrictivos.

مطلوب تفسير ديناميكي وليبرالي للحق في العمل

3. تشير اتفاقية اللاجئين إلى الإعلان العالمي لحقوق الإنسان في ديباجتها. لذلك يمكن القول إن اتفاقية اللاجئين توقعت تطوير معاهدات الأمم المتحدة الأساسية لحقوق الإنسان، ومنذ ذلك التطوير، لم تعد اتفاقية اللاجئين الإطار المرجعي الوحيد لتفسير أحكامها. ويجب النظر إلى اتفاقية اللاجئين الآن باعتبارها جزء من مجموعة قوانين حقوق الإنسان الدولية ويجب قراءتها مع معاهدات حقوق الإنسان الأخرى. حيث تُعد كل دولة طرف في واحد أو أكثر من هذه الصكوك، مما يضمن تطابقًا كبيرًا بين الدول الأطراف. وهي صكوك تكميلية بشكل مشترك، تتقاسم موضوع وهدف حماية حقوق الإنسان والحريات الأساسية.

4. تتطلب معاهدات حقوق الإنسان تفسيرًا ديناميكيًا في ضوء الظروف المتغيرة وتفسيرًا ليبراليًا يحمي صاحب الحقوق الفردية على أفضل وجه. ويُعزز هذا التفسير من خلال «شروط تحفظيه» مثل المادة 5 من اتفاقية اللاجئين، والتي تنص على: "لا يوجد في هذه الاتفاقية ما يعوق أي حقوق أو مزايا تمنحها دولة متعاقدة للاجئين بخلاف هذه الاتفاقية". وفي الحالات التي تكون فيها الدول أطرافًا في أكثر من معاهدة ذات صلة، وتحتوي المعاهدات على التزامات مختلفة، يستفيد اللاجئون من أكثر الأحكام سخاءً. وبالمثل، يجب أن تُفسَّر أي قيود على حقوق الإنسان بدقة. ويقع على عاتق الدولة عبء تبرير أي قيود وفقًا للمتطلبات المعتادة من الضرورة والشرعية والتناسب. وحيثما تؤكد الدول هدفًا مشروعًا لتقييد الحق في العمل، يجب أن تكون الوسائل المعتمدة لتحقيق هذا الهدف هي الأقل تقييدًا.

ТРЕБУЕТСЯ ДИНАМИЧЕСКОЕ И ЛИБЕРАЛЬНОЕ ТОЛКОВАНИЕ ПРАВА НА ТРУД

3. Конвенция о статусе беженцев в ее преамбуле ссылается на Всеобщую декларацию прав человека. Поэтому можно сказать, что Конвенция о статусе беженцев предусматривает развитие основных договоров ООН по правам человека, в результате чего эта Конвенция больше не является единственной основой для толкования положений. Конвенция о статусе беженцев должна теперь рассматриваться как часть международного права в области прав человека вместе с другими договорами по правам человека. Каждое государство является участником одного или нескольких таких договоров, обеспечивая согласованность среди государств-участников. Это - взаимодополняющие и усиливающие друг друга механизмы, которые объединяют защиту прав человека и основных свобод.

4. Договоры о правах человека требуют динамического толкования в свете меняющихся обстоятельств, а также либерального толкования, которое наилучшим образом защищает отдельного правообладателя. Такое толкование подкрепляется «договорными оговорками», такими как статья 5 Конвенции о статусе беженцев, которая гласит: «Ничто в настоящей Конвенции не нарушает никаких прав и преимуществ, предоставленных беженцам каким-либо Договаривающимся государством независимо от настоящей Конвенции». Если государства являются участниками более чем одного соответствующего договора, и в договорах содержатся различные обязательства, беженцы получают лучшие преимущества, которые указаны в этих договорах. Точно так же любые ограничения прав человека должны толковаться ограничительно. Государство обязано обосновать любые ограничения, опираясь на обычные требования необходимости, законности и соразмерности. Если государства отстаивают законную цель в ограничении права на труд, то средства, принятые для достижения этой цели, должны быть наименее ограничительными.

THE RIGHT TO WORK UNDER THE REFUGEE CONVENTION

5. The Refugee Convention divides the right to work among three articles: Article 17 (wage-earning employment); Article 18 (self-employment); and Article 19 (participation in the liberal professions). In each case, the right to work depends on a certain level of attachment to the country of refuge. Under Article 17, states parties are required to "accord to refugees *lawfully staying* in their territory the most favourable treatment accorded to nationals of a foreign country in the same circumstances, as regards the right to engage in wage-earning employment." Article 19 requires the same level of attachment as Article 17, while Article 18 simply requires lawful presence. Lawful stay is also required under Article 24 of the Refugee Convention, which concerns rights at work (employment conditions) and social security.

LE DROIT AU TRAVAIL AU SENS DE LA CONVENTION	**EL DERECHO AL TRABAJO EN VIRTUD DE LA CONVENCIÓN SOBRE EL ESTATUTO DE LOS REFUGIADOS**

5. Trois articles de la Convention protègent le droit au travail: l'article 17 (professions salariées), l'article 18 (professions non salariées) et l'article 19 (professions libérales). Dans chacune de ces hypothèses, l'étendue du droit au travail dépend du degré de connexion du réfugié avec le pays d'asile. Selon l'article 17, « les États contractants accorderont à tout réfugié *résidant régulièrement* sur leur territoire le traitement le plus favorable accordé, dans les mêmes circonstances, aux ressortissants d'un pays étranger en ce qui concerne l'exercice d'une activité professionnelle salariée ». L'article 19 requiert le même degré de connexion que l'article 17, tandis que l'article 18 se contente de ce que le réfugié réside régulièrement. L'article 24 de la Convention, relatif à la législation du travail (les conditions de travail) et à la sécurité sociale, concerne également les réfugiés qui résident régulièrement.

5. La Convención sobre el Estatuto de los Refugiados divide el derecho al trabajo en tres artículos: artículo 17 (empleo remunerado), artículo 18 (trabajo por cuenta propia) y artículo 19 (participación en las profesiones liberales). En cada caso, el derecho al trabajo depende de un cierto nivel de apego al país de acogida. Según el artículo 17, los estados partes deben "conceder a los refugiados que se encuentren legalmente en el territorio de tales Estados el trato más favorable concedido en las mismas circunstancias a los nacionales de países extranjeros respecto del derecho a participar en el empleo remunerado". El artículo 19 requiere el mismo nivel de apego que el artículo 17, mientras que el artículo 18 simplemente requiere presencia legal. También se exige la residencia legal en virtud del artículo 24 de la Convención sobre el Estatuto de los Refugiados, que se refiere a los derechos en el trabajo (condiciones de empleo) y el seguro social.

---

6. . . . National determination of refugee status is declaratory, not constitutive. While domestic law is the first point of reference, the meaning of the term 'lawful' in the Refugee Convention must refer ultimately to international law and the factual realities for the particular refugee.

6. La procédure de détermination du statut de réfugié est déclarative de droit, non constitutive de droit. Bien que le droit national constitue une référence pertinente, la signification du terme « régulier » au sens de la Convention doit d'abord se comprendre eu égard au droit international et aux réalités du réfugié concerné.

6. La determinación nacional de la condición de refugiado es declaratoria, no constitutiva. Si bien el derecho interno es el primer punto de referencia, el significado del término "legal" en la Convención sobre el Estatuto de los Refugiados debe referirse en última instancia al derecho internacional y a las realidades de los hechos para el refugiado en particular.

---

7. The meaning of the term 'lawful' must be ascertained in accordance with a good faith interpretation of the Refugee Convention, and in light of human rights treaties that protect rights on the basis of physical presence and the premise of equality. If a refugee's presence in the territory of a state party to the Convention is not unlawful, in that the state is aware, or should be aware, of the refugee's presence and the state is unable or unwilling to remove the refugee, then the refugee's presence may be regarded as lawful for the purposes of the Refugee Convention.

7. La signification du terme « régulier » doit être déterminée à partir d'une interprétation de bonne foi de la Convention et à la lumière des traités de protection des droits de l'homme, qui s'appliquent du seul fait de la présence physique sur le territoire et sont fondés sur un principe d'égalité. Si la présence d'un réfugié sur le territoire d'un État partie à la Convention n'est pas irrégulière, c'est-à-dire si l'État sait, ou devrait savoir, que le réfugié se trouve sur son territoire et n'est pas en mesure ou ne souhaite pas le renvoyer, alors sa présence peut être considérée comme régulière au sens de la Convention.

7. El significado del término "legal" debe determinarse de acuerdo con una interpretación de buena fe de la Convención sobre el Estatuto de los Refugiados y en vista de los tratados de derechos humanos que protegen los derechos sobre la base de la presencia física y la premisa de la igualdad. Si la presencia de un refugiado en el territorio de un estado parte de la Convención no es ilegal, en cuanto a que la nación tiene conocimiento, o debería tener conocimiento, de la presencia del refugiado y la nación no puede o no desea expulsar al refugiado, entonces la presencia del refugiado puede considerarse legal a los fines de la Convención sobre el Estatuto de los Refugiados.

الحق في العمل بموجب اتفاقية اللاجئين

5. تقسّم اتفاقية اللاجئين الحق في العمل بين ثلاث مواد: المادة 17 (العمل بأجر)؛ وال مادة١٨٥ (العمل الحر)؛ والمادة 19 (المشاركة في المهن الحرة). وفي كل حالة، يعتمد الحق في العمل على مستوى معين من التعلق ببلد اللجوء. بموجب المادة 17، يتعين على الدول الأطراف «منح اللاجئين المقيمين بصورة قانونية في إقليمها أفضل معاملة ممكنة تُمنح، في نفس الظروف، لمواطني بلد أجنبي فيما يتعلق بالحق في ممارسة عمل مأجور». وتقتضي المادة 19 نفس مستوى التعلق مثل المادة 17، بينما تتطلب المادة 18 ببساطة وجودًا قانونيًّا. ويلزم أيضًا إقامة قانونية بموجب المادة 24 من اتفاقية اللاجئين، التي تتعلق بالحقوق في العمل (شروط العمل) والضمان الاجتماعي.

6. . . . تحديد وضع اللاجئ على المستوى المحلي يكون بشكل بياني وليس تأسيسي. في حين أن القانون المحلي هو النقطة المرجعية الأولى، فإن معنى مصطلح "قانوني" في اتفاقية اللاجئين يجب أن يحيل في نهاية المطاف إلى القانون الدولي والحقائق الواقعية للاجئين المعينين.

7. ويجب التحقق من معنى مصطلح "قانوني" وفقًا لتفسير حسن النية لاتفاقية اللاجئين، وفي ضوء معاهدات حقوق الإنسان التي تحمي الحقوق على أساس الوجود المادي وفرضية المساواة. إذا كان وجود لاجئ في إقليم دولة طرف في الاتفاقية غير قانوني، فإن الدولة تدرك، أو يجب أن تدرك، وجود اللاجئ والدولة غير قادرة أو غير راغبة في إزالة اللاجئين، فإن وجود اللاجئين في هذه الحالة يمكن اعتباره مشروعًا لأغراض اتفاقية اللاجئين.

ПРАВО НА РАБОТУ В СООТВЕТСТВИИ С КОНВЕНЦИЕЙ О СТАТУСЕ БЕЖЕНЦЕВ

5. Конвенция о статусе беженцев определяет право на труд в трех статьях: статья 17 (работа по найму); статья 18 (работа в собственном предприятии); и статья 19 (свободные профессии). В каждом случае право на труд зависит от определенного уровня привязанности к стране, предоставившей убежище. Согласно статье 17, государства-участники обязаны «предоставлять беженцам, *законно* проживающим на их территории, в отношении их права работы по найму наиболее благоприятное правовое положение, которым пользуются граждане иностранных государств при тех же обстоятельствах». Статья 19 требует такого же уровня привязанности, что и статья 17, тогда как статья 18 просто требует законного пребывания. Законное пребывание также требуется в соответствии со статьей 24 Конвенции о статусе беженцев, которая касается трудового законодательства и социального обеспечения.

6. . . . Национальное определение статуса беженца является декларативным, а не правоустанавливающим. Хотя внутреннее право является точкой отсчета, значение термина «законный» в Конвенции о статусе беженцев должно, в конечном счете, относиться к международному праву и фактическим реалиям конкретного беженца.

7. Значение термина «законный» должно быть установлено в соответствии с добросовестным толкованием Конвенции о статусе беженцев и договоров по правам человека, которые защищают права на основе физического присутствия и предпосылки равенства. Если нахождение беженца на территории государства-участника Конвенции не является незаконным, поскольку государству известно или должно быть известно о нахождении беженца на его территории, и государство не может или не желает депортировать беженца, то согласно Конвенции о статусе беженцев его нахождение может считаться законным.

8. The term 'stay' distinguishes refugees who are present in the state on an ongoing basis from those in transit or who are merely visiting. Refugees 'lawfully staying' in states party to the Convention include those recognized as refugees through individual refugee status determinations (RSD) or as *prima facie* refugees (refugees whose status has been determined on a group basis) whether by the state or by UNHCR; asylum-seekers in a state that fails to determine or to comply with an RSD system or where the procedure is unduly prolonged; and refugees waiting for resettlement in another state.

8. Le terme « résider » implique une distinction entre les réfugiés qui sont présents sur le territoire de l'État de manière habituelle, d'une part, et ceux qui sont en transit ou en simple visite, d'autre part. Les réfugiés « qui résident régulièrement » sur le territoire des États parties à la Convention incluent ceux qui sont reconnus réfugiés à la suite d'une procédure de détermination du statut de réfugié ou *prima facie* (c'est-à-dire ceux dont le statut a été déterminé sur le fondement d'une évaluation de la situation de l'ensemble du groupe dont ils relèvent), que cette reconnaissance ait été réalisée par l'État ou par le H.C.R., de même que les demandeurs d'asile se trouvant sur le territoire d'un État qui n'applique pas de procédure de détermination du statut de réfugié, ceux dont la procédure est d'une durée excessive ou encore ceux qui attendent d'être réinstallés dans un autre État.

8. El término "residencia" distingue a los refugiados que están presentes en la nación de manera permanente de los que están en tránsito o simplemente de visita. Los refugiados que "residen legalmente" en los estados partes de la Convención incluyen a aquellos reconocidos como refugiados mediante determinaciones individuales de la condición de refugiado (DCR) o como refugiados *prima facie* (refugiados cuya condición ha sido determinada a nivel grupal) ya sea por la nación o por el ACNUR; solicitantes de asilo en una nación que no determine o no cumpla con un sistema de DCR o donde el procedimiento se prolongue indebidamente; y refugiados que esperan el reasentamiento en otra nación.

9. The Refugee Convention provides for a gradual integration of refugees into host communities, with a corresponding increase in protection of rights, imposing obligations to at least consider granting the most generous protection possible. Article 17(3) requires states parties to give 'sympathetic consideration' to granting the right to engage in wage-earning employment on the same basis as nationals. Articles 18 and 19 of the Refugee Convention provide for a standard of treatment "as favourable as possible and, in any event, not less favourable than that accorded to aliens generally in the same circumstances."

9. La Convention prévoit une intégration graduelle des réfugiés au sein de la communauté d'accueil, avec une augmentation progressive de la protection, tout en exigeant des États qu'ils envisagent d'octroyer la protection la plus généreuse possible. L'article 17, §3, de la Convention exige des États qu'ils « envisagent avec bienveillance » la possibilité d'octroyer aux réfugiés le droit d'exercer une profession salariée dans les mêmes conditions que leurs nationaux. Les articles 18 et 19 de la Convention exigent quant à eux « un traitement aussi favorable que possible et en tout cas un traitement non moins favorable que celui accordé dans les mêmes circonstances aux étrangers en général ».

9. La Convención sobre el Estatuto de los Refugiados prevé una integración gradual de los refugiados en las comunidades de acogida, con un aumento correspondiente en la protección de los derechos, imponiendo obligaciones para, al menos, considerar la concesión de la protección más favorecedora posible. El artículo 17 (3) exige que los estados partes otorguen "consideración favorable" a la concesión del derecho a participar en el empleo remunerado en las mismas condiciones que los ciudadanos. Los artículos 18 y 19 de la Convención sobre el Estatuto de los Refugiados establecen un estándar de trato para que sea "el trato más favorable posible y en ningún caso menos favorable que el concedido en las mismas circunstancias generalmente a los extranjeros".

10. Under Article 17(2) of the Refugee Convention, a refugee with three years of residence in a country of refuge or who has a spouse or child possessing the nationality of the country of refuge cannot be subjected to restrictive measures on aliens or the employment of aliens to protect the national labor market. The period of three years of residence commences once a person enters the country, rather than from the time of recognition as a refugee.

10. Conformément à l'article 17, §2, de la Convention, un réfugié qui réside depuis trois ans dans le pays ou dont le conjoint ou l'un des enfants possèdent la nationalité du pays d'asile, ne peut pas être soumis aux mesures restrictives imposées aux étrangers ou à l'emploi d'étrangers pour la protection du marché national du travail. La période de trois années de résidence commence à courir dès que l'individu pénètre sur le territoire du pays, et non à partir du moment où il est reconnu comme réfugié.

10. De conformidad con el artículo 17 (2) de la Convención sobre el Estatuto de los Refugiados, un refugiado con tres años de residencia en un país de acogida, o que tenga un cónyuge o un hijo que posea la nacionalidad del país de acogida, no puede ser sometido a medidas restrictivas contra extranjeros o el empleo de extranjeros para proteger el mercado laboral nacional. El período de tres años de residencia comienza una vez que la persona ingresa al país, y no desde el momento del reconocimiento como refugiado.

8. مصطلح "البقاء" يميز اللاجئين الموجودين في الدولة على أساس مستمر من أولئك الذين يعبرون أو يزورون فقط. يشمل اللاجئون «المقيمون بصورة قانونية» في الدول المتعاقدة في الاتفاقية الأشخاص المعترف بهم كلاجئين من خلال تحديد وضع اللاجئين بوصفهم لاجئين بصورة فردية أو بصورة بديهية (اللاجئين الذين تم تحديد وضعهم على أساس جماعي) سواء من قبل الدولة أو من قبل المفوضية السامية للأمم المتحدة لشؤون اللاجئين وطالبي اللجوء في دولة لا تحدد أو تلتزم بنظام تحديد وضع اللاجئين أو حيث يمتد الإجراء من دون مبرر واللاجئين الذين ينتظرون إعادة التوطين في دولة أخرى.

8. Термин «пребывание» отличает беженцев, которые постоянно находятся в государстве от тех, кто находится в пути или тех, кто просто посещают это государство. Беженцы, «законно пребывающие» в государствах-участниках Конвенции, включают лиц, которые были признаны беженцами с помощью индивидуального определения статуса беженца (ОСБ) или как *предположительные* беженцы (беженцы, статус которых определяется на групповой основе), будь то государством или Управлением Верховного комиссара ООН по делам беженцев (УВКБ); просителей убежища в государстве, которое не может определить или соблюдать систему ОСБ, или если процедура чрезмерно затягивается; а также беженцы, ожидающие переселения в другое государство.

9. تنص اتفاقية اللاجئين على الاندماج التدريجي للاجئين في المجتمعات المضيفة، مع زيادة مقابلة في حماية الحقوق، وتفرض التزامات بأن تنظر على الأقل في منح الحماية الأكثر سخاء. تلزم المادة 3 (17) الدول المتعاقدة أن تنظر «بعين العطف» لمنح الحق بالعمل المأجور على نفس الأساس الذي يتمتع به المواطنون. تنص المادتان 18 و19 من اتفاقية اللاجئين على أن تكون المعاملة «أفضل معاملة ممكنة، وعلى ألا تكون في أي حال أقل رعاية من المسنوحة للأجانب ناسلة في نفس الظروف».

9. Конвенция о статусе беженцев предусматривает их постепенную интеграцию в принимающие общины с соответствующим увеличением защиты прав, налагая обязательства, по крайней мере, рассмотреть возможность предоставления самой полной защиты. Статья 17(3) требует, чтобы государства-участники «благожелательно относились» к предоставлению права заниматься трудоустройством на тех же основах, что и граждане такого государства. В статьях 18 и 19 Конвенции о статусе беженцев предусмотрена стандартная форма обращения «как можно более благоприятная и, в любом случае, не менее благоприятная, чем та, которая предоставляется иностранцам, находящимся в тех же обстоятельствах».

10. وبموجب المادة 2 (17) من اتفاقية اللاجئين، لا يجوز إخضاع لاجئ استكمل ثلاث سنوات من الإقامة في بلد اللجوء أو من يكون له زوج أو طفل يحمل جنسية بلد اللجوء إلى تدابير تقييدية على الأجانب أو توظيف الأجانب لحماية سوق العمل الوطنية. وتبدأ فترة الإقامة لمدة ثلاث سنوات بمجرد دخول الشخص إلى البلد وليس من وقت الاعتراف به كلاجئ.

10. В соответствии со статьей 17(2) Конвенции о статусе беженцев, беженец, проживший в стране, предоставившей убежище, три года или имеющий супруга или ребенка, получившего гражданство этой страны, не может подвергаться ограничительным мерам в отношении иностранцев, которые направлены на защиту национального рынка труда. Отсчет трех лет проживания начинается после того, как человек въезжает в страну, а не с момента признания его беженцем.

11. Article 17(1) provides for a minimum standard of treatment with respect to wage-earning employment, namely the treatment accorded to most favored foreigners 'in the same circumstances.' According to Article 6 of the Refugee Convention, the phrase 'in the same circumstances' means that refugees must fulfill any conditions for the enjoyment of the right protected in Article 17 which a most favored foreigner would also have to meet in order to enjoy that right. The conditions are attached to enjoyment of the same rights as the most favored foreigner, not to the requirements for becoming a most favored foreigner. Refugees in countries that have treaties establishing access to the labor market for most favored foreigners in economic communities or common markets (such as the European Union or the Economic Community of West African States) must be accorded the same access to the labor market as non-nationals covered by these treaties. A liberal interpretation of the language 'most favourable treatment accorded to nationals of a foreign country' requires that if aliens who are permanent residents are authorized to work, refugees lawfully staying should be afforded the same authorization to work as permanent residents.

11. L'article 17, §1er, prévoit un minimum de protection en ce qui concerne l'exercice d'une profession salariée, à savoir le bénéfice du traitement le plus favorable accordé aux ressortissants d'un pays étrangers « dans les mêmes circonstances ». Selon l'article 6 de la Convention, l'expression « dans les mêmes circonstances » implique que les réfugiés soient soumis aux mêmes conditions d'accès aux droits protégés par l'article 17 que les étrangers bénéficiant du traitement le plus favorable. Il s'agit donc d'être soumis aux mêmes conditions d'accès au droit que les étrangers bénéficiant du traitement le plus favorable, et non d'être soumis aux mêmes conditions d'accès au statut d'étranger bénéficiant du traitement le plus favorable. Les réfugiés dans des pays qui sont liés par des traités autorisant l'accès au marché du travail pour certains étrangers dans le cadre de l'élaboration d'une communauté économique ou d'un marché commun (comme l'Union européenne ou la Communauté économique des États de l'Afrique de l'Ouest) doivent bénéficier du même accès au marché du travail que les non-nationaux relevant de ces traités. Une interprétation, orientée vers une protection effective, du terme « traitement le plus favorable accordé aux ressortissants d'un pays étrangers » implique que si les étrangers bénéficiant du statut de résident permanent ont un accès libre au marché du travail, il doit en aller de même pour les réfugiés résidant régulièrement sur le territoire de l'État.

11. El artículo 17 (1) establece un nivel mínimo de trato con respecto al empleo remunerado, concretamente en haciendo referencia al trato hacia los extranjeros más favorecidos "en las mismas circunstancias". Según el artículo 6 de la Convención sobre el Estatuto de los Refugiados, la frase "en las mismas circunstancias" significa que, para gozar del derecho protegido bajo el artículo 17, los refugiados deben cumplir las mismas condiciones que debería cumplir un extranjero más favorecido. Las condiciones están asociadas al goce de los mismos derechos que el extranjero más favorecido, no a los requisitos para convertirse en un extranjero favorecido. Los refugiados en países que cuentan con tratados que establecen el acceso al mercado laboral para los extranjeros más favorecidos en comunidades económicas o mercados comunes (como la Unión Europea o la Comunidad Económica de los Estados de África Occidental) deben contar con el mismo acceso al mercado laboral que los no ciudadanos amparados por estos tratados. Una interpretación liberal de la formulación "el trato más favorable concedido en las mismas circunstancias a los nacionales de países extranjeros" requiere que, si los extranjeros que son residentes permanentes están autorizados a trabajar, los refugiados que residan legalmente deberían contar con la misma autorización para trabajar como si fuesen residentes permanentes.

---

12. Article 6 of the Refugee Convention exempts refugees from conditions that are too onerous for refugees to meet. If a fee is required in order to obtain a work permit for most favored foreigners, states should waive the fee for refugees, in recognition of the generally limited nature of refugees' resources and their often precarious financial situations while they are seeking employment authorization. A case by case assessment may be required.

12. L'article 6 de la Convention exempt les réfugiés des conditions qu'ils ne peuvent pas remplir, en raison de la nature de ces conditions. Si les étrangers bénéficiant du traitement le plus favorable doivent payer une taxe pour obtenir un permis de travail, cette taxe ne devrait pas être exigée des réfugiés, en raison de leurs ressources généralement limitées et de leur situation financière généralement précaire tant qu'ils n'ont pas obtenu l'autorisation d'exercer un emploi. Une évaluation au cas par cas peut être nécessaire.

12. El artículo 6 de la Convención sobre el Estatuto de los Refugiados exime a los refugiados de condiciones cuyo cumplimiento sea demasiado oneroso. Si los extranjeros más favorecidos deben pagar una tasa para obtener un permiso de trabajo, las naciones deben eximir de dicho cargo a los refugiados, en reconocimiento de la naturaleza generalmente limitada de los recursos de dichas personas y sus situaciones financieras, que suelen ser precarias mientras buscan un permiso de empleo. Podría ser necesario realizar una evaluación de cada caso en particular.

11. وتنص المادة 17 (1) على حد أدنى من المعاملة فيما يتعلق بالعمل المأجور، أي المعاملة الممنوحة للأجانب الأكثر رعاية "في الظروف نفسها". وتنص المادة 6 من اتفاقية اللاجئين على أن عبارة "في الظروف نفسها" تعني أنه يتعين على اللاجئين أن يستوفوا كافة الشروط المنصوص عليها في المادة 17 للتمتع بالحق في الحماية التي سيتعين على الأجنبي الأكثر رعاية أن يستوفيها أيضًا من أجل التمتع بذلك الحق. وترتبط هذه الشروط بالتمتع بنفس الحقوق التي يتمتع بها الأجنبي الأكثر رعاية، وليس المتطلبات ليصبح الأجنبي الأكثر رعاية. ويجب منح اللاجئين في البلدان التي لديها معاهدات تتيح إمكانية الوصول إلى سوق العمل للأجانب الأكثر رعاية في المجتمعات الاقتصادية أو الأسواق المشتركة (مثل الاتحاد الأوروبي أو الجماعة الاقتصادية لدول غرب أفريقيا) نفس فرص الوصول إلى سوق العمل مثل المواطنين غير المواطنين الذين تشملهم هذه المعاهدات. والتفسير الليبرالي للغة "المعاملة الأكثر ملاءمة الممنوحة لمواطني بلد أجنبي" يتطلب أنه إذا أذن للأجانب المقيمين بصفة دائمة بالعمل، فإنه ينبغي منح اللاجئين المقيمين بصورة قانونية نفس الترخيص للعمل كمقيمين دائمين.

11. В статье 17(1) предусматривается минимальный стандарт обращения относительно занятости по найму, а именно обращение, предоставляемое большинству привилегированных иностранцев «в тех же обстоятельствах». Согласно статье 6 Конвенции о статусе беженцев фраза «в тех же обстоятельствах» означает, что беженцы должны соответствовать любым условиям для реализации права, защищенного статьей 17, которые должен получить наиболее привилегированный иностранец, который также соответствует требованиям. Условия относятся к возможности пользоваться теми же правами, что и наиболее привилегированный иностранец, а не возможности стать таким наиболее привилегированным иностранцем. Беженцы в странах, которые заключили договоры, регулирующие доступ к рынку труда для наиболее привилегированных иностранцев в экономических сообществах или на общих рынках (таких как Европейский союз или Экономическое сообщество западно-африканских государств), должны иметь такой же доступ к рынку труда, как и не имеющие гражданства лица, которые охватываются упомянутыми договорами. Либеральная интерпретация выражения «наиболее благоприятный режим, предоставляемый гражданам иностранного государства» требует, чтобы, если иностранцы, которые являются постоянными жителями, имеют право работать, то и законно проживающим беженцам, должно быть предоставлено такое же разрешение на постоянное проживание.

12. وتعفي المادة 6 من اتفاقية اللاجئين أيضًا اللاجئين من الظروف المرهقة التي لا يمكن أن يستوفيها اللاجئون. وإذا كانت هناك حاجة إلى رسم للحصول على تصريح عمل للأجانب الأكثر تفضيلا، ينبغي أن تتنازل الدول عن رسوم اللاجئين، اعترافا بالطبيعة المحدودة عموما لموارد اللاجئين وأوضاعهم المالية غير المستقرة في كثير من الأحيان في الوقت الذي يسعون فيه للحصول على تصريح العمل. وقد يتطلب الأمر إجراء تقييم لكل حالة على حدة.

12. Статья 6 Конвенции о статусе беженцев освобождает беженцев от слишком обременительных условий. Если за получение разрешения на работу для наиболее привилегированных иностранцев берется плата, государства должны отказаться от подобной платы за беженцев в знак признания ограниченного характера их ресурсов и часто нестабильной финансовой ситуации беженцев, когда они ожидают получения разрешения на работу. Может потребоваться отдельная оценка ситуации для каждого случая.

THE RIGHT TO WORK UNDER OTHER HUMAN RIGHTS INSTRUMENTS

13. Article 6 of the ICESCR protects every person's opportunity to gain a living by work which he or she freely chooses or accepts. All forms of work, including wage-earning employment, self-employment, and participation in the liberal professions are protected . . .

LE DROIT AU TRAVAIL AU SENS D'AUTRES INSTRUMENTS DE PROTECTION DES DROITS DE L'HOMME

13. L'article 6 du PIDESC protège le droit de toute personne d'obtenir la possibilité de gagner sa vie par un travail librement choisi ou accepté. Il protège toutes les formes de travail, en ce compris les professions salariées, non salariées ou libérales.

EL DERECHO AL TRABAJO EN VIRTUD DE OTROS INSTRUMENTOS DE DERECHOS HUMANOS

13. El artículo 6 del Pacto Internacional de Derechos Económicos, Sociales y Culturales (PIDESC) protege la oportunidad de cada persona de ganarse la vida mediante un trabajo que elija o acepte libremente. Todas las formas de trabajo, incluido el empleo remunerado, el empleo independiente y la participación en las profesiones liberales, están protegidas.

14. As described by the Committee on Economic, Social and Cultural Rights (CESCR), Article 6 of the ICESCR protects 'decent work': 'work that respects the fundamental rights of the human person as well as the rights of workers in terms of conditions of work safety and remuneration. [Such work] also provides an income allowing workers to support themselves and their families as highlighted in article 7 of the Covenant. These fundamental rights also include respect for the physical and mental integrity of the worker in the exercise of his/her employment.'

14. Comme affirmé par le Comité des droits économiques, sociaux et culturels, l'article 6 protège le droit à un « travail décent », à savoir un travail qui « respecte les droits fondamentaux de la personne humaine ainsi que les droits des travailleurs concernant les conditions de sécurité au travail et de rémunération. (. . .) (Pareil travail) assure aussi un revenu permettant au travailleur de vivre et de faire vivre sa famille, conformément à l'article 7 du Pacte. Parmi ces droits fondamentaux figurent le respect de l'intégrité physique et mentale du travailleur dans l'exercice de son activité ».

14. Tal como lo describe el Comité de Derechos Económicos, Sociales y Culturales (CDESC), el artículo 6 del PIDESC protege el "trabajo decente": "un trabajo que respeta los derechos fundamentales de la persona humana y los derechos de los trabajadores en términos de condiciones de seguridad laboral y remuneración. [Dicho trabajo] también proporciona un ingreso que permite a los trabajadores mantenerse a sí mismos y a sus familias, como se destaca en el artículo 7 del Pacto. Estos derechos fundamentales también incluyen el respeto por la integridad física y mental del trabajador en el ejercicio de su empleo".

15. Article 6 of the ICESCR protects all individuals within a state's territory or jurisdiction on a non-discriminatory basis. 'The Covenant rights apply to everyone including non-nationals, such as refugees, asylum-seekers, stateless persons, migrant workers and victims of international trafficking, regardless of legal status and documentation.' . . .

15. L'article 6 du PIDESC protège de manière indiscriminée tous les individus se trouvant sur le territoire d'un État ou relevant de sa juridiction. « Les droits visés par le Pacte s'appliquent à chacun, y compris les non-ressortissants, dont font partie notamment les réfugiés, les demandeurs d'asile, les apatrides, les travailleurs migrants et les victimes de la traite internationale de personnes, indépendamment de leurs statut juridique et titres d'identité ».

15. El artículo 6 del PIDESC protege a todas las personas dentro del territorio o la jurisdicción de una nación sobre una base de no discriminación. "Los derechos del Pacto se aplican a todas las personas, incluso a las que no sean ciudadanas, como los refugiados, los solicitantes de asilo, los apátridas, los trabajadores migrantes y las víctimas de trata internacional, independientemente de su condición legal y documentación".

الحق في العمل بموجب صكوك حقوق الإنسان الأخرى

ПРАВО НА РАБОТУ В СООТВЕТСТВИИ С ДРУГИМИ МЕЖДУНАРОДНО-ПРАВОВЫМИ НОРМАМИ В ОБЛАСТИ ПРАВ ЧЕЛОВЕКА

13. تحمي المادة 6 من العهد الدولي للحقوق الاقتصادية والاجتماعية والثقافية فرصة كل شخص لكسب رزقه عن طريق العمل الذي اختاره أو قبله بحرية. ويتم حماية جميع أشكال العمل، بما في ذلك العمل المأجور والعمل الحر والمشاركة في المهن الحرة ...

13. Статья 6 Международного пакта об экономических, социальных и культурных правах (МПЭСКП) защищает возможность каждого человека зарабатывать на жизнь работой, которую он или она свободно выбирает или принимает. Все формы работы, в том числе работа по найму, самозанятость и участие в свободных профессиях, защищены.

14. وعلى نحو ما وصفته اللجنة المعنية بالحقوق الاقتصادية والاجتماعية والثقافية، تحمي المادة 6 من العهد الدولي للحقوق الاقتصادية والاجتماعية والثقافية "العمل اللائق": "العمل الذي يحترم الحقوق الأساسية للإنسان وكذلك حقوق العمال من حيث شروط العمل الآمنة والمكافآت. ويوفر هذا العمل أيضًا دخلا يتيح للعمال إعالة أنفسهم وأسرهم على النحو المبين في المادة 7 من العهد. وتشمل هذه الحقوق الأساسية أيضًا احترام السلامة الجسدية والعقلية للعامل في ممارسة وظيفته".

14. Как указано Комитетом по экономическим, социальным и культурным правам (КЭСКП), статья 6 МПЭСКП защищает «достойную работу»: «работу, которая уважает основные права человеческой личности, а также права трудящихся с точки зрения условий безопасность труда и вознаграждения. [Такая работа] также обеспечивает доход, позволяющий работникам поддерживать себя и свои семьи, как это подчеркивается в статье 7 пакта. Эти основополагающие права также включают уважение физической и умственной неприкосновенности работника при выполнении работы».

15. تحمي المادة 6 من العهد الدولي للحقوق الاقتصادية والاجتماعية والثقافية جميع الأفراد الموجودين في إقليم أو ولاية الدولة على أساس غير تمييزي. «تنطبق الحقوق المنصوص عليها في العهد على الجميع بمن فيهم غير المواطنين مثل اللاجئين وطالبي اللجوء وعديمي الجنسية والعمال المهاجرين وضحايا الاتجار الدولي بغض النظر عن وضعهم القانوني ووثائقهم». ...

15. Статья 6 МПЭСКП защищает всех лиц на территории или юрисдикции государства на недискриминационной основе. «Права Пакта распространяются на всех, включая неграждан, например, беженцев, просителей убежища, лиц без гражданства, трудящихся-мигрантов и жертв международной торговли, независимо от правового статуса и документации».

16. As recognized by the Committee on the Elimination of Racial Discrimination in General Recommendation No. XXX and the CESCR in General Comment No. 20, differential treatment based on a prohibited ground (such as nationality) will be discriminatory unless the justification for the distinction is reasonable and objective. Similar analysis is required under the free-standing protection of equality under Article 26 of the ICCPR. Under the ICESCR, this requires 'an assessment as to whether the aim and effects of the measures or omissions are legitimate, compatible with the nature of the Covenant rights and solely for the purpose of promoting the general welfare in a democratic society. In addition, there must be a clear and reasonable relationship of proportionality between the aim sought to be realized and the measures or omissions and their effects.' Covenant rights, including the right to work, cannot be denied or limited solely on the basis of refugee status.

16. Comme affirmé par le Comité pour l'élimination de la discrimination raciale dans son observation générale n° XXX et par le Comité des droits économiques, sociaux et culturels dans son observation générale n° 20, un traitement différencié fondé sur un motif prohibé, comme la nationalité, doit être considéré comme discriminatoire à moins que la distinction opérée soit fondée sur une justification objective et raisonnable. Une exigence similaire se déduit de l'article 26 du PIDCP. Le PIDESC requiert quant à lui d'évaluer « si les objectifs et les effets des mesures ou des omissions sont légitimes, s'ils sont compatibles avec le caractère des droits énoncés dans le Pacte, et s'ils n'ont pour but que de promouvoir l'intérêt général dans le cadre d'une société démocratique. En outre, il doit exister un lien clair et raisonnable de proportionnalité entre l'objectif que l'on cherche à atteindre et les mesures ou omissions et leurs effets ». Les droits consacrés par le Pacte, en ce compris le droit au travail, ne peuvent pas être refusés ou limités au seul motif que le bénéficiaire est titulaire du statut de réfugié.

16. Según lo reconocido por el Comité para la Eliminación de la Discriminación Racial en la Recomendación general N.° XXX y el CDESC en la Observación general N.° 20, el trato diferenciado que se base en un motivo prohibido (como la nacionalidad) será discriminatorio a menos que la justificación para la distinción sea razonable y objetiva. Se requiere un análisis similar conforme a la protección independiente de la igualdad en virtud del artículo 26 del PIDCP. Según el PIDESC, esto requiere "una evaluación sobre si el objetivo y los efectos de las medidas u omisiones son legítimos, compatibles con la naturaleza de los derechos del Pacto y únicamente con el propósito de promover el bienestar general en una sociedad democrática. Además, debe existir una relación clara y razonable de proporcionalidad entre el objetivo que se pretende alcanzar y las medidas u omisiones y sus efectos". Los derechos del Pacto, incluido el derecho al trabajo, no se pueden denegar ni limitar únicamente sobre la base de la condición de refugiado.

---

17. In addition to refugees, others protected by *non-refoulement* obligations have the right to work. This includes persons entitled to complementary forms of protection under, *inter alia*, Article 3 of the Convention Against Torture and Other Cruel, Inhuman or Degrading Treatment or Punishment and Articles 6 and 7 of the ICCPR.

17. Outre les réfugiés, les autres personnes protégées par le principe de non-refoulement ont le droit au travail. Cela inclut les personnes éligibles à des formes complémentaires de protection, en vertu entre autres de l'article 3 de la Convention contre la torture et autres peines ou traitements cruels, inhumains et dégradants et les articles 6 et 7 du PIDCP.

17. Además de los refugiados, otros individuos protegidos por las obligaciones de no devolución tienen derecho a trabajar. Esto incluye a las personas con derecho a formas complementarias de protección en virtud de, entre otros, el artículo 3 de la Convención contra la Tortura y Otros Tratos o Penas Crueles, Inhumanos o Degradantes y los artículos 6 y 7 del PIDCP.

16. وكما اعترفت به لجنة القضاء على التمييز العنصري في التوصية العامة رقم ثلاثون واللجنة المعنية بالحقوق الاقتصادية والاجتماعية والثقافية في التعليق العام رقم 20، فإن المعاملة التفضيلية القائمة على أساس محظور (مثل الجنسية) ستكون تمييزية ما لم يكن تبرير التمييز معقولًا وهادفًا. ويلزم إجراء تحليل مماثل بموجب حماية المساواة القائمة بذاتها بموجب المادة 26 من العهد الدولي الخاص بالحقوق المدنية والسياسية. بموجب العهد الدولي للحقوق الاقتصادية والاجتماعية والثقافية، يتطلب ذلك "إجراء تقييم لما إذا كان هدف وآثار التدابير أو الامتناع عن العمل مشروعة، ومتوافقة مع طبيعة الحقوق المنصوص عليها في العهد، وذلك فقط لغرض تعزيز الرفاهية العامة في مجتمع ديمقراطي. بالإضافة إلى ذلك، يجب أن تكون هناك علاقة واضحة ومعقولة من التناسب بين الهدف الذي ينبغي تحقيقه والتدابير والامتناع عن العمل وآثارها". لا يمكن إنكار الحقوق المنصوص عليها في العهد، بما في ذلك الحق في العمل، أو قصرها على أساس وضع اللاجئ فقط.

16. Как было признано Комитетом по ликвидации расовой дискриминации в Общей рекомендации № XXX и Комитетом по экономическим, социальным и культурным правам (КЭСКП) в Замечании общего порядка № 20, дифференцированный режим, основанный на запрещенном основании (например, гражданство), будет дискриминационным, если обоснование такого разделения не будет разумным и объективным. Подобный анализ необходим в рамках независимой защиты равенства в соответствии со статьей 26 Международного пакта о гражданских и политических правах (МПГПП). В соответствии с МПЭСКП это требует «оценки того, являются ли цель и последствия мер или упущений законными, совместимыми с характером прав, закрепленных в Пакте, служащим исключительно целям содействия всеобщему благосостоянию в демократическом обществе. Кроме того, должны быть четкие и разумные отношения пропорциональности между целью, которая должна быть реализована, и мерами или упущениями и их последствиями». Права, указанные в Пакте, включая право на труд, не могут отрицаться или ограничиваться исключительно на основе статуса беженца.

17. بالإضافة إلى اللاجئين، يكون للأشخاص الآخرين المحميين بموجب التزامات عدم الإعادة القسرية الحق في العمل. ويشمل ذلك الأشخاص الذين يحق لهم الحصول على أشكال الحماية التكميلية، في جملة أمور، بموجب المادة 3 من اتفاقية مناهضة التعذيب وغيره من ضروب المعاملة أو العقوبة القاسية أو اللاإنسانية أو المهينة، والمادتين 6 و7 من العهد الدولي الخاص بالحقوق المدنية والسياسية.

17. В дополнение к беженцам другие лица, защищенные обязательствами по *принципу невысылки*, имеют право на труд. Сюда входят лица, имеющие право на дополнительные формы защиты, *в частности*, Статьи 3 Конвенции против пыток и других жестоких, бесчеловечных или унижающих достоинство видов обращения и наказания, и статей 6 и 7 МПГПП.

18. The ICCPR and ICESCR also require protection of the right to work for persons who for administrative or practical reasons cannot be returned or for whom return is unreasonably prolonged. In such cases, limitations may apply—for example, if return becomes practical, restrictions on freedom of movement, such as reporting requirements, may need to be imposed in order to facilitate return. However, limitations must in all cases comply with international legal standards. Article 4 of the ICESCR establishes requirements of legality, compatibility with the nature of the rights and promotion of the general welfare in a democratic society. A policy of enforced destitution is incompatible with human rights.

18. Le PIDCP et le PIDESC requièrent également la protection du droit au travail des personnes qui ne peuvent pas retourner ou dont le retour est prolongé pour une durée déraisonnable, en raison de motifs administratifs ou pratiques. En pareil cas, des limitations peuvent trouver à s'appliquer – par exemple des restrictions à la liberté de circulation, comme l'obligation de signaler régulièrement sa présence auprès des autorités, peuvent être imposées afin de faciliter le retour dans l'hypothèse où il deviendrait envisageable. L'article 4 du PIDESC exige par ailleurs de ces limitations qu'elles soient établies par la loi, compatibles avec la nature des droits et entendent favoriser le bien-être général. Une politique contraignant à la précarité n'est pas compatible avec les droits fondamentaux.

18. El PIDCP y el PIDESC también exigen la protección del derecho al trabajo para las personas que por razones administrativas o prácticas no puedan regresar o para quienes el regreso se prolongue de manera injustificada. En tales casos, pueden aplicarse limitaciones. Por ejemplo, si el retorno se torna práctico, podría ser necesario imponer restricciones a la libertad de circulación, como requisitos de presentación de informes, para facilitar el retorno. Sin embargo, las limitaciones deben cumplir con las normas legales internacionales en todos los casos. El artículo 4 del PIDESC establece requisitos de legalidad, compatibilidad con la naturaleza de los derechos y promoción del bienestar general en una sociedad democrática. Una política de destitución forzada es incompatible con los derechos humanos.

THE RIGHT TO SOCIAL SECURITY AND SOCIAL ASSISTANCE

19. The right to social security and social assistance is another basic right that is particularly important to refugees and others who are unemployed, unable to work, or underemployed. Article 24 of the Refugee Convention guarantees social security to lawfully staying refugees, while Article 9 of the ICESCR is a universal entitlement to social assistance. States must account for the problems that contributory schemes of social security may impose for refugees and similarly situated people. The right to social assistance in Article 9 of the ICESCR is interdependent with Article 11 of the ICESCR—a universal entitlement to an adequate standard of living—and many other rights, including, most notably, the right to life.

LE DROIT À LA SÉCURITÉ SOCIALE

19. Le droit à la sécurité sociale et à l'assistance publique est un autre droit fondamental qui est particulièrement important pour les réfugiés et les autres personnes qui sont sans emploi, incapables d'exercer un emploi ou sous-employées. L'article 24 de la Convention garantit le droit à la sécurité sociale aux réfugiés qui résident régulièrement sur le territoire des États parties, tandis que l'article 9 du PIDESC consacre un droit général à la sécurité sociale. Les États doivent prendre en considération les difficultés que des systèmes de sécurité sociale contributifs peuvent produire pour les réfugiés et d'autres personnes dans une situation similaire. Le droit à la sécurité sociale tel que consacré par l'article 9 du PIDESC est interdépendant avec l'article 11 du PIDESC, lequel consacre un droit universel à bénéficier d'un niveau de vie adéquat, et de nombreux autres droits, en ce compris le droit à la vie.

EL DERECHO AL SEGURO SOCIAL Y LA ASISTENCIA SOCIAL

19. El derecho al seguro social y la asistencia social es otro derecho básico que es particularmente importante para los refugiados y otras personas que estén desempleadas, no puedan trabajar o estén subempleadas. El artículo 24 de la Convención sobre el Estatuto de los Refugiados garantiza el seguro social a los refugiados que residan legalmente, mientras que el artículo 9 del PIDESC es un derecho universal a la asistencia social. Las naciones deben dar cuenta de los problemas que los regímenes contributivos de los seguros sociales pueden imponer a los refugiados y las personas en situaciones similares. El derecho a la asistencia social en el artículo 9 del PIDESC es interdependiente con el artículo 11 del PIDESC—un derecho universal a un nivel de vida adecuado— y muchos otros derechos, incluido, sobre todo, el derecho a la vida.

18. كما يتطلب العهد الدولي الخاص بالحقوق المدنية والسياسية والعهد الدولي للحقوق الاقتصادية والاجتماعية والثقافية حماية الحق في العمل للأشخاص الذين لا يمكن إعادتهم لأسباب إدارية أو عملية أو الذين تخطت مدة عودتهم مدة معقولة. في مثل هذه الحالات، قد تنطبق القيود، إذا أصبحت العودة عملية، على سبيل المثال، قد يلزم فرض قيود على حرية التنقل، مثل متطلبات الإبلاغ، من أجل تيسير العودة. ولكن، يجب أن تتوافق القيود في جميع الحالات مع المعايير القانونية الدولية. تنص المادة 4 من العهد الدولي للحقوق الاقتصادية والاجتماعية والثقافية على شروط الشرعية والتوافق مع طبيعة الحقوق وتعزيز الرفاهية العامة في مجتمع ديمقراطي. لا تتفق سياسة العوز القسري مع حقوق الإنسان.

18. МПГПП и МПЭСКП также требуют защиты права на труд для лиц, которые по административным или практическим причинам не могут быть возвращены на родину или для которых возвращение необоснованно затягивается. В таких случаях могут применяться ограничения: например, если возвращение становится практическим, для того, чтобы облегчить возвращение, потребуется наложение ограничения на свободу передвижения или предоставление информации о местоположении. Тем не менее, во всех случаях ограничения должны соответствовать международно-правовым стандартам. Статья 4 МПЭСКП устанавливает требования законности и совместимости с характером прав и поощрения всеобщего благосостояния в демократическом обществе. Политика принудительной нищеты несовместима с правами человека.

الحق في الضمان الاجتماعي والمساعدة الاجتماعية

19. الحق في الضمان الاجتماعي والمساعدة الاجتماعية هو حق أساسي آخر له أهمية خاصة بالنسبة للاجئين وغيرهم من العاطلين عن العمل أو غير القادرين على العمل أو العاطلين جزئيا عن العمل. تكفل المادة 24 من اتفاقية اللاجئين الضمان الاجتماعي للاجئين المقيمين بصورة قانونية، في حين أن المادة 9 من العهد الدولي للحقوق الاقتصادية والاجتماعية والثقافية هي حق عام في الحصول على المساعدة الاجتماعية. يجب على الدول مراعاة المشاكل التي قد تفرضها مخططات الضمان الاجتماعي للاشتراكات على اللاجئين والأشخاص ذوي الأوضاع المماثلة. يرتبط الحق في المساعدة الاجتماعية في المادة 9 من العهد الدولي للحقوق الاقتصادية والاجتماعية والثقافية بالمادة 11 من العهد الدولي للحقوق الاقتصادية والاجتماعية والثقافية - استحقاق عالمي بمستوى معيشي لائق - وحقوق أخرى، وتشمل بشكل خاص، الحق في الحياة.

ПРАВО НА СОЦИАЛЬНОЕ ОБЕСПЕЧЕНИЕ И СОЦИАЛЬНУЮ ПОМОЩЬ

19. Право на социальное обеспечение и социальную помощь является еще одним основным правом, которое особенно важно для беженцев и других лиц, которые являются безработными, частично безработными или не могут работать. Статья 24 Конвенции о статусе беженцев гарантирует социальное обеспечение законного пребывания беженцев, а статья 9 МПЭСКП указывает на всеобщее право на социальную помощь. Государства должны учитывать проблемы, которые могут влиять на социальное обеспечение беженцев и людей в подобном положении. Право на социальную помощь в статье 9 МПЭСКП является взаимозависимым со статьей 11 МПЭСКП — универсальным правом на достаточный жизненный уровень и многими другими правами, в том числе, правом на жизнь.

SAFEGUARDING THE RIGHT TO SEEK ASYLUM

20. Good faith compliance with the obligations in the Refugee Convention requires that asylum-seekers are able to access prompt and fair RSD (unless asylum-seekers are assumed to be refugees without the necessity of any individual or group determination), as well as respect for their human rights. This includes the right to an adequate standard of living. State policies or conduct contrary to fundamental rights carry the risk that an asylum-seeker will be compelled to return to a place of persecution, thereby violating the obligation of *non-refoulement*.

GARANTIR LE DROIT À DEMANDER L'ASILE

20. Le respect de bonne foi des obligations consacrées par la Convention implique que les demandeurs d'asile bénéficient d'un accès rapide à une procédure de détermination du statut de réfugié loyale (à moins que les demandeurs d'asile ne soient considérés comme des réfugiés sans qu'il ne soit nécessaire de réaliser un examen du risque individuel ou relatif à la situation du groupe dont ils relèvent), de même que le respect de leurs droits fondamentaux. Cela inclut le droit à un niveau de vie adéquat. Les politiques étatiques ou les comportements contraires aux droits fondamentaux provoquent le risque que le demandeur d'asile se trouve contraint de retourner là où il risque la persécution, en violation du principe de non-refoulement.

PROTECCIÓN DEL DERECHO A BUSCAR ASILO

20. El cumplimiento de buena fe de las obligaciones de la Convención sobre el Estatuto de los Refugiados requiere que los solicitantes de asilo puedan acceder a una DCR rápida y equitativa (a menos que se suponga que los solicitantes de asilo son refugiados sin necesidad de una determinación individual o grupal), así como al respeto de sus derechos humanos. Esto incluye el derecho a un nivel de vida adecuado. Las políticas o conductas estatales contrarias a los derechos fundamentales conllevan el riesgo de que un solicitante de asilo se vea obligado a regresar a un lugar de persecución, lo cual incumple la obligación de no devolución.

---

21. Article 6 of the ICESCR is a universal entitlement, protected on a non-discriminatory basis. Work is a means to ensure asylum-seekers' survival, self-reliance and dignity . . .

21. L'article 6 du PIDESC consacre un droit universel, protégé sans discriminations. Le travail est un moyen permettant d'assurer la survie, l'autonomie et la dignité des demandeurs d'asile.

21. El artículo 6 del PIDESC es un derecho universal, protegido sobre una base no discriminatoria. El trabajo es un medio para garantizar la supervivencia, la autosuficiencia y la dignidad de los solicitantes de asilo.

---

22. However, it may be difficult for asylum-seekers to obtain work and states must, in any event, provide adequate levels of social assistance in accordance with Articles 9 and 11 of the ICESCR, as well as other interdependent rights such as the right to the highest standard of mental and physical health, the right to life, and the prohibition on inhuman or degrading treatment . . .

22. Il peut toutefois être difficile pour les demandeurs d'asile de trouver un travail, et les États doivent, dans tous les cas, fournir une assistance adéquate conformément aux articles 9 et 11 du PIDESC, de même que d'autres droits interdépendants comme le droit de bénéficier du meilleur état de santé physique et mentale, le droit à la vie et l'interdiction des traitements inhumains et dégradants.

22. Sin embargo, a los solicitantes de asilo les puede resultar difícil conseguir trabajo y las naciones deben, en cualquier caso, proporcionar niveles adecuados de asistencia social de conformidad con los artículos 9 y 11 del PIDESC, así como también otros derechos interdependientes, como el derecho al más elevado nivel de salud mental y física, el derecho a la vida y la prohibición de los tratos inhumanos o degradantes.

OBLIGATIONS WITH RESPECT TO REFUGEES' RIGHT TO WORK

23. . . . States have obligations to respect, protect, and fulfill the right to work so that refugees may exercise their rights to decent work under the Refugee Convention, the ICESCR, and other human rights treaties . . .

LES OBLIGATIONS RELATIVES AU DROIT AU TRAVAIL DES RÉFUGIÉS

23. Les États ont l'obligation de respecter, de protéger et de mettre en œuvre le droit au travail, de manière telle qu'ils puissent exercer leur droit à un travail décent tel qu'il ressort de la Convention, du PIDESC et d'autres traités de protection des droits de l'homme.

OBLIGACIONES CON RESPECTO AL DERECHO A TRABAJAR DE LOS REFUGIADOS

23. Las naciones tienen la obligación de respetar, proteger y cumplir el derecho al trabajo para que los refugiados puedan ejercer sus derechos al empleo decente en virtud de la Convención sobre el Estatuto de los Refugiados, el PIDESC y otros tratados de derechos humanos.

ЗАЩИТА ПРАВА НА УБЕЖИЩЕ

20. Соблюдение обязательств в Конвенции о статусе беженцев требует, чтобы просители убежища имели возможность получить доступ к оперативному и справедливому определению статуса беженца (за исключением случаев, когда просители убежища считаются беженцами без какого-либо индивидуального или группового определения), а также уважения прав человека, включая право на адекватный жизненный уровень. Государственная политика или поведение, противоречащее основополагающим правам, повышают риск того, что проситель убежища будет вынужден вернуться туда, где его преследовали, что нарушает положение *принципа невысылки*.

21. Статья 6 МПЭСКП является универсальным правом, защищенным на недискриминационной основе. Работа — это средство обеспечения выживания, уверенности в себе и достоинства просителей убежища.

22. Однако просителям убежища может быть не просто получить работу, и государства должны в любом случае обеспечить адекватный уровень социальной помощи в соответствии со статьями 9 и 11 МПЭСКП, а также другие взаимозависимые права, такие как право на хорошее психическое и физическое здоровье, право на жизнь и запрет на бесчеловечное или унижающее достоинство обращение.

ОБЯЗАТЕЛЬСТВА В ОТНОШЕНИИ ПРАВА БЕЖЕНЦЕВ НА РАБОТУ

23. . . . Государства обязаны уважать, защищать и осуществлять право на труд, для того, чтобы беженцы могли реализовывать свои права на достойный труд в соответствии с Конвенцией о статусе беженцев, МПЭСКП и другими договорами по правам человека.

حماية الحق في طلب اللجوء

20. يتطلب الامتثال بحسن نية للالتزامات المقررة في اتفاقية اللاجئين أن يكون طالبو اللجوء قادرين على الوصول السريع والعادل إلى مراكز اللاجئين (ما لم يفترض أن يكون طالبو اللجوء لاجئين دون الحاجة إلى تحديد أي فرد أو جماعة)، بالإضافة إلى احترام حقوق الإنسان. يشمل هذا الحق في مستوى معيشي لائق. تتحمل سياسات الدولة أو السلوك المخالف للحقوق الأساسية خطر إلزام طالب اللجوء بالعودة إلى مكان الاضطهاد، مما ينتهك الالتزام بعدم الإعادة القسرية.

21. المادة 6 من العهد الدولي للحقوق الاقتصادية والاجتماعية والثقافية هي استحقاق عالمي محمي على أساس غير تمييزي. والعمل هو وسيلة لضمان بقاء طالبي اللجوء واعتمادهم على الذات والكرامة . . .

22. ومع ذلك، قد يكون من الصعب على طالبي اللجوء الحصول على عمل ويجب على الدول، في جميع الأحوال، توفير مستويات كافية من المساعدة الاجتماعية وفقًا للمادتين 9 و11 من العهد الدولي للحقوق الاقتصادية والاجتماعية والثقافية، فضلًا عن حقوق أخرى مترابطة مثل الحق في أعلى مستوى من الصحة النفسية والجسدية والحق في الحياة وحظر المعاملة اللاإنسانية أو المهينة . . .

الالتزامات المتعلقة بحق اللاجئين في العمل

23. . . . ويقع على عاتق الدول التزامات باحترام الحق في العمل وحمايته وتحقيقه حتى يتمكن اللاجئون من ممارسة حقوقهم في العمل اللائق موجب اتفاقية اللاجئين والعهد الدولي للحقوق الاقتصادية والاجتماعية والثقافية وغيرها من معاهدات حقوق الإنسان . . .

24. Obligations to Respect: In order to make the right to work meaningful, states have an obligation to provide a secure legal status and associated documentation to protect refugees from penalization for working without proper authorization and in order to minimize the risk of exploitation by unscrupulous employers. Where refugees are found working in the informal sector, their rights at work, including rights protected by relevant ILO conventions, such as fair wages and equal remuneration, must be respected. Refugees must be provided with information in an accessible language and all necessary guidance and facilities with respect to the procedure for acquiring a secure legal status and associated documentation. Any fees should be waived. States must review laws to ensure that they do not discriminate on prohibited grounds such as nationality, thereby limiting employment opportunities for refugees. They must provide effective remedies for any violations of the right to work. States must also respect, protect, and fulfill other interdependent rights, such as the right to housing.

24. L'obligation de respecter: Afin que le droit au travail soit effectif, les États ont l'obligation de garantir aux réfugiés un statut juridique solide et de leur fournir les documents nécessaires pour les préserver de poursuites au motif qu'ils travailleraient sans disposer des autorisations requises et afin de minimiser les risques d'exploitation et d'abus par des employeurs sans scrupules. S'il s'avère que des réfugiés travaillent dans le secteur informel, leurs droits au travail, en ce compris les droits protégés par les Convention de l'O.I.T. pertinentes, comme le droit à une rémunération équitable et égale, doivent être respectés. Les réfugiés doivent être informés dans une langue qu'ils comprennent et doivent bénéficier de toute l'assistance et de toutes les facilités nécessaires pour accéder aux procédures leur permettant de bénéficier d'un statut juridique solide et des documents nécessaires. Ils ne devraient payer aucune taxe pour accéder à ce statut et se procurer ces documents. Les États doivent évaluer leurs règlementations afin de s'assurer qu'il n'en résulte pas de discrimination pour un motif prohibé, comme la nationalité, de nature à limiter les opportunités d'emploi pour les réfugiés. Ils doivent fournir des recours effectifs contre les violations du droit au travail. Les États doivent également respecter, protéger et mettre en œuvre d'autres droits interdépendants, comme le droit à un logement.

24. Obligaciones de respeto: Para hacer que el derecho al trabajo sea significativo, las naciones tienen la obligación de proporcionar una condición legal segura y la documentación asociada para proteger a los refugiados de la penalización por trabajar sin la debida autorización y para minimizar el riesgo de explotación por parte de empleadores inescrupulosos. En casos en los que se descubra que los refugiados trabajen en el sector informal, deberán respetarse sus derechos en el trabajo, incluidos los derechos protegidos por los convenios pertinentes de la OIT, como los salarios justos y la igualdad de remuneración. Los refugiados deben recibir información en un idioma accesible y todas las guías e instalaciones necesarias con respecto al procedimiento para adquirir una condición legal segura y la documentación asociada. No se debe cobrar ningún cargo aplicable. Las naciones deben revisar las leyes para garantizar que no discriminen por motivos prohibidos como la nacionalidad, ya que esto limita las oportunidades de empleo de los refugiados. Deben proporcionar medidas compensatorias efectivas ante cualquier violación del derecho al trabajo. Las naciones también deben respetar, proteger y cumplir otros derechos interdependientes, como el derecho a la vivienda.

25. Obligations to Protect: The obligation to protect requires states to take positive measures for the realization of the right to work. States must protect refugees from violations of their right to work and rights at work by private actors, including private employers. States must protect refugees from direct and indirect discrimination on the basis of, *inter alia*, race, nationality, or refugee status, and combat the multiple levels of discrimination affecting refugees . . . States must ensure protection against exploitation by private employers through, *inter alia*, the provision of a secure legal status and enforcement of basic labor standards. Identification of a person as a refugee in any documentation that confirms the entitlement to work should be avoided. States must take account of the fact that temporary residence permits may discourage employers from hiring refugees, thereby interfering with the ability to exercise the right to work to its fullest . . .

25. L'obligation de protéger: L'obligation de protéger implique que les États doivent adopter diverses mesures visant à réaliser le droit au travail. Les États doivent protéger les réfugiés contre toutes violations de leurs droits au travail et relatifs à leurs conditions de travail qui seraient commises par des acteurs privés, en ce compris des employeurs privés. Les États doivent protéger les réfugiés contre toute discrimination directe et indirecte sur le fondement, entre autres, de la race, de la nationalité, du statut de réfugié, et combattre les discriminations susceptibles d'affecter certains d'entre eux en particulier. Les États doivent garantir une protection contre l'exploitation par des employeurs privés en prévoyant un statut légal solide et en faisant respecter les standards minimaux de protection des travailleurs notamment. Les documents établissant le droit de travailler devraient éviter de mentionner la circonstance que la personne qui en dispose bénéficie du statut de réfugié. Les États doivent prendre en considération la circonstance que des autorisations au séjour temporaires pourraient avoir pour effet de décourager les employeurs d'engager des réfugiés, ce qui constitue un obstacle à l'exercice intégral de leur droit au travail.

25. Obligaciones en cuanto a proteger: La obligación de proteger exige que las naciones tomen medidas en pro del respeto del derecho al trabajo. Las naciones deben proteger a los refugiados de violaciones de su derecho al trabajo y los derechos en el trabajo por parte de actores privados, incluidos empleadores privados. Las naciones deben proteger a los refugiados de la discriminación directa e indirecta sobre la base de, entre otros, raza, nacionalidad o condición de refugiado, y combatir los múltiples niveles de discriminación que los afectan. Las naciones deben asegurarse de proteger contra la explotación por parte de empleadores privados a través de, entre otros, la provisión de una condición legal segura y el cumplimiento de las normas laborales básicas. No se debe identificar a una persona como refugiado en ningún documento que confirme su derecho a trabajar. Las naciones deben tener en cuenta que los permisos de residencia temporales pueden contribuir a que los empleadores opten por no contratar refugiados, lo que interfiere con la capacidad de ejercer el derecho al trabajo al máximo.

٢٤. الالتزامات بالاحترام: من أجل جعل الحق في العمل ذا مغزى، فإنه يتعين على الدول الالتزام بتوفير وضع قانوني آمن وما يرتبط به من وثائق لحماية اللاجئين من المعاقبة على العمل من دون الحصول على تصريح سليم ومن أجل التقليل إلى أدنى حد من خطر الاستغلال من جانب أرباب العمل عديمي الضمير. وحيثما وُجد اللاجئون العاملون في القطاع غير الرسمي، يجب احترام حقوقهم في العمل، بما في ذلك الحقوق التي تحميها اتفاقيات منظمة العمل الدولية ذات الصلة، مثل الأجور العادلة والأجر المتساوي. يجب تزويد اللاجئين بالمعلومات بلغة سهلة الفهم وجميع التوجيهات والتسهيلات اللازمة فيما يتعلق بإجراءات الحصول على وضع قانوني آمن والوثائق المرتبطة بها. وينبغي إلغاء أي رسوم. يجب على الدول مراجعة القوانين لضمان عدم تمييزها على أسس محظورة مثل الجنسية، مما يحد من فرص العمل للاجئين. ويجب أن توفر سبل انتصاف فعالة لأي انتهاكات للحق في العمل. كما يجب على الدول أيضًا أن تحترم وتحمي وتحقق حقوقًا أخرى مترابطة، مثل الحق في السكن.

24. Обязательства, требующие соблюдения: Для того, чтобы право на труд имело смысл, государства обязаны обеспечивать безопасный правовой статус и соответствующую документацию для защиты беженцев от наказания за работу без надлежащего разрешения, а также свести к минимуму риск эксплуатации беженцев недобросовестными работодателями. В тех случаях, когда беженцы работают в неформальном секторе, должны соблюдаться их права на рабочем месте, включая права, защищенные соответствующими конвенциями МОТ, такие как справедливая заработная плата и равное вознаграждение. Беженцам должна быть предоставлена информация на доступном языке и все необходимые указания и возможности в отношении процедуры получения законного юридического статуса и соответствующей документации. Должны быть отменены любые сборы. Государства должны пересмотреть законы, связанные с дискриминацией по таким запрещенным признакам как гражданство, так как это ограничивает возможность трудоустройства беженцев. Они должны предоставлять эффективные средства правовой защиты для любых нарушений права на труд. Государства должны также уважать, защищать и выполнять другие взаимозависимые права, такие как право на жилище.

---

٢٥. الالتزامات بالحماية: يتطلب الالتزام بالحماية من الدول اتخاذ تدابير إيجابية لإعمال الحق في العمل. ويجب على الدول حماية اللاجئين من انتهاكات حقوقهم في العمل والحقوق في العمل من قبل جهات فاعلة خاصة، بما في ذلك أرباب العمل من القطاع الخاص. ويجب على الدول حماية اللاجئين من التمييز المباشر وغير المباشر على أساس، في جملة أمور، العرق أو الجنسية أو وضع اللاجئ ومكافحة مستويات التمييز المتعددة التي تؤثر على اللاجئين . . . . ويجب على الدول أن تكفل الحماية من الاستغلال من جانب أرباب العمل من القطاع الخاص من خلال، في جملة أمور، وتوفير وضع قانوني آمن وإنفاذ معايير العمل الأساسية. وينبغي تفادي تحديد هوية الشخص كلاجئ في أي وثائق تؤكد الحق في العمل. ويجب على الدول مراعاة أن تصاريح الإقامة المؤقتة قد تثني أرباب العمل عن توظيف اللاجئين، مما يتعارض مع القدرة على ممارسة الحق في العمل على أكمل وجه . . .

25. Обязательства по защите: Обязательства по защите требуют от государства принимать позитивные меры для реализации права на труд. Государства должны защищать беженцев от нарушений их права на труд и права на работу, как частных субъектов, в том числе частных работодателей. Государства должны защищать беженцев от прямой и косвенной дискриминации на основе, *в частности*, расы, национальности или статуса беженца и бороться с множественными уровнями дискриминации, затрагивающими беженцев. Государства должны обеспечить защиту от эксплуатации частными работодателями посредством, *в частности*, обеспечения безопасного правового статуса и соблюдения основных трудовых норм. Следует избегать идентификации лица в качестве беженца в любой документации, подтверждающей право на работу. Государства должны учитывать тот факт, что временное разрешение на жительство может препятствовать найму беженцев работодателями, тем самым препятствуя их возможности в полной мере осуществлять право на труд.

26. Obligations to Fulfill: States must take further steps to fulfill refugees' rights to work, including measures such as: development of necessary infrastructure, including, for example, employment offices; language and skills training; loans and grants for small businesses; funding for non-governmental organizations that support refugees' employment; recognition of the equivalency of foreign academic, professional and vocational diplomas, certificates and degrees; fee waivers and assistance for conversion tests that enable professional recognition; and incentives for employers to employ refugees. States should also develop and implement public education campaigns concerning the rights of refugees and their economic and other contributions to countries of refuge.

26. L'obligation de réaliser: Les États doivent prendre des mesures pour réaliser le droit au travail des réfugiés, en ce compris des mesures visant à développer l'infrastructure nécessaire, incluant par exemple la mise en place d'agences pour l'emploi, de formations en langue et autres qualifications professionnelles, des prêts et des financements pour les petites entreprises, le financement d'organisations non gouvernementales qui soutiennent l'accès au travail des réfugiés, la reconnaissance de l'équivalence des diplômes et certificats académiques, professionnels et des formations professionnelles, la levée des frais d'inscription et l'assistance pour présenter les tests d'équivalence qui permettent d'obtenir la reconnaissance des qualifications et des incitants pour les employeurs de réfugiés. Les États devraient également développer et mettre en œuvre des campagnes d'éducation publique relativement aux droits des réfugiés et à leur contribution au pays d'accueil, en ce compris sur le plan économique.

26. Obligaciones a cumplir: Las naciones deben tomar nuevas medidas para respetar los derechos al trabajo de los refugiados, lo cual incluye medidas tales como: desarrollo de la infraestructura necesaria, incluidas, por ejemplo, oficinas de empleo; capacitación en relación con el dominio de idiomas y habilidades; préstamos y subvenciones para pequeñas empresas; financiación para organizaciones no gubernamentales que apoyan el empleo de los refugiados; reconocimiento de la equivalencia de diplomas, certificados y títulos académicos y profesionales extranjeros; exención de tasas y asistencia para pruebas de conversión que permitan el reconocimiento profesional; e incentivos para que los empleadores contraten refugiados. Las naciones también deberían desarrollar y lanzar campañas de educación pública sobre los derechos de los refugiados y sus contribuciones económicas y de otro tipo para los países de acogida.

27. Obligations of International Cooperation: Under Articles 55(c) and 56 of the U.N. Charter, all U.N. members pledge to cooperate in order to achieve 'universal respect for, and observance of, human rights and fundamental freedoms for all.' Article 2(1) of the ICESCR also imposes on state parties obligations of international assistance and cooperation . . . The preamble to the Refugee Convention and Recommendation D of the Final Act of the Conference of Plenipotentiaries which adopted the Refugee Convention also recognize the obligation to cooperate. International assistance and cooperation in the refugee context may take the form, *inter alia*, of resettlement of refugees, financial assistance, and technical assistance. It may also take the form of family reunification, labor migration programs, and development assistance.

27. Les obligations de coopération internationale: Conformément aux articles 55, c, et 56 de la Charte des Nations unies, les États membres des Nations unies s'engage à coopérer afin de garantir « le respect universel et effectif des droits de l'homme et des libertés fondamentales pour tous ». L'article 2, §1er, du PIDESC impose également une obligation d'assistance et de coopération internationale. Le préambule de la Convention et la recommandation D de l'acte final de la conférence des plénipotentiaires, qui ont adopté la Convention, consacrent également une obligation de coopération. La coopération et l'assistance internationale en matière d'asile peut notamment se concrétiser par des programmes de réinstallation des réfugiés et l'apport d'une assistance financière et technique. Elle peut également s'exercer au travers du regroupement familial, des programmes d'immigration économique et de l'aide au développement.

27. Obligaciones de cooperación internacional: De conformidad con los artículos 55 (c) y 56 de la Carta de las Naciones Unidas, todos los miembros de la ONU se comprometen a cooperar para alcanzar "el respeto universal de los derechos humanos y las libertades fundamentales de todos". El artículo 2 (1) del PIDESC también impone a los estados partes obligaciones de asistencia y cooperación internacionales. El preámbulo de la Convención sobre el Estatuto de los Refugiados y la Recomendación D del Acta Final de la Conferencia de Plenipotenciarios que adoptó la Convención sobre el Estatuto de los Refugiados también reconocen la obligación de cooperar. La asistencia y cooperación internacionales en el contexto de los refugiados pueden concretarse, entre otras cosas, mediante el reasentamiento de refugiados, asistencia financiera y asistencia técnica. También puede suceder en acciones destinadas a la reunificación familiar, programas de migración laboral y asistencia para el desarrollo.

٢٦. الالتزامات بالإنفاذ: يجب على الدول أن تتخذ المزيد من الخطوات لتحقيق حقوق اللاجئين في العمل، بما في ذلك تدابير مثل: تطوير البنى التحتية اللازمة، بما في ذلك، على سبيل المثال، مكاتب التوظيف، والتدريب على المهارات اللغوية، والقروض والمنح للمؤسسات الصغيرة، وتمويل المنظمات غير الحكومية التي تدعم عمالة اللاجئين، والاعتراف بمعادلة الشهادات الأكاديمية والمهنية والشهادات والدرجات العلمية، والإعفاء من الرسوم والمساعدة في اختبارات التحويل التي تمكن الاعتراف المهني، وحوافز لأرباب العمل لتوظيف اللاجئين. وينبغي على الدول أيضًا أن تضع وتنفذ حملات توعية عامة بشأن حقوق اللاجئين ومساهماتهم الاقتصادية وغيرها من المساهمات في بلدان اللجوء.

26. Обязательства для выполнения: Государства должны предпринимать дальнейшие шаги для реализации прав беженцев на работу, включая такие меры, как: развитие необходимой инфраструктуры, в том числе, бюро по трудоустройству; обучение языкам и навыкам; кредиты и гранты для малого бизнеса; финансирование неправительственных организаций, которые поддерживают работу беженцев; признание эквивалентности иностранных академических, профессиональных и профессиональных дипломов, сертификатов и степеней; отказ от платы и помощь в проведении экзаменов на профессиональную переквалификацию; а также меры стимулирования работодателей в найме беженцев. Государствам следует также разрабатывать и осуществлять просветительские кампании в отношении прав беженцев, их экономического вклада и других видов вкладов в развитие принимающей страны.

٢٧. الالتزامات بالتعاون الدولي: بموجب المادتين ٥٥(ج) و٥٦ من ميثاق الأمم المتحدة، يتعهد جميع الدول الأعضاء في الأمم المتحدة بالتعاون من أجل تحقيق «الاحترام العالمي لحقوق الإنسان والحريات الأساسية للجميع ومراعاتها». وتنص المادة ٢ (١) من العهد الدولي للحقوق الاقتصادية والاجتماعية والثقافية أيضًا على التزامات الدول المتعاقدة بالمساعدة والتعاون الدوليين . . . وتعترف ديباجة اتفاقية اللاجئين والتوصية (د) من الوثيقة الختامية لمؤتمر المفوضين التي اعتمدت اتفاقية اللاجئين أيضًا بالالتزام بالتعاون. وقد تتخذ المساعدة والتعاون الدوليين فيما يتعلق بشئون اللاجئين عدة صور منها، إعادة توطين اللاجئين وتقديم المساعدة المالية والمساعدة التقنية. وقد تتخذ أيضا شكل لمّ شمل الأسر وبرامج هجرة اليد العاملة والمساعدة الإنمائية.

27. Обязательства международного сотрудничества: В соответствии со статьями 55(с) и 56 Устава ООН все члены ООН обязуются сотрудничать в вопросах достижения «всеобщего уважения и соблюдения прав человека и основных свобод для всех». Статья 2(1) МПЭСКП также налагает обязательства на государства-участники относительно международной помощи и сотрудничества . . . Преамбула Конвенции о статусе беженцев и Рекомендация D Заключительного акта Конференции полномочных представителей, которая приняла Конвенцию о статусе беженцев, также признают обязательства относительно сотрудничества. Международная помощь и сотрудничество в контексте беженцев могут, *в частности*, распространяться на переселение беженцев, оказание им финансовой и технической помощи. Помощь также может распространяться на воссоединение семей, программу трудовой миграции и целевое развитие.

MASS INFLUX

28. Situations of mass influx may raise particularly acute problems with respect to protection of refugee rights . . . [I]nadequate absorption or response capacity serves to distinguish the situation of developing countries from developed countries. Developed countries are generally able to cope with a rapid influx of large numbers of asylum-seekers or refugees.

L'AFFLUX MASSIF

28. Les situations d'afflux massif peuvent soulever des défis particulièrement importants pour la protection des droits des réfugiés. [L'existence] d'une capacité d'absorption ou de réponse inadéquate permet d'opérer une distinction entre les pays développés et les pays en voie de développement. Les pays développés sont généralement en mesure de faire face à un afflux d'un grand nombre de demandeurs d'asile ou de réfugiés concentré sur une courte période.

AFLUENCIA MASIVA

28. Las situaciones de afluencia masiva pueden plantear problemas particularmente graves con respecto a la protección de los derechos de los refugiados. La capacidad de absorción o respuesta (in)adecuada sirve para distinguir la situación de los países en desarrollo de la de los países desarrollados. Los países desarrollados en general pueden hacer frente a la rápida afluencia de una gran cantidad de solicitantes de asilo o refugiados.

---

29. There is no general derogation clause in either the Refugee Convention or the ICESCR. '[I]n time of war or other grave and exceptional circumstances,' Article 9 of the Refugee Convention allows, in individual cases, provisional measures essential to national security 'pending a determination . . . that that person is in fact a refugee and that the continuance of such measures is necessary in his case in the interests of national security.' A situation of mass influx does not, in and of itself, trigger the ability to impose provisional measures under Article 9 . . .

29. Ni la Convention ni le PIDESC ne contiennent de clause de dérogation de portée générale. « En temps de guerre ou dans d'autres circonstances graves et exceptionnelles », l'article 9 de la Convention autorise l'adoption, dans certains cas individuels, de mesures provisoires essentielles à la sécurité nationale « en attendant qu'il soit établi par ledit État contractant que cette personne est effectivement un réfugié et que le maintien desdites mesures est nécessaire à son égard dans l'intérêt de sa sécurité nationale ». Une situation d'afflux massif ne suffit pas, en soi, pour que les États puissent imposer des mesures provisoires en application de l'article 9.

29. No existe una cláusula de derogación general en la Convención sobre el Estatuto de los Refugiados ni en el PIDESC. "En tiempos de guerra u otras circunstancias graves y excepcionales", el artículo 9 de la Convención sobre el Estatuto de los Refugiados permite, en casos individuales, medidas transitorias esenciales para la seguridad nacional "a la espera de una determinación [. . .] de que esa persona sea, en realidad, un refugiado y que la continuación de tales medidas sea necesaria en su caso en aras de la seguridad nacional". Una situación de afluencia masiva en sí misma no permite imponer medidas transitorias en virtud del artículo 9.

---

30. . . . As far as the right to work is concerned, refugees will not, in the initial phases, be 'lawfully staying' for the purposes of Article 17 of the Refugee Convention. However, under the Refugee Convention, the right to engage in self-employment adheres at the early stage of 'lawful presence.' The impact on state resources may be such that states' ability to fulfill the right to work under the ICESCR may be weakened. Under the ICESCR, however, states parties must always meet the minimum core content of rights under the Covenant and 'take steps' towards the realization of all rights, with international assistance, if necessary.

30. En ce qui concerne le droit au travail, il ne peut pas être considéré à ce stade que les réfugiés « résident régulièrement » au sens de l'article 17 de la Convention. Toutefois, la Convention consacre le droit d'exercer une profession non salariée dès que le réfugié est « régulièrement présent ». Les effets sur les ressources étatiques peuvent être telles que la capacité des États de réaliser le droit au travail conformément au PIDESC peut se trouver affaiblie. Le PIDESC oblige toutefois les États à toujours respecter le minimum des droits consacrés par le Pacte et à prendre des mesures permettant la réalisation de ceux-ci, si nécessaire avec l'assistance de la communauté internationale.

30. En lo que respecta al derecho al trabajo, en las fases iniciales los refugiados no estarán "residiendo legalmente" a los efectos del artículo 17 de la Convención sobre el Estatuto de los Refugiados. Sin embargo, según la Convención sobre el Estatuto de los Refugiados, el derecho al empleo independiente se adhiere a la etapa temprana de "presencia legal". El impacto en los recursos de la nación puede ser tal que la capacidad de las naciones para cumplir con el derecho al trabajo en virtud del PIDESC puede verse debilitada. Sin embargo, según el Pacto Internacional de Derechos Económicos, Sociales y Culturales, los estados partes deben respetar siempre el contenido básico mínimo de los derechos en virtud del Pacto y "tomar medidas" para que se respeten todos los derechos, solicitando asistencia internacional en caso de que sea necesario.

МАССОВЫЙ ПРИТОК БЕЖЕНЦЕВ

28. Ситуации с массовым притоком могут вызвать особенно острые проблемы в отношении защиты прав беженцев. Возможности по поглощению или реагированию отличают ситуацию в развивающихся странах от развитых стран. Развитые страны, как правило, могут справиться с быстрым притоком большого числа просителей убежища или беженцев.

29. В Конвенции о статусе беженцев или МПЭСКП нет общего положения об отклонении вопроса. «Во время войны или других серьезных и исключительных обстоятельствах», Статья 9 Конвенции о статусе беженцев допускает, в отдельных случаях, временные меры, необходимые для обеспечения национальной безопасности «до принятия решения, является ли лицо беженцем фактически, при этом применение таких мер необходимо в интересах национальной безопасности». Ситуация с массовым притоком сама по себе не дает возможности налагать временные меры в соответствии со Статьей 9.

30. . . . Что касается права на труд, то беженцы на начальных этапах не будут считаться «законно проживающими» в стране, согласно статье 17 Конвенции о статусе беженцев. Однако в соответствии с Конвенцией о статусе беженцев право на самостоятельную занятость приобретается на ранней стадии «законного проживания». Влияние на государственные ресурсы может быть таковым, что способность государства обеспечивать право на работу в рамках МПЭСКП может быть ослаблена. Однако в соответствии с МПЭСКП государства-участники всегда должны соответствовать минимальному основному содержанию прав в соответствии с Пактом и «предпринимать шаги» по реализации всех прав международной помощи, если это необходимо.

التدفق الجماعي

28. قد تثير حالات التدفق الجماعي مشاكل حادة بصفة خاصة فيما يتعلق بحماية حقوق اللاجئين . . . [1] إن عدم كفاية القدرة على الاستيعاب أو الاستجابة ينتج عنه التمييز بين حالة البلدان النامية والبلدان المتقدمة. حيث تكون البلدان المتقدمة قادرة عمومًا على مواجهة التدفق السريع لأعداد كبيرة من طالبي اللجوء أو اللاجئين.

29. لا يوجد شرط عام للتقييد في اتفاقية اللاجئين أو العهد الدولي للحقوق الاقتصادية والاجتماعية والثقافية. «[في] وقت الحرب أو غيرها من الظروف الخطيرة والاستثنائية»، تسمح المادة 9 من اتفاقية اللاجئين، في حالات فردية، باتخاذ التدابير المؤقتة الضرورية للأمن القومي «ريثما يتم البت فيها . . . أن هذا الشخص في الواقع لاجئ وأن استمرار هذه التدابير ضروري في قضيته لمصلحة الأمن القومي». ولا تؤدي حالة التدفق الجماعي، في حد ذاتها، إلى القدرة على فرض تدابير مؤقتة بموجب المادة 9 . . .

30. . . . وفيما يتعلق بالحق في العمل، فإن اللاجئين لن يكونوا في المراحل الأولى «مقيمين بصورة قانونية» لأغراض المادة 17 من اتفاقية اللاجئين. ومع ذلك، بموجب اتفاقية اللاجئين، يلتزم الحق بالانخراط في العمل الحر في المرحلة المبكرة من «الوجود القانوني». وقد يكون التأثير على موارد الدولة من شأنه أن يضعف قدرة الدول على الوفاء بالحق في العمل بموجب العهد الدولي للحقوق الاقتصادية والاجتماعية والثقافية. ولكن بموجب العهد الدولي للحقوق الاقتصادية والاجتماعية والثقافية، يجب على الدول الأطراف دائمًا أن تفي بالحد الأدنى من المضمون الأساسي للحقوق المنصوص عليها في العهد وأن «تتخذ خطوات» نحو إعمال جميع الحقوق، بمساعدة دولية، إذا لزم الأمر.

31. States and other actors must assist those states faced with a mass influx in accordance with the obligation of international cooperation. This includes 'the provision of financial and in-kind assistance in support of refugee populations and host communities to promote refugee self-reliance, as appropriate, thus enhancing the sustainability of any future durable solution and relieving the burden on countries of first asylum': UNHCR Executive Committee Conclusion No. 100 (LV).

31. Les États et les autres acteurs concernés doivent assister les États qui font face à un afflux massif, conformément à l'obligation de coopération internationale. Cela inclut « la fourniture d'une assistance financière et en nature au bénéfice des populations réfugiées et des communautés hôtes, lorsque cela semble nécessaire, pour promouvoir l'autonomie des réfugiés, ce qui renforce la viabilité de toute solution durable éventuelle et allège le fardeau assumé par les pays de premier asile » : Conclusion No. 100 (LV), Comité exécutif du Programme du Haut Comissaire pour les réfugies.

31. Las naciones y otros actores deben ayudar a las naciones que enfrentan una afluencia masiva de conformidad con la obligación de cooperación internacional. Esto incluye "la provisión de asistencia financiera y en especie para apoyar a las poblaciones de refugiados y comunidades de acogida para promover la autosuficiencia de los refugiados, según corresponda, y así mejorar la sostenibilidad de cualquier solución duradera futura y aliviar la carga de los países de primer asilo": Conclusión N.° 100 (LV) del Comité Ejecutivo del ACNUR.

These Guidelines reflect the consensus of all the participants at the Fifth Michigan Colloquium on Challenges in International Refugee Law, held in Ann Arbor, Michigan, USA, on November 13–15, 2009.

Penelope Mathew
Colloquium Convener and Chair
University of Michigan/
The Australian National University

Ryszard Cholewinski
International Organization for
*   Migration (personal capacity)*

Matthew Craven
University of London

Alice Edwards
University of Oxford

Kate Jastram
University of California, Berkeley

Jonathan Klaaren
University of Witwatersrand, Johannesburg

Bernard Ryan
University of Kent

Adam Weiss
The AIRE Centre

Rebecca Cohen
Colloquium Rapporteur
University of Michigan alumna

Fiona le Diraison
Colloquium Rapporteur
Visiting Scholar
University of Michigan

Caroline Aiello
Student
University of Michigan

Jillian Blake
Student
University of Michigan

Uzma Burney
Student
University of Michigan

Jessika Croizat
Student
University of Michigan

Jonah Eaton
Student
University of Michigan

Samantha Funk
Student
University of Michigan

Su Kim
Student
University of Michigan

Raphaëlle Monty
Student
University of Michigan

Juliana Vengoechea Barrios
Student
University of Michigan

Nina Zelic
Student
University of Michigan

The Colloquium deliberations benefited from the counsel of Dr. Kees Wouters, Division of International Protection, United Nations High Commissioner for Refugees.

31. يجب على الدول والجهات الفاعلة الأخرى أن تساعد تلك الدول التي تواجه تدفق جماعي وفقًا لالتزام التعاون الدولي. ويشمل ذلك «تقديم مساعدة مالية وعينية دعمًا لمجموعات اللاجئين والمجتمعات المضيفة لها تعزيزًا لاعتماد اللاجئين على أنفسهم، حسب الاقتضاء، مما يزيد مناستدامة ما قد يتم التوصل إليه مستقبلًا من حلول مستديمة ويخفف الأعباء على بلدان اللجوء الأول»: استنتاج اللجنة التنفيذية للمفوضية السامية للأمم المتحدة لشؤون اللاجئين رقم 100 (LV).

31. Государства и другие субъекты должны оказывать помощь тем государствам, которые столкнулись с массовым притоком в соответствии с обязательством международного сотрудничества. Это включает в себя «предоставление финансовой и натуральной помощи в поддержку беженцев и принимающих общин в целях содействия самообеспечению беженцев, повышения надежности любого будущего долговременного решения и облегчения бремени для стран первого убежища»: Вывод Исполнительного комитета УВКБ № 100 (LV).

Article 1(F)(a) of the Convention relating to the Status of Refugees ('Convention') requires the exclusion from refugee status of '. . . any person with respect to whom there are serious reasons for considering that . . . he has committed a crime against peace, a war crime, or a crime against humanity, as defined in the international instruments drawn up to make provision in respect of such crimes.'

LES RECOMMANDATIONS DE MICHIGAN SUR L'EXCLUSION DES AUTEURS DE CRIMES INTERNATIONAUX

L'article 1, F, a, de la Convention relative au statut des réfugiés (« la Convention ») prévoit l'exclusion du statut de réfugié des « personnes dont on aura des raisons sérieuses de penser (. . .) qu'elles ont commis un crime contre la paix, un crime de guerre ou un crime contre l'humanité, au sens des instruments internationaux élaborés pour prévoir des dispositions relatives à ces crimes ».

DIRECTRICES DE MICHIGAN SOBRE LA EXCLUSIÓN DE LOS CRIMINALES INTERNACIONALES

El artículo 1(F)(a) de la Convención sobre el Estatuto de los Refugiados ("la Convención") exige la exclusión de la condición de refugiado a "cualquier persona respecto de la cual existan motivos fundados para considerar que ha cometido un crimen contra la paz, un crimen de guerra o un crimen de lesa humanidad según lo definido en los instrumentos internacionales elaborados para adoptar disposiciones respecto de tales delitos".

Current state practice relating to Article 1(F)(a) exclusion fails to draw consistently on international criminal law, as is mandated by the Convention's text. The process of drawing on international criminal law is in any event complex given both the continuing evolution of international criminal law and normative divergence among the interpretations adopted by courts and national authorities. Most important, there has been a failure to recognize that international criminal law must be drawn upon in a way that takes full account of key differences between the purpose and structure of international criminal law and those of international refugee law. In the result, Article 1(F)(a) is prone to misapplication, leading to unwarranted denials of protection.

La pratique actuelle des États relative à l'application de la clause d'exclusion de l'article 1, F, a, échoue à s'appuyer de manière cohérente sur le droit pénal international, comme cela est pourtant requis par le texte de la Convention. Il est, en outre, difficile de se référer au droit pénal international, compte tenu tant de sa nature évolutive que des divergences d'interprétation entre les autorités nationales et les cours et tribunaux. De manière plus préoccupante, il n'est pas suffisamment admis que le droit pénal international ne constitue une référence d'interprétation pertinente qu'à la condition qu'il soit pleinement tenu compte de ce que ses objectifs et sa structure diffèrent de celles du droit international des réfugiés. Il en résulte que l'article 1, F, a, est souvent mal appliqué, ce qui mène à des refus d'accorder une protection contraire à la Convention.

La práctica actual de los Estados con respecto a la exclusión establecida en el artículo 1(F)(a) no realiza un uso consistente del derecho penal internacional, como lo manda el texto de la Convención. El proceso de hacer uso del derecho penal internacional es, en todo caso, muy complejo dada la continua evolución del derecho penal internacional y la discrepancia normativa de las interpretaciones adoptadas por los tribunales y las autoridades nacionales. Sobre todo, vale destacar que no se ha reconocido que el derecho penal internacional debe utilizarse de manera tal que tenga plenamente en cuenta las diferencias fundamentales entre el propósito y la estructura del derecho penal internacional y los del derecho internacional de los refugiados. En consecuencia, el artículo 1(F)(a) es susceptible al uso incorrecto, lo que deriva en la denegación de protección en forma arbitraria.

МИЧИГАНСКИЕ РУКОВОДЯЩИЕ ПРИНЦИПЫ ИСКЛЮЧЕНИЯ МЕЖДУНАРОДНЫХ ПРЕСТУПНИКОВ

Статья 1(F)(a) Конвенции о статусе беженцев («Конвенция») требует исключения из статуса беженца « . . . любого лица, в отношении которого имеются серьезные основания считать, что . . . оно совершило преступление против мира, военное преступление или преступление против человечества, как это определено в международных документах, разработанных с целью предотвращения таких преступлений».

دليل جامعة ميشيغان الإرشادي بشأن استبعاد المجرمين الدوليين

بموجب المادة 1(و)(أ) من الاتفاقية الخاصة بوضع اللاجئين («الاتفاقية») لا تنطبق وضع اللاجئ على « . . . أي شخص تتوفر أسباب جدية للاعتقاد بأنه . . . ارتكب جريمة ضد السلام أو جريمة حرب أو جريمة ضد الإنسانية، بالمعنى المستخدم لهذه الجرائم في الصكوك الدولية الموضوعة للنص على أحكام بشأنها».

Текущая практика государств, относящаяся к статье 1(F)(a), показывает, что исключение не может быть всегда связано с международным уголовным правом, как это предусмотрено в тексте Конвенции. Процесс привлечения международного уголовного права в любом случае является комплексным, с учетом не только постоянной эволюции международного уголовного права, но и нормативного расхождения между толкованиями, принятыми судами и национальными властями. Особенно важно то, что отсутствует признание того, что международное уголовное право должно быть построено таким образом, чтобы в полной мере учитывать основные различия между целью и структурой международного уголовного права и международными правами беженцев. В результате статья 1(F)(a) часто применяется неправильно, что приводит к необоснованному отказу в защите.

تختلف الممارسة الحالية للدولة فيما يتعلق بالمادة 1(و)(أ) من الاستبعاد بصورة متسقة بشأن القانون الجنائي الدولي، على النحو الذي ينص عليه نص الاتفاقية. وتبدو عملية الاستناد على القانون الجنائي الدولي معقدة على أي حال نظرًا إلى التطور المستمر للقانون الجنائي الدولي والاختلاف المعياري بين التفسيرات التي تعتمدها المحاكم والسلطات الوطنية. والأهم من ذلك أن هناك إخفاقًا في الاعتراف بأن القانون الجنائي الدولي يجب أن يُستند إليه على نحو داعٍ، تمامًا الاختلافات الرئيسية بين غرض القانون الجنائي الدولي وهيكلته وقانون اللاجئين الدولي. نتيجة لذلك، تكون المادة 1(و)(أ) عرضة لسوء التطبيق، مما يؤدي إلى إنكار الحماية دون مبرر.

With a view to promoting a shared understanding of the proper approach to Article 1(F)(a) exclusion from refugee status, we have engaged in sustained collaborative study and reflection on relevant norms and state practice. Our research was debated and refined at the Sixth Colloquium on Challenges in International Refugee Law, convened in March 2013 by the University of Michigan's Program in Refugee and Asylum Law. These Guidelines are the product of that endeavor, and reflect the consensus of Colloquium participants on how decision makers can best ensure the application of Article 1(F)(a) in a manner that conforms to international legal principles.

Afin de promouvoir une interprétation commune de l'approche à suivre pour appliquer la clause d'exclusion du statut de réfugié consacrée par l'article 1, F, a, de la Convention, nous avons entrepris une étude et une réflexion approfondie et commune relativement aux normes et aux pratiques étatiques pertinentes. Les résultats de notre recherche ont été débattus et affinés à l'occasion du sixième colloque sur les défis du droit international des réfugiés, organisé en mars 2013 par le programme de droit d'asile et des réfugiés de l'université du Michigan. Ces recommandations sont le résultat de cette entreprise et reflètent le consensus des participants au colloque au sujet d'une application de l'article 1, F, a, qui respecte les principes de droit international.

Con el objetivo de promover un enfoque apropiado y compartido del artículo 1(F)(a) sobre la exclusión de la condición de refugiado, nos hemos dedicado a un estudio colaborativo profundo y a la reflexión sobre las normas relevantes y la práctica de los Estados. Nuestra investigación fue debatida y perfeccionada en el Sexto Coloquio sobre los Desafíos en el Derecho Internacional de los Refugiados, convocado en marzo del año 2013 por el Programa de Legislación sobre Refugiados y Asilo de la Universidad de Michigan. Estas Directrices son el producto de ese esfuerzo, y reflejan el consenso de los participantes del Coloquio sobre cómo los encargados de tomar decisiones pueden asegurarse de que el artículo 1(F)(a) se aplique de la mejor manera en virtud de los principios del derecho internacional.

GENERAL CONSIDERATIONS

1. A person who falls afoul of Article 1(F)(a) of the Convention must not be recognized as a refugee, even assuming that he or she faces a well-founded fear of being persecuted. Because of the seriousness of a decision to deny protection to a person shown or assumed to face the risk of persecution, Article 1(F)(a), like all exclusion clauses, should be applied with caution.

CONSIDÉRATIONS GÉNÉRALES

1. Une personne qui a commis un acte relevant de l'article 1, F, a, de la Convention ne doit pas être reconnue comme réfugiée quand bien même elle éprouve une crainte fondée d'être persécutée. Refuser la protection à une personne qui risque la persécution revêt de graves conséquences, ce qui implique que l'article 1, F, a, comme les autres clauses d'exclusion, soit appliqué avec prudence.

CONSIDERACIONES GENERALES

1. Una persona que no se encuentre bajo los supuestos señalados en el artículo 1(F)(a) de la Convención no puede ser reconocida como refugiada, incluso aunque tenga un temor bien fundado a ser perseguida. Debido a la gravedad de la decisión de denegar la protección a una persona que se haya confirmado o se sospeche que esté en riesgo de sufrir una persecución, el artículo 1(F)(a), como todas las cláusulas de exclusión, se debe aplicar de manera prudente.

2. Decision makers moreover have a duty in good faith to interpret the text of Article 1(F)(a) not by reference to text alone, but rather in a manner consistent with the context, object, and purpose of that article and of the Convention as a whole.

2. L'article 1, F, a, doit être interprété de bonne foi, sans uniquement se référer à son texte, mais en prenant également en considération le contexte, l'objet et l'objectif, de cette disposition et de la Convention dans son ensemble.

2. Los responsables de tomar decisiones tienen el deber de interpretar el texto del artículo 1(F)(a) de buena fe, no solo haciendo referencia al texto del artículo, sino más bien teniendo en cuenta el contexto, objeto y fin del artículo y de la Convención en conjunto.

ومن أجل تعزيز فهم مشترك للنهج السليم للمادة 1(و)(أ) الاستبعاد من وضع اللاجئ، شاركنا في دراسة تعاونية مستمرة والتفكير في القواعد ذات الصلة وممارسات الدول. تمت مناقشة وصقل بحثنا في الندوة السادسة حول التحديات في قانون اللاجئين الدولي، والتي عقدت في مارس 2013 من قبل برنامج جامعة ميشيغان حول قانون اللاجئين واللجوء. وتأتي هذه المبادئ التوجيهية نتيجة هذا المسعى، والتي تعكس توافق آراء المشاركين في الندوة حول كيفية ضمان قيام صانعي القرار بأفضل تطبيق للمادة 1(و)(أ) على نحو يتفق مع المبادئ القانونية الدولية.

В целях содействия пониманию надлежащего подхода к статье 1(F)(a) относительно исключения из статуса беженца, мы проводили постоянные совместные исследования и анализ соответствующих норм и практики государств. Наши исследования обсуждались и уточнялись на шестом коллоквиуме по проблемам международных прав беженцев, который проходил в марте 2013 года по Программе Мичиганского университета в области законодательства о беженцах и убежище. Данные Руководящие принципы являются результатом этих усилий и отражают единое мнение участников коллоквиума о том, что лица, принимающие решения, могут обеспечить наиболее правильное применение статьи 1(F)(a) в соответствии с международно-правовыми принципами.

الاعتبارات العامة

1. يجب ألا يُعترف، بالشخص الذي ينتقص من المادة 1(و)(أ) من الاتفاقية كلاجئ، حتى على افتراض أنه يواجه خوفًا مبررًا له من التعرض للاضطهاد. وبسبب خطورة قرار حرمان الشخص الذي يظهر أو يفترض أنه يواجه خطر التعرض للاضطهاد، يجب تطبيق المادة 1(و)(أ)، مثل جميع شروط الاستبعاد، بحذر.

ОБЩИЕ ПОЛОЖЕНИЯ

1. Лицо, которое подпадает под действие статьи 1(F)(a) Конвенции, не должно признаваться беженцем, даже если предположить, что ему грозит вполне обоснованная опасность преследования. Из-за серьезности решения об отказе в защите лица, которое доказано или предположительно сталкивается с риском преследования, статью 1(F)(a), как и все положения об исключении, следует применять с осторожностью.

2. علاوة على ذلك، يجب على صانعي القرارات أن يقوموا بتفسير نص المادة 1(و)(أ) بحسن نية، وليس بالاعتماد على النص وحده بل بطريقة تتفق مع سياق هذه المادة وموضوعها والغرض منها والاتفاقية ككل.

2. Кроме того, лица, принимающие решения, должны добросовестно толковать статью 1(F)(a) не только по тексту, а скорее в соответствии с контекстом, объектом и целью этой статьи и Конвенции в целом.

3. The context of Article 1(F)(a) includes, in particular, the fact that decisions on refugee exclusion are binary: an individual either is, or is not, excluded from refugee status. In contrast, the ramifications of a finding of guilt in the context of international criminal law can be tempered by the sentencing process – an option not available to the refugee decision maker. This contextual difference should be recognized and, to the greatest extent possible, accommodated in the assessment of criminal responsibility for purposes of exclusion from refugee status.

3. Le contexte de l'article 1, F, a, comprend, en particulier, la circonstance que les décisions relatives à l'exclusion du statut de réfugié sont binaires: un individu est exclu du statut de réfugié ou ne l'est pas. Il n'en va pas de même des conséquences résultant d'un verdict de culpabilité en droit pénal international, qui peuvent être tempérées par la détermination de la peine – ce qui n'est pas possible en droit des réfugiés. Cette différence contextuelle devrait être reconnue et, dans la mesure du possible, prise en considération lorsqu'il s'agit d'évaluer la responsabilité criminelle aux fins d'exclure du statut de réfugié.

3. En particular, el contexto del artículo 1(F)(a) incluye el hecho de que las decisiones sobre la exclusión de los refugiados son binarias: o se excluye a un individuo de la condición de refugiado, o no se lo excluye. En contraste, las ramificaciones de un hallazgo de culpabilidad en el contexto del derecho penal internacional pueden verse atenuadas por el proceso de sentencia, una opción que no está disponible para el tomador de decisiones sobre refugiados. Esta diferencia contextual debe ser reconocida y, en la medida de lo posible, considerada en la evaluación de la responsabilidad penal a los fines de excluir a un individuo de la condición de refugiado.

4. The fundamental object and purpose of Article 1(F)(a) is to exclude persons whose international criminal conduct means that their admission as a refugee threatens the integrity of the international refugee regime. This goal is to be distinguished from the advancement of host state safety and security, a matter addressed by Article 33(2) of the Convention. Nor is Article 1(F)(a) exclusion required to ensure the punishment of international criminals. Like all other persons, refugees suspected of having committed an international crime are subject to the duty of states to either prosecute or extradite ('*aut dedere aut judicare*'), this being the appropriate means of ensuring accountability for unexpiated international criminality.

4. L'objet et l'objectif fondamentaux de l'article 1, F, a, consistent à exclure du statut de réfugié les individus qui, en raison de leur comportement criminel au regard du droit international, ne peuvent se voir reconnaître la qualité de réfugié sans menacer l'intégrité du régime international de protection des réfugiés. Cet objectif doit être distingué de la protection du pays d'accueil contre un danger pour sa sécurité ou une menace pour sa communauté, poursuivi par l'article 33, §2, de la Convention. En outre, la clause d'exclusion de l'article 1, F, a, n'entend pas sanctionner les auteurs de crimes de droit pénal international. Les États ont l'obligation de droit international de poursuivre ou d'extrader (« *aut dedere aut judicare* ») les réfugiés suspectés d'avoir commis un crime de droit pénal international, au même titre que toute autre personne, puisqu'il s'agit là du mode approprié pour garantir que des crimes de droit international ne demeurent pas impunis.

4. El objeto y el fin primordiales del artículo 1(F)(a) es la exclusión de personas cuya conducta analizada por el derecho penal internacional implique que su admisión al país como refugiado amenaza la integridad del régimen internacional de los refugiados. Este objetivo debe distinguirse de la promoción de la seguridad del Estado anfitrión, materia que se rige por el artículo 33(2) de la Convención. La norma de exclusión contenida en el artículo 1(F)(a) tampoco es necesaria para evitar que los criminales internacionales gocen de impunidad. Como todas las personas, los refugiados bajo sospecha de haber cometido un delito internacional se encuentran sujetos al deber de los Estados de procesar o extraditar ("*aut dedere aut judicare*"), siendo estos los medios apropiados para garantizar la rendición de cuentas por delitos penales internacionales no expiados.

A CRIME AS DEFINED IN THE INTERNATIONAL INSTRUMENTS

5. Article 1(F)(a) requires that exclusion be grounded in international criminal law instruments that define crimes against peace, war crimes, and crimes against humanity. The express reference to "international instruments" mandates reliance on codified standards of international, not domestic, law. This open-ended framing moreover requires that account be taken of international criminal law instruments that have come into force in the years since the Convention's drafting.

UN CRIME AU SENS DES INSTRUMENTS INTERNATIONAUX

5. L'article 1, F, a, requiert que l'exclusion soit fondée sur les instruments de droit pénal international qui définissent les crimes contre la paix, les crimes de guerre et les crimes contre l'humanité. La référence expresse aux « instruments internationaux » implique qu'il soit fait application des normes codifiées de droit pénal international et non de celles de droit national. L'usage d'une formulation ouverte par la Convention implique également qu'il soit tenu compte des instruments de droit pénal international qui sont entrés en vigueur après l'élaboration de la Convention.

UN CRIMEN SEGÚN LO DEFINIDO EN LOS INSTRUMENTOS INTERNACIONALES

5. El artículo 1(F)(a) exige que la exclusión esté fundamentada en los instrumentos del derecho penal internacional que definan los crímenes contra la paz, de guerra y de lesa humanidad. La referencia expresa a "los instrumentos internacionales" ordena basarse en las normas codificadas en el derecho internacional, y no en la legislación nacional. Además, esta formulación abierta exige que se consideren los instrumentos del derecho penal internacional que han entrado en vigencia después de la elaboración de la Convención.

3. Контекст статьи 1(F)(a) включает, в частности, тот факт, что решения об исключении беженцев являются двойным: физическое лицо либо лишается, либо не лишается статуса беженца. Напротив, последствия признания вины в контексте международного уголовного права могут быть смягчены в процессе вынесения приговора — вариант, недоступный для лица, принимающего решение о предоставлении убежища. Указанную контекстуальную разницу следует признать и, насколько это возможно, учитывать при оценке уголовной ответственности при лишении статуса беженца.

4. والغرض الأساسي من المادة 1(و)(أ) هو استبعاد الأشخاص الذين يعني سلوكهم الجنائي الدولي أن قبولهم كلاجئ يهدد سلامة نظام اللاجئين الدوليين. يجب التمييز بين هذا الهدف وبين النهوض، بسلامة وأمن الدولة المضيفة، وهي مسألة تتناولها القانون33 (2) من الاتفاقية. كما أن المادة 1(و)(أ) لا تلزم ضمان معاقبة المجرمين الدوليين. ومثل جميع الأشخاص الآخرين، فإن اللاجئين المشتبه في ارتكابهم لجرعة دولية يخضعون لواجب الدول إما للمحاكمة أو التسليم («مبدأ تسليم المجرم أو محاكمته»)، وهي الوسيلة المناسبة لضمان المساءلة عن الإجرام الدولي غير المنفذ.

4. Основной задачей и целью статьи 1(F)(a) является исключение лиц, чье международное преступное поведение означает, что предоставление им статуса беженца угрожает целостности международного режима относительно беженцев. Эту цель следует отличать от обеспечения охраны и безопасности государства пребывания, вопрос, рассматриваемый в статье 33(2) Конвенции. Также статья 1(F)(a) не предусматривает исключения, требуемого для обеспечения наказания международных преступников. Как и все другие лица, беженцы, подозреваемые в совершении международного преступления, подпадают под действия государств в виде преследования в судебном порядке либо выдачи («*требование об обязательной выдаче или привлечении к суду*»), что является надлежащим средством обеспечения ответственности за международные преступления, которые не были искуплены.

الجرعة كما تعرفها العهود الدولية

5. تلزم المادة 1(و)(أ) بأن يستند الاستبعاد إلى مواد القانون الجنائي الدولي التي تعرف الجرائم ضد السلام وجرائم الحرب والجرائم المرتكبة ضد الإنسانية. والإشارة الصريحة إلى «العهود الدولية» تتطلب الاعتماد على مواد القانون الدولي وليس القانون المحلي. علاوة على ذلك، فإن هذا الإطار يتطلب مراعاة مواد القانون الجنائي الدولي التي دخلت حيز التنفيذ في السنوات التي تلت صياغة الاتفاقية.

ПРЕСТУПЛЕНИЕ, ОПРЕДЕЛЯЕМОЕ В МЕЖДУНАРОДНЫХ НОРМАХ

5. Статья 1(F)(a) требует, чтобы исключение было основано на международных нормах уголовного права, которые определяют преступления против мира, военные преступления и преступления против человечества. Четкая ссылка на «международные нормы» предусматривает использование кодифицированных стандартов международного, а не внутреннего законодательства. Кроме того, это открытое обрамление требует учета международных инструментов уголовного права, которые вступили в силу в годы, прошедшие после разработки Конвенции.

6. Given the plurality of international criminal law instruments, a decision maker contemplating exclusion under Article 1(F)(a) should first identify those instruments that are most substantively relevant to the criminal conduct alleged. As leading courts interpreting Art. 1(F)(a) have recognized, the Rome Statute of the International Criminal Court is particularly relevant in light of its recent vintage, detailed definitions of relevant crimes, and global scope of application.

6. Étant donné qu'il existe plusieurs instruments de droit pénal international, l'application de l'article 1, F, a, suppose d'identifier au préalable les instruments les plus pertinents eu égard au comportement reproché. Comme cela a été reconnu par les principales cours amenées à interpréter l'article 1, F, a, le Statut de Rome de la Cour pénale internationale est particulièrement pertinent en ce qu'il est relativement récent, qu'il contient une définition détaillée des crimes pertinents et qu'il revêt un champ d'application universel.

6. Debido a la pluralidad de los instrumentos internacionales, el responsable de tomar una decisión de conformidad con la exclusión establecida en el artículo 1(F)(a), en primer lugar deberá identificar los instrumentos con el mayor grado de relevancia sustantiva en cuanto a la presunta conducta criminal. Tal y como ha sido reconocido por los más altos tribunales que interpretan el artículo 1(F)(a), el Estatuto de Roma de la Corte Penal Internacional es particularmente relevante en vista de su reciente adopción, sus definiciones detalladas respecto a delitos pertinentes y su alcance de aplicación global.

---

7. In addition to analysis of the text of relevant international criminal law instruments, account should be taken of persuasive interpretations of such instruments rendered by both international tribunals and national courts. Interpretations that offer an authoritative and cogent understanding of how international criminal norms apply in comparable factual circumstances are of particular value.

7. En plus d'une analyse du texte des instruments de droit pénal international pertinents, il convient d'également prendre en considération les interprétations convaincantes développées par les cours et tribunaux nationaux et internationaux. Les interprétations relatives à la manière dont les normes de droit pénal international s'appliquent à des circonstances de fait similaires, qui font autorité et sont cohérentes, doivent se voir accorder une attention particulière.

7. Además del análisis del texto de los instrumentos relevantes del derecho penal internacional, se deben tener en cuenta las interpretaciones convincentes de dichos instrumentos pronunciadas por los tribunales internacionales y los tribunales nacionales. Se debe dar un valor particular a las interpretaciones que ofrecen una comprensión fidedigna y contundente de cómo se aplican las normas del derecho penal internacional en circunstancias de hecho comparables.

HAS COMMITTED A CRIME

8. The phrase "he has committed a crime" makes clear the importance of finding individual criminal responsibility in relation to an enumerated crime before refusing to recognize refugee status in a particular case. The decision maker must first identify the pertinent mode of liability, and then carefully assess the applicable *actus reus*, *mens rea*, and defences.

A COMMIS UN CRIME

8. Il ressort clairement de la formulation « a commis un crime » qu'il est essentiel de déterminer la responsabilité pénale individuelle pour un des crimes énumérés par l'article 1, F, a, avant de refuser de reconnaître la qualité de réfugié dans un cas spécifique. Il convient d'abord d'établir les causes de responsabilité pertinentes, puis d'analyser attentivement l'*actus reus,* le *mens rea* et les moyens de défense.

HA COMETIDO UN DELITO

8. La frase "ha cometido un delito" hace hincapié en la importancia de establecer la responsabilidad penal individual en relación con uno de los delitos enumerados antes de denegar el reconocimiento de la condición de refugiado en un caso concreto. El responsable de tomar la decisión debe primero identificar la causal de responsabilidad penal pertinente, y después analizar cuidadosamente posibles aplicaciones de *actus reus*, *mens rea*, y causas para excluir la responsabilidad penal.

6. نظرا لتعدد عهود القانون الجنائي الدولي، يجب على صانعي القرار الذين يفكرون في الاستبعاد بموجب المادة 1(و)(أ) أن يحددوا أولًا المواد ذات الصلة بموضوع السلوك الإجرامي المزعوم. فكما أوضحت المحاكم الرائدة عند تفسير المادة1(و)(أ)، فإن نظام روما الأساسي للمحكمة الجنائية الدولية له أهمية خاصة في ضوء تعريفاته الأخيرة المفصلة والمتكررة للجرائم ذات الصلة والنطاق العالمي للتطبيق.

6. Учитывая множество международных норм в области уголовного права, лицо, принимающее решение, которое предусматривает исключение согласно статье 1(F)(a), должно сначала определить нормы, которые в наибольшей степени сохранили свою актуальность для предполагаемого уголовного преступления. Ведущие суды, интерпретирующие статью 1(F)(a) признают, что Римский статут Международного уголовного суда особенно актуален в свете его недавних подробных определений соответствующих преступлений и общей сферы применения.

---

7. بالإضافة إلى تحليل نص مواد القانون الجنائي الدولي ذات الصلة، ينبغي مراعاة التفسيرات المقنعة لتلك المواد التي تصدرها المحاكم الدولية والمحاكم المحلية على حد سواء. إن التفسيرات التي توفر فهمًا موثوقًا ومقنعًا لكيفية تطبيق القواعد الجنائية الدولية في ظروف واقعية مماثلة ذات قيمة خاصة.

7. В дополнение к анализу текста соответствующих международных документов по уголовному праву следует учитывать убедительные толкования таких документов, как международными трибуналами, так и национальными судами. Особое значение имеют толкования, которые предлагают авторитетное и убедительное понимание того, как применяются международные уголовные нормы в сопоставимых фактических обстоятельствах.

إرتكاب جريمة

8. توضح عبارة «أنه ارتكب جريمة» أهمية إيجاد المسؤولية الجنائية الفردية فيما يتعلق بجريمة تم ذكرها قبل رفض الاعتراف بوضع اللاجئ في حالة معينة. ويجب على صانع القرار أولًا تحديد ارتباط أسلوب المسؤولية، ثم تقييم دقيق للفعل الإجرامي والقصد الجنائي والدفاعات المطبقة.

СОВЕРШЕНИЕ ПРЕСТУПЛЕНИЯ

8. Фраза «он совершил преступление» четко указывает на необходимость установления уголовной ответственности в отношении указанного преступления, до отказа в признании статуса беженца в конкретном случае. Лицо, ответственное за принятие решений, должно сначала определить соответствующий режим ответственности, а затем тщательно оценить *actus reus, mens rea* (*состав преступления, преступный умысел)* и защиту.

9. The modes of liability that will be most apposite to Article 1(F)(a) exclusion are those that clearly specify a particular person's direct role in the crime: committing the crime; ordering, soliciting, or inducing the crime; and aiding, abetting, or otherwise assisting in the commission of the crime. Modes of liability predicated on more attenuated forms of involvement require a decision maker to undertake especially careful analysis before concluding that the individual concerned 'has committed' an enumerated crime.

9. Les causes de responsabilité les plus pertinentes pour appliquer la clause d'exclusion de l'article 1, F, a, sont celles qui permettent d'identifier précisément le rôle direct d'un individu donné: commettre le crime; ordonner, solliciter ou susciter le crime; être complice, encourager ou assister de toute autre manière dans la commission du crime. Les causes de responsabilité reposant sur des formes d'implications moindres impliquent de réaliser une analyse particulièrement attentive avant de conclure qu'un individu « a commis » un des crimes énumérés par l'article 1, F, a.

9. Las causales de responsabilidad penal más apropiadas en función de la cláusula de exclusión contenida en el artículo 1(F)(a) son aquellas que precisan claramente el rol directo del individuo involucrado en el delito: cometer el delito; ordenar, proponer o inducir la comisión del delito; y ser cómplice o encubridor o colaborar de algún modo en la comisión del delito. Las causales de responsabilidad penal que presuponen formas de participación más atenuadas requieren que el responsable de tomar la decisión se comprometa a un análisis especialmente cuidadoso antes de concluir que el individuo "ha cometido" uno de los delitos enumerados.

10. In keeping with general principles of criminal law, an individual can only have 'committed a crime' if the relevant conduct was criminal at the time of its commission. The definition of a crime should moreover be strictly construed, with ambiguity resolved in favor of the person being considered for exclusion from refugee status and consideration given to whether an action that is truly *de minimis* evinces the moral responsibility required for commission of an international crime.

10. Conformément aux principes généraux de droit pénal international, il ne peut être considéré qu'un individu « a commis un crime » que si sa conduite était criminelle au moment où elle a été commise. Un crime doit, en outre, être défini strictement, les ambiguïtés devant bénéficier à la personne dont l'exclusion du statut de réfugié est envisagée, de même que la circonstance que son implication est tellement minimale que la responsabilité morale requise pour la commission d'un crime de droit international n'est pas rencontrée.

10. De conformidad con los principios generales del derecho penal, un individuo sólo puede haber "cometido un delito" si la conducta en cuestión constituía un crimen en el momento de su comisión. La definición de un delito además se debe interpretar de manera estricta, y cualquier ambigüedad se debe resolver a favor de la persona bajo consideración para la exclusión de la condición de refugiado y considerando la posibilidad de que el acto sea verdaderamente *de minimis,* en cuyo caso no existe la responsabilidad moral que se requiere en relación con la comisión de un delito internacional.

11. Exclusion under Article 1(F)(a) should not be ordered where the facts suggest a plausible defence, since a person entitled to the benefit of a relevant defence has not 'committed a crime.' In keeping with the approach codified in Article 31 of the Rome Statute, a broad range of substantively relevant defences should be considered. To accommodate the important contextual difference between international criminal law and international refugee law noted in para. 3 above, relevant defences should be understood to include not simply pure defences, but also factors that can variably be invoked as either a defence or a mitigating factor.

11. L'exclusion en application de l'article 1, F, a, ne devrait pas être décidée quand les moyens de défense sont vraisemblables eu égard aux faits de l'espèce, puisqu'en pareil cas un crime n'a pas « été commis ». Conformément à l'approche codifiée par l'article 31 du Statut de Rome, divers moyens de défense doivent être pris en considération. Afin de tenir compte de l'importante différence contextuelle entre le droit pénal international et le droit international des réfugiés telle que soulignée par le paragraphe 3 ci-dessus, les moyens de défense pertinents doivent être compris comme ne comprenant pas exclusivement les motifs d'exonération de responsabilité, mais également les éléments pouvant être invoqués à la fois comme motif d'exonération de responsabilité ou comme circonstances atténuantes.

11. La exclusión en virtud del artículo 1(F)(a) no se debe aplicar cuando los hechos del caso indiquen que existe una causa razonable de exoneración de la responsabilidad penal, ya que una persona con el derecho al beneficio de una causa de exoneración no "ha cometido un delito". En consonancia con el enfoque codificado en el artículo 31 del Estatuto de Roma, se debe considerar una amplia variedad de causas sustantivas de exoneración de la responsabilidad penal. A fin de tener en cuenta la diferencia contextual entre el derecho penal internacional y el derecho internacional de los refugiados al que se hace referencia en el párrafo 3 anterior, se debe entender que las causas apropiadas para excluir la responsabilidad penal deben incluir no solo las causas de exención per se, sino también otros factores que pueden ser invocados, ya sea una causa de exoneración o una circunstancia atenuante.

9. أساليب المسؤولية التي ستكون أكثر ملاءمة لاستبعاد المادة 1(و)(أ) هي تلك التي تحدد بوضوح الدور المباشر لشخص معين في الجريمة سواء كانت: ارتكاب الجريمة أو طلبها أو التماسها أو التحريض عليها والمساعدة أو التحريض على ارتكابها. مما يتطلب من صانع القرار تحليلًا دقيقًا بالغ العناية قبل أن يستنتج المعني «قد ارتكب» جريمة محددة وذلك باستخدام الصيغة الأخف عند تفسير العلاقة بين الشخص والجريمة.

9. Способы ответственности, которые являются наиболее уместными для исключений из статьи 1(F)(a), это те, которые четко определяют прямую роль конкретного лица в совершении преступления: совершение преступления; заказ или побуждение к преступлению; пособничество, подстрекательство или иное содействие в совершении преступления. Режимы ответственности, основанные на более ослабленных формах участия, требуют от лица, принимающего решения, особо тщательного анализа, перед принятием решения о том, что соответствующее лицо «совершило» указанное преступление.

10. تماشيًا مع المبادئ العامة للقانون الجنائي، لا يجوز لأي فرد أن «يرتكب جريمة» إلا إذا كان السلوك المعني جنائيًا وقت ارتكابه. يجب أيضًا أن يكون تفسير تعريف الجريمة دقيقًا، مع تفسير مواضع الغموض فيها لصالح الشخص الذي يُجرى النظر فيه من أجل الاستبعاد من وضع اللاجئ، والنظر فيما إذا كان الفعل حقًا يبرهن الحد الأدنى من المسؤولية الأخلاقية المطلوبة لارتكاب جريمة دولية.

10. В соответствии с общими принципами уголовного права человек может «совершить преступление» только в том случае, если соответствующее поведение было преступным во время его совершения. Более того, определение преступления должно быть истолковано таким образом, чтобы неоднозначность решалась в пользу лица, в отношении которого рассматривается вопрос о лишении статуса беженца, и рассмотрение вопроса о том, действительно ли указанное действие *минимально* определяет моральную ответственность, необходимую для совершения международного преступления.

11. وينبغي ألا يصدر أمر الاستبعاد بموجب المادة 1(و)(أ) عندما تشير الوقائع إلى وجود دفاع معقول، لأن الشخص الذي يحق له الاستفادة من دفاع ذي صلة لا يكون قد «ارتكب جريمة». تماشيًا مع النهج المدون في المادة 31 من نظام روما الأساسي، ينبغي النظر في نطاق واسع من الدفاعات ذات الصلة بالموضوع. لاستيعاب الاختلاف الظرفي عند تفسير القانون الجنائي الدولي أو قانون اللاجئين الدولي المشار إليه في الفقرة 3 أعلاه، يجب فهم الدفاعات ذات الصلة على أنها ليست مجرد دفاعات بحتة، بل أيضًا عوامل يمكن الاستناد إليها على نحو متغير إما كدفاع أو كعامل مخفف.

11. Исключение в соответствии со статьей 1(F)(a) не следует использовать, если факты указывают на убедительные доводы в защиту такого лица, поскольку лицо, имеющее право на соответствующую защиту, «не совершило преступления». В соответствии с подходом, закрепленным в статье 31 Римского статута, следует рассмотреть широкий спектр соответствующих аспектов защиты. Для учета важной контекстуальной разницы между международным уголовным правом и международным правом беженцев, указанными выше в п. 3, следует понимать, что соответствующая защита должна включать не просто саму защиту, но также факторы, которые можно в определенных случаях использовать как защиту или смягчающий фактор.

SERIOUS REASONS FOR CONSIDERING

12. The text of Article 1(F)(a) directs decision makers to exclude an individual from refugee status only where there are "serious reasons for considering" that he or she has committed a crime against peace, a war crime, or a crime against humanity. "Serious reasons" sets the standard in both fact and law that must be met in an exclusion decision, and thus has both an evidentiary and a substantive role.

LES RAISONS SÉRIEUSES DE PENSER

12. Le texte de l'article 1, F, a, invite à n'exclure un individu du statut de réfugié que s'il existe des « raisons sérieuses de penser » qu'il a commis un crime contre la paix, un crime de guerre ou un crime contre l'humanité. « Les raisons sérieuses » constituent le degré de certitude qui doit être rencontré en droit et en fait pour qu'il puisse être conclu à l'exclusion du statut de réfugié, ce qui revêt des implications en termes à la fois de preuves et de conditions de fond.

MOTIVOS FUNDADOS PARA CONSIDERAR

12. El texto del artículo 1(F)(a) ordena a los responsables de tomar decisiones excluir a una persona de la condición de refugiado solo cuando existan "motivos fundados para considerar" que haya cometido un crimen contra la paz, un crimen de guerra o un crimen de lesa humanidad. "Motivos fundados" define los criterios de derecho y de hecho que deben cumplirse para dictar una decisión de exclusión, y por lo tanto juega un papel tanto probatorio como sustantivo.

---

13. As an evidentiary matter, the 'serious reasons' standard is generally understood to be a means of accommodating the practical constraints of access to less evidence than is normally available in a criminal trial. The decision maker must nonetheless be satisfied that there is clear and convincing evidence that a crime has been committed by the individual before finding the person to be excluded under Article 1(F)(a).

13. En termes de preuves, l'exigence de « raisons sérieuses » est généralement comprise comme un moyen de faciliter les aspects pratiques d'accès aux preuves, moins nombreuses que dans un procès pénal. L'autorité de décision doit toutefois estimer qu'il y a des éléments clairs et convaincants permettant de considérer qu'un crime a été commis par une personne avant de conclure à son exclusion du statut de réfugié en vertu de l'article 1, F, A.

13. Como tema probatorio, el estándar "motivos fundados" generalmente se entiende como el medio para satisfacer las limitaciones prácticas relativas al acceso a menos evidencia de la que normalmente suele estar disponible en un proceso penal. No obstante, el responsable de tomar la decisión debe estar convencido de que existen pruebas claras y convincentes de que esa persona ha cometido un delito antes de determinar su exclusión de conformidad con el artículo 1(F)(a).

---

14. As a substantive matter, the 'serious reasons' standard requires that exclusion decisions be based upon settled norms of international criminal law. Where an individual's conduct meets the standard for liability under such a settled norm, he or she should be excluded from refugee status.

14. En termes de contenu, l'exigence de « raisons sérieuses » implique que les décisions d'exclusion soient fondées sur les normes bien établies de droit international. Lorsque la conduite d'un individu rencontre les conditions d'établissement de la responsabilité consacrées par ces normes établies, il doit être exclu du statut de réfugié.

14. Como asunto sustantivo, el estándar "motivos fundados" exige que las decisiones de exclusión se basen en normas del derecho penal internacional establecidas. Cuando la conducta de un individuo cumpla con los criterios de responsabilidad establecidos en dichas normas, dicho individuo debe ser excluido de la condición de refugiado.

СЕРЬЕЗНЫЕ ОСНОВАНИЯ ПРЕДПОЛАГАТЬ

12. يوجه نص المادة 1 (و) (أ) صانعي القرار إلى استبعاد الفرد من وضع اللاجئ فقط عندما تكون هناك "أسباب جدية تبعث على الاعتقاد" أنه ارتكب جريمة ضد السلام أو جريمة حرب أو جريمة ضد إنسانية. تحدد «الأسباب الجدية» المعيار في كل من الواقع والقانون الذي يجب الاستناد إليه في قرار الاستبعاد، وبالتالي يكون له دور استدلالي وموضوعي.

12. Текст статьи 1(F)(a) рекомендует лицам, принимающим решения, лишать человека статуса беженца только там, где есть «серьезные основания предполагать», что он совершил преступление против мира, военное преступление или преступление против человечества. «Серьезные причины» определяют стандарт, как в отношении фактов, которые необходимо установить, так и закона, который должен выполняться при принятии решения о лишении статуса беженца, и, следовательно, играет как доказательную, так и значимую роль.

13. كدليل على ذلك، يُفهم بشكل عام أن معيار «الأسباب الجدية» هو وسيلة لتيسير القيود العملية التي تحول دون الحصول على أدلة أقل مما هو متاح عادة في محاكمة جنائية. لذلك يجب أن يكون صانع القرار مقتنعًا بأن هناك أدلة واضحة ومقنعة على ارتكاب جريمة من قبل الفرد قبل العثور على الشخص الذي سيتم استبعاده بموجب المادة 1(و)(أ).

13. В качестве доказательства, стандарт доказывания «серьезных причин» обычно понимается как средство удовлетворения практических ограничений доступа к меньшим доказательствам, чем обычно доступно в уголовном процессе. Тем не менее, лицо, принимающее решения, должно удостовериться в наличии четких и убедительных доказательств того, что преступление было совершено этим человеком, до того, как принять решение о лишении его статуса беженца по статье 1(F)(a).

14. يتطلب معيار «الأسباب الجدية» كمسألة موضوعية، أن تستند قرارات الاستبعاد إلى المعايير القائمة في القانون الجنائي الدولي. عندما يستوفي سلوك الفرد معيار المسؤولية بموجب هذه المعايير القائمة، ينبغي استبعاده من وضع اللاجئ.

14. В качестве значимого факта, стандартный уровень «серьезных причин» требует, чтобы решения о лишении статуса основывались на установленных нормах международного уголовного права. Если поведение лица соответствует стандарту ответственности в соответствии с этой установленной нормой, он или она должны быть лишены статуса беженца.

15. There may, however, be a material conflict among authoritative understandings of relevant international criminal law instruments. Because there are not 'serious reasons' for considering an individual to have 'committed a crime' where the relevant criteria for imposition of criminal liability are contested, the 'serious reasons for considering' standard should be understood to require the decision maker to give effect to the relevant norm that most restricts criminal responsibility. Thus, where the standards for the imposition of liability (modes of liability, *actus reus*, and *mens rea*) are contested, the most constrained authoritative interpretation of relevant instruments should be relied upon. Similarly, where the standards for invocation of a relevant defence are contested, the most generous authoritative reading of plausible defences should be adopted.

15. Il se peut, toutefois, qu'une incompatibilité matérielle surgisse entre différentes interprétations, qui font autorité, des instruments de droit pénal international pertinents. Étant donné qu'il ne peut y avoir de « raisons sérieuses » de penser qu'un individu a « commis un crime » lorsque les critères relatifs à l'établissement de la responsabilité pénale sont contestés, l'exigence de « raisons sérieuses de penser » devrait être comprise comme impliquant qu'il soit tenu compte des normes les plus strictes en termes d'établissement de la responsabilité pénale. En conséquence, s'il s'avère que les critères permettant d'établir la responsabilité pénale (degré de responsabilité, *actus reus* et *mens rea*) sont contestés, l'interprétation la plus stricte parmi celles qui font autorité doit prévaloir. De même, à l'inverse, lorsque la possibilité d'invoquer certains moyens de défense est contestée, il convient de suivre l'interprétation faisant autorité la plus généreuse quant aux moyens de défense admissibles.

15. Sin embargo, puede existir un conflicto material entre las interpretaciones vinculantes de los instrumentos de derecho penal internacional. Como no se puede decir que haya "motivos fundados" para considerar que un individuo "ha cometido un delito" cuando los criterios relevantes de responsabilidad penal son impugnados, el estándar de "motivos fundados para considerar" exige que el responsable de tomar la decisión actúe en función de la norma relevante que más limite la responsabilidad penal. En consecuencia, cuando los estándares para la asignación de responsabilidad (formas de responsabilidad, *actus reus* y *mens rea*) son impugnados, se debe aplicar la interpretación vinculante más fidedigna. Asimismo, cuando los estándares para la invocación de una defensa son impugnados, se debe adoptar la interpretación vinculante más amplia.

These Guidelines reflect the consensus of all the participants at the Sixth Colloquium on Challenges in Refugee Law, held at Ann Arbor, Michigan, USA, on March 22–24, 2013.

James C. Hathaway
Convener and Chair
University of Michigan

Jennifer Bond
Research Director
University of Ottawa

Michel Bastarache
Supreme Court of Canada (ret.)

Won Kidane
Seattle University

Audrey Macklin
University of Toronto

William Schabas
Middlesex University

James Sloan
University of Glasgow

Elies van Sliedregt
Vrije Universiteit Amsterdam

Matthew Zagor
Australian National University

Meredith Garry
Student
University of Michigan

Pauline Hilmy
Student
University of Michigan

Palmer Lawrence
Student
University of Michigan

Sarah Oliai
Student
University of Michigan

Johnny Pinjuv
Student
University of Michigan

Jessica Soley
Student
University of Michigan

Robby Staley
Student
University of Michigan

Alisa Whitfield
Student
University of Michigan

Betsy Fisher
Co-Rapporteur
University of Michigan

Timothy Shoffner
Co-Rapporteur
University of Michigan

The Colloquium deliberations benefited from the counsel of Sibylle Kapferer, Senior Legal Officer, Division of International Protection, United Nations High Commissioner for Refugees.

15. لكن قد يكون هناك تعارض مادي بين التفاهمات الموثوقة لصكوك القانون الجنائي الدولي ذات الصلة. لأنه لا توجد «أسباب جدية» للاعتقاد بأن الفرد قد «ارتكب جريمة» حيث يتم الطعن في المعايير ذات الصلة لفرض المسؤولية الجنائية، ينبغي فهم معيار «الأسباب الجدية للاعتقاد» الذي يلزم صانع القرار بتنفيذ القاعدة ذات الصلة التي تقيّد معظم المسؤولية الجنائية. لذا، عندما تكون معايير فرض المسؤولية (أساليب المسؤولية والفعل الإجرامي والنية الجرمية) متنازع عليها، يجب الاعتماد على التفسر الرسمي الأكثر تقييدًا للصكوك ذات الصلة. بالمثل، حيثما يتم الاعتراض على معايير الاحتجاج بدفاع ذي صلة، ينبغي اعتماد القراءة الأكثر سخاء الموثوقة للدفاعات المعقولة.

15. Однако может возникнуть существенный конфликт между авторитетным пониманием соответствующих международных документов в области уголовного права. Поскольку нет «серьезных причин» предполагать, что лицо «совершило преступление», когда оспариваются соответствующие критерии для привлечения к уголовной ответственности, следует понимать, что стандарт определения «серьезных причин предполагать» требует от лица, принимающего решение, ввести в действие соответствующую норму, которая в большинстве случаев ограничивает уголовную ответственность. Таким образом, если стандарты для установления ответственности (виды ответственности, *состав преступления*, *преступный умысел*) оспариваются, следует полагаться на наиболее ограничительную авторитетную интерпретацию соответствующих норм. Аналогичным образом, когда оспариваются стандартные условия обращения к соответствующей защите, следует принять самое полное авторитетное подтверждение убедительных соображений.

The Convention relating to the Status of Refugees ('Convention') recognizes as refugees those who, owing to a well-founded fear of being persecuted on the basis of *inter alia* 'political opinion,' are unable or unwilling to avail themselves of the protection of their home country.

LES RECOMMANDATIONS DE MICHIGAN SUR LE RISQUE EN RAISON D'OPINIONS POLITIQUES

La Convention relative au statut des réfugiés (« la Convention ») reconnaît comme réfugiés ceux qui, craignant avec raison d'être persécutés notamment du fait des « opinions politiques, » ne peuvent ou ne veulent se réclamer de la protection de leur pays d'origine.

LAS DIRECTRICES DE MICHIGAN SOBRE EL RIESGO POR RAZONES DE OPINIÓN POLÍTICA

La Convención sobre el Estatuto de los Refugiados (en adelante, la "Convención") reconoce como refugiados a aquellos que, debido a un temor fundado de ser perseguidos sobre la base de, entre otras cosas, "la opinión política", no pueden o no desean beneficiarse de la protección de su país de origen.

State practice acknowledges that protection based on 'political opinion' should not be limited to those individuals at risk by reason of their views about partisan politics. Beyond this, the absence of an authoritative definition of 'political opinion' in either the Convention or international law more generally has allowed interpretive inconsistencies to emerge, both within and among jurisdictions. Further complicating the search for a consistent approach is a lack of clarity about how best to ensure that the social and political context of the country of origin is meaningfully taken into account in assessing the existence of a 'political opinion.'

La pratique des États reconnaît que la protection du fait des « opinions politiques » ne devrait pas être limitée aux individus courant un risque en raison de leurs vues sur la politique partisane. Au-delà de ceci, l'absence d'une définition faisant autorité de ce que constitue une « opinion politique » dans la Convention ou dans le droit international général a conduit à l'émergence des divergences d'interprétation à la fois au sein et entre les juridictions. Le manque de clarté sur la meilleure manière d'assurer la prise en considération sérieuse du contexte social et politique du pays d'origine dans l'évaluation de l'existence d'une « opinion politique » complique encore davantage la recherche d'une approche cohérente.

La práctica de las naciones reconoce que la protección basada en la "opinión política" no debe limitarse a las personas en situación de riesgo con motivo de sus opiniones sobre la política partidista. Más allá de esto, la ausencia de una definición autorizada de "opinión política" en la Convención o en el derecho internacional en términos más generales ha permitido la aparición de inconsistencias interpretativas, tanto dentro de las jurisdicciones como entre ellas. Lo que complica aún más la búsqueda de un enfoque coherente es la falta de claridad sobre la mejor manera de garantizar que el contexto social y político del país de origen se tenga en cuenta de manera significativa al evaluar la existencia de una "opinión política".

With a view to promoting a shared understanding of the proper interpretation of 'political opinion' within the context of Article 1(A)(2) of the Convention, we have engaged in sustained collaborative study and reflection on relevant norms and state practice. Our research was debated and refined at the Seventh Colloquium on Challenges in International Refugee Law, convened in March 2015 by the University of Michigan's Program in Refugee and Asylum Law. These Guidelines are the product of that endeavor, and reflect the consensus of Colloquium participants on how best to interpret 'political opinion' in a manner that ensures both fidelity to international law and the continuing vitality of the Convention.

Afin de promouvoir une approche commune sur l'interprétation correcte de « opinions politiques » dans le contexte de l'article 1(A)(2) de la Convention, nous avons entrepris une étude et une réflexion systématique et approfondie sur les normes pertinentes et la pratique étatique. Notre recherche fut débattue et affinée au cours du septième colloque sur les défis en droit international des réfugiés organisé en mars 2015 par le Programme en droit d'asile et des réfugiés de l'université du Michigan. Ces présentes Recommandations sont le résultat de cette entreprise et reflètent le consensus des participants au colloque sur la meilleure façon d'interpréter la notion d'« opinions politiques » d'une manière qui assure à la fois la fidélité au droit international et la vitalité continue de la Convention.

Con miras a promover una comprensión compartida de la interpretación adecuada de la "opinión política" en el contexto del artículo 1 (A) (2) de la Convención, hemos realizado un estudio y una reflexión sostenidos y colaborativos sobre las normas y la práctica estatal pertinentes. Nuestra investigación se debatió y se perfeccionó en el Séptimo Coloquio sobre Desafíos en el Derecho Internacional de los Refugiados, celebrado en marzo de 2015 por el Programa de Legislación en materia de Refugio y Asilo de la Universidad de Michigan. Estas directrices son el producto de ese esfuerzo y reflejan el consenso de los participantes del coloquio sobre la mejor manera de interpretar la "opinión política" de manera tal que garantice tanto la fidelidad al derecho internacional como la vitalidad continua de la Convención.

МИЧИГАНСКИЕ РУКОВОДЯЩИЕ ПРИНЦИПЫ ОТНОСИТЕЛЬНО РИСКА ПРИЧИН ПОЛИТИЧЕСКОГО МНЕНИЯ

Конвенция о статусе беженцев («Конвенция») признает беженцами тех, кто из-за вполне обоснованного опасения подвергнуться преследованию на основании, в частности, «политического мнения», не может или не желает пользоваться защитой своей родной страны.

دليل جامعة ميتشغان الإرشادي حول التعرض للخطر بسبب الرأي السياسي
تعترف اتفاقية تحديد وضعية اللاجئين (الاتفاقية) بأن اللاجئين هم الأشخاص، وبسبب «الرأي السياسي» أو أي من الأسباب الأخرى لديهم خوف مبرر من الاضطهاد وغير قادرين أو راغبين بسبب ذلك الخوف من التمتع بحماية أوطنهم.

Государственная практика признает, что защита на основании «политического мнения», не должна ограничиваться теми лицами, которые подвержены риску из-за своих взглядов на политику оппонентов. Помимо этого, отсутствие авторитетного определения «политического мнения» в рамках Конвенции или международного права в более общем плане допускало возникновение противоречивых толкований как внутри одной юрисдикции, так и между юрисдикциями. Дальнейшее усложнение поиска последовательного подхода заключается в отсутствии ясности в отношении того, как наилучшим образом обеспечить, чтобы социальные и политические особенности страны происхождения обоснованно учитывались при оценке наличия «политического мнения».

تقر ممارسات الدول بأن توفير الحماية بناء على «الرأي السياسي» لا تقتصر على الأفراد المعرضين للخطر بسبب آرائهم بشأن السياسات الحزبية. علاوة على ذلك، فإن عدم وجود تعريف رسمي «للرأي السياسي» في الاتفاقية أو القانون الدولي بشكل عام، سمح بوجود تناقضات تفسيرية سواء داخل أو فيما بين جهات الولاية القانونية. ومما يزيد من تعقيد البحث عن نهج متسق هو عدم وضوح أفضل السبل لضمان مراعاة السياق الاجتماعي والسياسي لبلد المنشأ على نحوٍ مجدٍ في تقييم وجود «رأي سياسي».

Стремясь обеспечить понимание правильной интерпретации термина «Политическое мнение» в контексте статьи 1(А)(2) Конвенции, мы проводили последовательное совместное изучение и сопоставление соответствующих норм и государственной практики. Эти исследования обсуждались и уточнялись на шестом коллоквиуме по проблемам международного права беженцев, который проходил в марте 2015 года по Программе Мичиганского университета в области законодательства о беженцах и убежище. Данные Руководящие принципы являются результатом указанных усилий и отражают единое мнение участников коллоквиума относительно того, как лучше всего интерпретировать «политическое мнение», чтобы обеспечить как приверженность международному праву, так и сохранить жизнеспособность Конвенции.

ومن أجل تعزيز رؤية واضحة وفهم مشترك لما يعنيه مصطلح «رأي سياسي» في سياق المادة 1 (أ) (2) من الاتفاقية، تشاركنا في دراسة تعاونية مستمرة للتفكير في المعايير ذات الصلة وممارسات الدول. وقد نوقش بحثنا وصُقل في الندوة السابعة حول التحديات في قانون اللاجئين الدولي، والتي عقدها برنامج جامعة ميشيغان حول قانون اللاجئين واللجوء في مارس 2015. وهذه المبادئ التوجيهية هي نتاج هذه الجهود، وتعكس توافق آراء المشاركين في الندوة حول أفضل طريقة لتفسير «الرأي السياسي» بطريقة تضمن الحفاظ على روح القانون الدولي واستمرارية الاتفاقية كنص حيوي.

GENERAL CONSIDERATIONS

1. As Article 1(A)(2) of the Convention sets a uniform standard for recognition of refugee status, it is desirable to seek consistency of interpretation both within and among states. Yet because a 'political opinion' is informed by time and place, the search for consistency must not be an excuse for interpretive inflexibility. More generally, the Vienna Convention on the Law of Treaties requires that the text be interpreted in good faith, and in a manner that is consistent with the context, object, and purpose of the Convention as a whole.

CONSIDÉRATIONS GÉNÉRALES

1. Puisque l'article 1(A)(2) de la Convention établit un standard commun de reconnaissance du statut de réfugié, il est souhaitable de chercher la cohérence dans l'interprétation à la fois au sein des États et entre eux. Cependant, puisqu'une « opinion politique » est fonction de moment et de lieu, la recherche de cette cohérence ne devrait pas être une excuse d'inflexibilité dans l'interprétation. Plus généralement, la Convention de Vienne sur le droit des traités exige que le texte soit interprété de bonne foi, dans son contexte et à la lumière de son objet et de son but.

CONSIDERACIONES GENERALES

1. Dado que el artículo 1 (A) (2) de la Convención establece un estándar uniforme para el reconocimiento de la condición de refugiado, es deseable lograr la uniformidad en la interpretación tanto dentro como entre las naciones. Sin embargo, debido a que una "opinión política" se informa por un momento y un lugar, la búsqueda de uniformidad no debe ser una excusa para la falta de flexibilidad a la hora de interpretarla. En términos más generales, la Convención de Viena sobre el Derecho de los Tratados exige que el texto se interprete de buena fe y de manera coherente con el contexto, el objeto y el propósito de la Convención en su conjunto.

---

2. It is thus especially important that interpretation of 'political opinion' align with the purpose of the Convention's nexus ('for reasons of') clause, which establishes a principled delimitation of persons at risk of being persecuted. 'Political opinion' is one of five enumerated grounds for the recognition of refugee status, each of which is derived from non-discrimination principles and is to be understood in light of international human rights law.

2. Il est de ce fait particulièrement important que l'interprétation de la notion d'« opinions politiques » se fasse en accord avec le lien de causalité (« du fait de ») de la Convention qui établit une délimitation de principe des personnes courant le risque d'être persécutées. L'« opinion politique » constitue l'une des cinq raisons énumérées pour la reconnaissance du statut de réfugié, chacune d'elles étant dérivée du principe de non-discrimination et devant être interprétée à la lumière du droit international des droits de l'homme.

2. Por lo tanto, es especialmente importante que la interpretación de la "opinión política" se alinee con el propósito de la cláusula nexo de la Convención ("con motivo de"), que establece una delimitación basada en principios de las personas en riesgo de ser perseguidas. La "opinión política" es uno de los cinco motivos enumerados para el reconocimiento de la condición de refugiado, cada uno de los cuales se deriva de los principios de no discriminación y debe entenderse en vista del derecho internacional de los derechos humanos.

'OPINION'

3. A decision maker should first turn her mind to the question of whether there is evidence of an 'opinion.'

« OPINION »

3. L'autorité habilitée à prendre une décision devrait en premier lieu examiner la question de savoir s'il y a preuve d'une « opinion. »

"OPINIÓN"

3. Un responsable de tomar decisiones primero debe enfocarse en si existe evidencia de una "opinión".

---

4. An 'opinion' is a conscious choice or stance.

4. Une « opinion » est un choix conscient ou une position.

4. Una "opinión" es una elección o postura consciente.

---

5. An expressed choice or stance necessarily constitutes an 'opinion'; an applicant may, however, hold an 'opinion' without having expressed it.

5. Un choix exprimé ou une position constitue nécessairement une « opinion »; un demandeur pourrait, cependant, avoir une « opinion » sans pourtant l'avoir exprimée.

5. Una elección o postura expresada necesariamente constituye una "opinión". No obstante, un solicitante puede mantener una "opinión" y no haberla expresado.

ОБЩИЕ ПОЛОЖЕНИЯ

1. Поскольку статья 1(А)(2) Конвенции задает единый стандарт признания статуса беженца, желательно добиваться согласованности толкования как внутри страны, так и между государствами. Тем не менее, поскольку «политическое мнение» связано со временем и местом, поиск согласованности не должен служить оправданием для негибкого толкования. В более общем плане Венская конвенция о праве международных договоров требует, чтобы текст был истолкован добросовестно и соответствовал контексту, объекту и цели Конвенции в целом.

2. Таким образом, особенно важно, чтобы толкование «политического мнения» соответствовало целям конвенции («по причинам»), которая устанавливает принципиальное разграничение лиц, подвергающихся риску подвергнуться преследованию. «Политическое мнение» является одним из пяти перечисленных оснований для признания статуса беженца, каждый из которых вытекает из принципа недискриминации и должен пониматься в свете международных норм в области прав человека.

«МНЕНИЕ»

3. Лицо, принимающее решение, должно сначала обратиться к вопросу о том, имеются ли доказательства в отношении наличия «мнения».

4. «Мнение» — это сознательный выбор или позиция.

5. Выраженный выбор или позиция обязательно представляют собой «мнение»; заявитель может, однако, придерживаться «мнения», не выражая его.

الاعتبارات العامة

1. وبما أن المادة 1 (أ)(2) من الاتفاقية تضع معيارًا موحدًا للاعتراف بوضع اللاجئ، فمن الأفضل السعي إلى اتساق التفسير فيما بين الدول وفي سياستها الداخلية. ومع ذلك، ونظرًا لأن «الرأي السياسي» مرتبط بزمان ومكان محددين، فإن البحث عن الاتساق يجب ألا يكون عذرًا لعدم المرونة التفسيرية. فبشكل عام، تقضي اتفاقية فيينا لقانون المعاهدات بأن يُفسر النص بحسن نية وتماشيًا مع سياق الاتفاقية وموضوعها والغرض منها ككل.

2. ولذا وجب أن يتم تفسير «الرأي السياسي» متماشيًا مع الهدف الأساسي للاتفاقية الذي يقوم على السببية في تحديد الأشخاص المعرضين لخطر الاضطهاد. «الرأي السياسي» هو واحد من خمسة أسباب محددة للاعتراف بوضع اللاجئ، كل سها مستمد من مبادئ عدم التمييز، ويجب فهمه في ضوء القانون الدولي لحقوق الإنسان.

«الرأي»

3. يجب على صانع القرار أولًا أن يلفت نظره إلى ما إذا كان هناك دليل على «الرأي».

4. «الرأي» هو خيار أو موقف واع.

5. ويشكل الخيار أو الموقف المعبر عنه بالضرورة «رأي»؛ إلا أن مقدم الطلب قد يكون له «رأي» دون أن يُعبر عنه.

6. Even if not actually held, a choice or stance may be attributed to an applicant by the agent of harm or by the state failing or refusing to protect on the basis of her action, specifiable inaction, status, or other characteristic.

6. Même s'il n'est pas effectivement exprimé, un choix ou une position peut être attribué à un demandeur par l'agent de persécution ou par l'Etat incapable ou refusant d'assurer la protection du fait de son action, de son inaction, de son statut, ou d'autres caractéristiques.

6. Incluso si no se mantiene realmente, el agente causante de daños puede atribuir una elección o una posición a un solicitante, o la nación puede hacerlo si no logra o se niega a proteger sobre la base de su acción, inacción, condición u otra característica que se pueda especificar

'POLITICAL' OPINION

7. Once an opinion is identified, the decision maker must determine whether it is a 'political' opinion.

OPINION « POLITIQUE »

7. Une fois qu'une opinion est identifiée, l'autorité compétente doit déterminer s'il s'agit d'une opinion « politique ».

OPINIÓN "POLÍTICA"

7. Una vez que se identifica una opinión, el responsable de la toma de decisiones debe determinar si se trata de una opinión "política".

8. A 'political' opinion is an opinion about the nature, policies, or practices of a state or of an entity that has the capacity, legitimately or otherwise, to exercise societal power or authority. A relevant non-state entity is one that is institutionalized, formalized, or informally systematized and which is shown by evidence of pattern or practice to exercise *de facto* societal power or authority.

8. Une opinion «politique » est une opinion sur la nature, les politiques ou les pratiques d'un État ou d'une entité ayant la capacité, légitimement ou non, d'exercer un pouvoir ou une autorité sociétale. Une entité non étatique pertinente est celle qui est institutionnalisée, formalisée, ou informellement systématisée, et qui démontre, sur la base de comportements ou pratiques établis, exercer de fait un pouvoir ou une autorité sociétal.

8. Una opinión "política" es una opinión sobre la naturaleza, las políticas o las prácticas de una nación o de una entidad que tiene la capacidad, en forma legítima o no, de ejercer poder o autoridad social. Una entidad no estatal relevante es aquella que está institucionalizada, formalizada o sistematizada de manera informal y que se muestra por evidencia de patrón o práctica para ejercer poder o autoridad social *de facto*.

9. It is immaterial whether the nature, policies, or practices to which the opinion relates are extant, obsolete, or desired.

9. Il n'est pas nécessaire de savoir si la nature, les politiques ou les pratiques auxquelles s'applique l'opinion sont d'actualité, désuètes, ou prospectives.

9. Es irrelevante si la naturaleza, las políticas o las prácticas a las que se refiere la opinión son existentes, obsoletas o deseadas.

10. An opinion need not be oppositional in order to be 'political.'

10. Une opinion ne devrait pas forcement s'opposer à quelque chose afin d'être considérée comme « politique. »

10. No es necesario que una opinión sea opositora para ser "política".

11. An opinion does not cease to be 'political' because it advances the self-interest of the person seeking recognition of refugee status. It must, however, speak to a matter that has a broader societal or collective impact.

11. Une opinion ne perd pas son caractère « politique » parce qu'elle avance l'intérêt propre de la personne demandant la reconnaissance du statut de réfugié. Elle doit, cependant, porter sur une question dont l'effet sur la société ou le collectif est plus large.

11. Una opinión no dejará de ser "política" por promover el interés propio de la persona que busca el reconocimiento de la condición de refugiado. Sin embargo, deberá referirse a un asunto que tenga un impacto social o colectivo más amplio.

6. Даже если при отсутствии такового, выбор или позиция заявителя могут приписываться ему агентом преследования либо государством, неспособным или не желающим предоставлять защиту этому лицу, на основании его действия, конкретного бездействия, статуса или другого признака.

٦. حتى وإن لم يكن قد تم بالفعل، فإن الخيار أو الموقف ممكن أن يعزى إلى مقدم الطلب من قبل وكيل الضرر أو من قبل الدولة التي تفشل أو ترفض الحماية على أساس عملها أو التقاعس المحدد أو الوضع أو سمة أخرى.

«ПОЛИТИЧЕСКОЕ» МНЕНИЕ

7. После определения наличия "мнения" лицо, принимающее решения, должно определить, является ли указанное мнение «политическим».

رأي «سياسي»

٧. حالما يتم تحديد رأي، يجب على صانع القرار تحديد ما إذا كان رأي «سياسي».

8. «Политическое» мнение — это мнение о природе, политике или практике какого-либо государства или субъекта, который обладает возможностью законным или иным образом применять общественную власть или полномочия. Соответствующий негосударственный субъект является институционализированным, формализованным или неофициально систематизированным, что подтверждается свидетельством характера или практики осуществления *фактической* социальной власти или полномочий.

٨. الرأي «السياسي» هو رأي حول طبيعة أو سياسات أو ممارسات الدولة أو كيان يتمتع، سواء بشكل قانوني أو غير ذلك، بسلطات مجتمعية نافذة. وهذه الكيانات، منظمه بشكل مؤسسي أو بشكل غير رسمي وتظهر في صورة ممارسات معينه تؤكد سلطتها المجتمعية.

9. Неважно, если характер, политика или практика, к которым относится мнение, являются устоявшимися, устаревшими или желательными.

٩. ومن غير المهم ما إذا كانت الطبيعة أو السياسات أو الممارسات التي يتعلق بها الرأي موجودة أو عفا عليها الزمن أو مرغوبة.

10. Для того, чтобы быть «политическим», мнение не должно быть оппозиционным.

١٠. ولا يحتاج الرأي إلى أن يكون معارضًا لكي يكون «سياسي».

11. Мнение не перестает быть «политическим», если оно способствует личным интересам человека, который хочет получить статус беженца. Однако оно должно отражать то, что имеет более широкое общественное или коллективное воздействие.

١١. ولا يتوقف الرأي عن كونه «سياسي» لأنه يخدم المصلحة الذاتية للشخص الذي يسعى للحصول على صفة اللاجئ. غير أنه يجب أن يتناول مسألة ذات أثر اجتماعي أو جماعي أوسع.

12. An opinion may be 'political' even if arising from, or associated with, an applicant's employment, profession, or other societal role.

12. Une opinion peut être « politique » même si elle résulte ou est le complément du travail, de la profession, ou de quelque autre rôle social du demandeur.

12. Una opinión puede ser "política" incluso si surge de, o está asociada con, el empleo, la profesión u otra función social del solicitante.

13. The meaning of a 'political' opinion should not be constrained by importing an understanding of 'political' that is contextually incongruous. For example, the notion of a non-"political" crime that circumscribes exclusion under Article 1(F)(b) derives meaning from its criminal context, whereas interpretation of the nexus clause must be informed by its non-discrimination context.

13. Le sens d'une opinion « politique » ne devrait pas être restreint par l'importation d'une interprétation contextuellement incongrue de ce qui est « politique. » Par exemple, le sens de la notion de crime non « politique » à laquelle se limite l'exclusion sous l'article 1(F)(b) provient de son contexte pénal, alors que l'interprétation du lien de causalité doit prendre en compte son contexte de non-discrimination.

13. El significado de una opinión "política" no debe restringirse importando una comprensión de "política" que sea contextualmente incongruente. Por ejemplo, el sentido de la noción de delito no "político" que circunscribe la exclusión en virtud del artículo 1 (F) (b) proviene de su contexto delictivo, mientras que la interpretación de la cláusula nexo debe ser informada por su contexto de no discriminación.

CONTEXTUAL CONSTRAINTS

14. Refugee status is not to be recognized simply because a risk of being persecuted co-exists with an actual or attributed 'political opinion.' The Convention rather requires a finding that the risk be 'for reasons of . . . political opinion.' The requisite causal link may be located in the reason an applicant is at risk of harm, or in the motivation of the state that fails to protect the applicant from that risk. A risk arising in a politicized context but which has no causal connection to an attribute of the kind protected by non-discrimination principles will not fulfill this requirement.

LIMITES CONTEXTUELLES

14. Le statut de réfugié ne devrait pas être reconnu simplement parce qu'un risque d'être persécuté coexiste avec une « opinion politique » réelle ou attribuée. La Convention exige plutôt d'établir que le risque est « de fait des. . . . opinions politiques. » Le lien de causalité requis peut se trouver dans la raison pour laquelle un demandeur court le risque d'être persécuté, ou dans la motivation de l'État qui n'est pas à même de protéger le demandeur de ce risque. Un risque émanant d'un contexte politisé, mais qui ne se rattache pas à une caractéristique du type de celles protégées par le principe de non-discrimination, ne satisfera pas à cette exigence.

RESTRICCIONES CONTEXTUALES

14. La condición de refugiado no debe reconocerse simplemente porque el riesgo de ser perseguido coexiste con una "opinión política" real o atribuida. La Convención más bien requiere una conclusión de que el riesgo sea "por razones de [. . .] opinión política". El vínculo causal requerido puede encontrarse en la razón por la cual un solicitante está en riesgo de sufrir daños, o en la motivación de la nación que no protege al solicitante de ese riesgo. Un riesgo que surja en un contexto politizado pero que no tenga conexión causal con un atributo del tipo protegido por principios de no discriminación no cumplirá este requisito.

15. The scope of a 'political opinion' as defined in paras. 3-13 of these Guidelines should not be constrained to ensure that the Convention is not brought into disrepute by recognizing the refugee status of an undeserving person. In particular, risk arising from a criminal prosecution that is conceived and conducted in accordance with international law does not amount to a risk of being persecuted, and will therefore not be the basis for recognition of refugee status. Decision makers must moreover exclude serious criminals and others deemed undeserving of protection on the terms mandated by Article 1(F) of the Convention. The combination of these safeguards suffices to protect the integrity of the Convention.

15. Le champ de cette notion d'« opinion politique » tel que défini aux points 3-13 des présentes Recommandations ne devrait pas être forcé afin de garantir que la Convention ne perde pas de sa valeur en reconnaissant le statut de réfugié à une personne qui ne le mérite pas. En particulier, le risque résultant des poursuites pénales conformes au droit international n'équivaut pas à un risque de persécution, et ne devrait par conséquent servir de fondement à la reconnaissance du statut de réfugié. Qui plus est, les autorités compétentes doivent exclure les criminels sérieux et autres personnes jugées indignes de protection selon les termes de l'article 1(F) de la Convention. La combinaison de ces sauvegardes suffit à protéger l'intégrité de la Convention.

15. El alcance de una "opinión política" tal como se define en los párrafos 3 a 13 de estas directrices no debe restringirse para garantizar que la Convención no sea desacreditada al reconocer la condición de refugiado de una persona no merecedora de la misma. En particular, el riesgo derivado de un proceso penal concebido y llevado a cabo de conformidad con el derecho internacional no equivale a un riesgo de ser perseguido y, por lo tanto, no será la base para el reconocimiento de la condición de refugiado. Los responsables de la toma de decisiones también deben excluir a los culpables de delitos graves y a otros que no merecen protección en los términos estipulados en el artículo 1 (F) de la Convención. La combinación de estas garantías es suficiente para proteger la integridad de la Convención.

12. Мнение может быть «политическим», даже если оно связано с занятостью заявителя, его профессией или другой общественной ролью.

.12 قد يكون الرأي «سياسي» حتى لو كان ناشئًا عن، أو مرتبط بعمل مقدم الطلب أو مهنته أو دوره المجتمعي.

13. Значение «политического» мнения не должно ограничиваться пониманием «политики», которое является контекстуально несоответствующим. Например, понятие «политическое» преступление, которое ограничивает исключение в соответствии со статьей 1(F)(b), приобретает значение из его уголовного контекста, тогда как интерпретация положения о взаимосвязи следует понимать в недискриминационном контексте.

.13 ولا يجب تقييد معنى الرأي «السياسي» باستخدام تعريف لكلمة «سياسي» متناقض مع السياق. على سبيل المثال، مفهوم الجرمة غير السياسية التي تقيد الاستبعاد بوجب المادة 1(و) (ب) يستمد معناه من سياقه الإجرامي، في حين أن تفسير شرط العلاقة يجب أن يسترشد به سياق عدم التمييز.

КОНТЕКСТУАЛЫІЫЕ ОГРАНИЧЕНИЯ

14. Статус беженца не следует признавать просто потому, что риск подвергнуться преследованию сосуществует с фактическим или приписываемым «политическим мнением». Конвенция скорее требует понимания того, что риск возникает «из-за наличия политического мнения». Необходимая причинно-следственная связь может быть установлена как следствие того, что заявитель подвергается риску получения вреда, или как мотивация государства, которое не защищает заявителя от этого риска. Риск, возникающий в политизированном контексте, но не имеющий причинно-следственной связи с определением, защищенным принципами недискриминации, не будет соответствовать данному требованию.

المحددات الظرفية

.14 لا يجب الاعتراف بوضع اللاجئ لمجرد أن خطر التعرض للاضطهاد يتعارض مع «رأي سياسي» فعلي أو منسوب للشخص. وتقتضي الاتفاقية، بدلا من ذلك، التوصل إلى نتيجة مفادها أن الخطر «لأسباب تتعلق، . . . برأي سياسي». وهكن إيجاد الصلة السببية المطلوبة في سبب تعرض مقدم الطلب لخطر الضرر، أو في الظروف التي أدت أن تخفق الدولة في حماية مقدم الطلب من هذا الخطر. ولا ينطبق هذا الشرط على الخطر الذي ينشأ في ظرف سياسي بدون أن يرتبط بأي من الصور التي يحميها مبدأ عدم التمييز.

15. Рамки «политического мнения», как это определено в пунктах 3–13 настоящих Руководящих принципов не должны ограничиваться гарантией того, что Конвенция не приобретет плохую репутацию после предоставления статуса беженца недостойному лицу. В частности, риск, связанный с уголовным преследованием, которое инициировано и проведено в соответствии с международным правом, не является риском подвергнуться преследованию и, следовательно, не станет основанием для признания статуса беженца. Кроме того, лица, принимающие решения, могут лишить статуса беженцев серьезных преступников и других лиц, которые считаются недостойными защиты на условиях, предусмотренных в статье 1(F) Конвенции. Для защиты целостности Конвенции достаточно сочетания этих гарантий.

.15 فتعريف «الرأي السياسي» المحدد الفقرات من 3 ل 13 في هذه الوثيقة ينبغي ألا يقيد قدرة الاتفاقية على عدم منح وضع اللاجئ لمن لا يستحقه. وعلى وجه الخصوص، لا تشكل المخاطر الناشئة عن الملاحقة الجنائية التي تصاغ وتجري وفقًا للقانون الدولي خطر التعرض للاضطهاد، وبالتالي لن تكون أساسًا للاعتراف بوضع اللاجئ. كما يجب على صانعي القرار استبعاد المجرمين الخطيرين وغيرهم ممن يعتبرون غير مستحقين للحماية بموجب الشروط المنصوص عليها في المادة 1(و) من الاتفاقية. ويكفي الجمع بين هذه الضمانات لحماية سلامة الاتفاقية.

These Guidelines reflect the consensus of the undersigned, each of whom participated in their personal capacity in the Seventh Colloquium on Challenges in International Refugee Law, held at Ann Arbor, Michigan, USA, on March 27–29, 2015.

James C. Hathaway
Convener and Chair
University of Michigan

Catherine Dauvergne
Research Director
University of British Columbia

Thomas Gammeltoft-Hansen
Danish Institute for Human Rights

Mark Gibney
UNC-Asheville and Lund University

David Kosař
Masaryk University

Susan Kneebone
University of Melbourne

Hélène Lambert
University of Westminster

Hugo Storey
United Kingdom Upper Tribunal

Adrienne Boyd
Student
University of Michigan

Elizabeth Bundy
Student
University of Michigan

Cari Carson
Student
University of Michigan

Julie Kornfeld
Student
University of Michigan

Katie Mullins
Student
University of Michigan

Anne Recinos
Student
University of Michigan

Gracie Willis
Student
University of Michigan

Emad Ansari
Co-Rapporteur
University of Michigan

Rosalind Elphick
Co-Rapporteur
University of Michigan

The Colloquium deliberations benefited from the counsel of Cornelis (Kees) Wouters, Senior Refugee Law Advisor, Division of International Protection, United Nations High Commissioner for Refugees.

Freedom of movement is essential for refugees to enjoy meaningful protection against the risk of being persecuted, and enables them to establish themselves socially and economically as foreseen by the Convention relating to the Status of Refugees ('Convention').

LES RECOMMANDATIONS DE MICHIGAN SUR LA LIBERTÉ DE CIRCULATION DES RÉFUGIÉS

La liberté de circulation des réfugiés est essentielle à la jouissance d'une protection effective contre la persécution. Elle offre aux réfugiés les moyens de s'établir socialement et économiquement, conformément à la Convention relative au statut des réfugiés (« la Convention »).

LAS DIRECTRICES DE MICHIGAN SOBRE LA LIBERTAD DE CIRCULACIÓN DE LOS REFUGIADOS

La libertad de circulación es esencial para que los refugiados gocen de una protección significativa contra el riesgo de ser perseguidos y les permite establecerse a nivel social y económico como lo prevé la Convención sobre el Estatuto de los Refugiados (en adelante, la "Convención").

The very structure of the Convention presumes the right to leave in search of protection, since a refugee is defined as an at-risk person who is 'outside' his or her own country. Once outside the home state, the Convention makes express provision for rights not to be sent away (*non-refoulement*), to enjoy liberty upon arrival, to benefit from freedom of movement and residence once lawfully present, to travel once lawfully staying, and ultimately to return to the home state if and when conditions allow. Respect for refugee freedom of movement in its various forms is thus central to good faith implementation of the Convention.

Le droit de quitter afin d'obtenir une protection relève des fondements mêmes de la Convention, qui définit le réfugié comme toute personne craignant avec raison d'être persécutée et qui se trouve hors de son propre pays. Lorsque le réfugié a quitté son pays d'origine, la Convention lui reconnait explicitement le droit de ne pas être expulsé ou refoulé (principe de non-refoulement), de jouir des droits et libertés, de circuler librement et de choisir son lieu de résidence lorsqu'il séjourne régulièrement, de voyager lorsqu'il réside régulièrement et finalement de retourner dans son pays d'origine si et lorsque les conditions qui y prévalent le permettent. Le respect de la liberté de circulation des réfugiés dans ses diverses expressions est donc indispensable à une mise en œuvre de bonne foi de la Convention.

La misma estructura de la Convención presupone el derecho a irse en busca de protección, ya que un refugiado se define como una persona en riesgo que se encuentra "fuera" de su propio país. Una vez fuera de la nación de origen, la Convención establece una disposición expresa para gozar de los derechos a no ser deportados (no devolución), a disfrutar de la libertad a su llegada, a beneficiarse de la libertad de circulación y residencia una vez que estén establecidos en el territorio de manera legal, a viajar una vez que residan legalmente y, en última instancia, a regresar a la nación de origen, siempre y cuando las condiciones lo permitan. El respeto de la libertad de circulación de los refugiados en sus diversas formas es, por tanto, fundamental para aplicación de buena fe de la Convención.

The right of refugees to move has moreover been reinforced by the advent of general human rights norms in the years since the Convention's drafting. Of particular importance is the International Covenant on Civil and Political Rights ('ICCPR'), the relevant provisions of which have been authoritatively interpreted to apply equally to citizens and non-citizens, including refugees.

La liberté de circulation des réfugiés a, en outre, été renforcée par l'avènement de diverses normes de droit international général depuis la rédaction de la Convention. Le Pacte international relatif aux droits civils et politiques (PIDCP), dont les dispositions relatives à la liberté de circulation ont été interprétées comme s'appliquant également aux citoyens et aux non-citoyens, en ce compris les réfugiés, revêt une importance particulière.

El derecho de los refugiados a trasladarse se ha visto reforzado por el advenimiento de las normas generales de derechos humanos en los años siguientes a la redacción de la Convención. De particular importancia es el Pacto Internacional de Derechos Civiles y Políticos («PIDCP»), cuyas disposiciones pertinentes han sido interpretadas de manera absoluta para aplicarse por igual a ciudadanos y no ciudadanos, incluidos los refugiados.

МИЧИГАНСКИЕ РУКОВОДЯЩИЕ ПРИНЦИПЫ СВОБОДЫ ПЕРЕДВИЖЕНИЯ БЕЖЕНЦЕВ

حرية النقل ضرورية لكي يتمتع اللاجئون بحمايه فعليه من خطر التعرض للاضطهاد، وتمكنهم من إقامة أنفسهم اجتماعيًّا واقتصاديًّا على النحو الذي أقرته الاتفاقية الخاصة بوضع اللاجئين («الاتفاقية»).

Свобода передвижения имеет большое значение для предоставления беженцам значимой защиты от риска подвергнуться преследованию, и позволяет им организовать себя социально и экономически, как это предусмотрено Конвенцией о статусе беженцев («Конвенция»).

ويؤكد نص الاتفاقية بوضوح على الحق في المغادرة بحثًا عن الحماية، حيث يعرف اللاجئ بأنه شخص معرض للخطر "خارج" دولة الموطن. وعند مغادرة الشخص لدولة الموطن، تنص الاتفاقية صراحة على الحق في عدم الاستبعاد (عدم الإعادة القسرية)، والتمتع بالحرية عند الوصول والاستفادة من حرية التنقل والإقامة بمجرد وجوده بصورة قانونية وحرية السفر عند تمتعه بإقامه قانونيه أو أن يعود إلى دولة الموطن في نهاية المطاف إذا سمحت الظروف بذلك. لذا، فإن احترام حرية اللاجئين في التنقل بأشكاله المختلفة هو أمر أساسي لتنفيذ الاتفاقية بحسن نية.

Сама структура Конвенции предполагает право на выезд в поисках защиты, поскольку беженец определяется как лицо, которое подвергается риску, и находится «вне» своей страны. Будучи вне своего родного государства, Конвенция четко заявляет о ненарушении *принципа невысылки*, возможности пользоваться свободой по прибытии, свободой передвижения и проживания после получения статуса законного нахождения в стране и, в конечном итоге, возвращения в родную страну, если и когда для этого возникнут соответствующие условия. Таким образом, уважение свободы передвижения беженцев в его различных формах является основным условием добросовестного осуществления Конвенции.

علاوة على ذلك، فإن حق اللاجئين في التحرك تعززه اتفاقيات ومواثيق حقوق الإنسان التي ظهرت في السنوات التي تلت صياغة الاتفاقية. ومن المواثيق ذات ت الأهمية الخاصة الاتفاقية الدولية للحقوق المدنية والسياسية، الذي تفسر أحكامها ذات الصلة على نحو يطبق بالتساوي على المواطنين وغير المواطنين، بمن فيهم اللاجئون.

Кроме того, право беженцев на перемещение подкрепляется появлением общих норм в области прав человека за годы, прошедшие после создания Конвенции. Особое значение имеет Международный пакт о гражданских и политических правах («МПГПП»), соответствующие положения которого представляют собой авторитетное толкование и могут применяться в равной степени, как к гражданам, так и к негражданам, включая беженцев.

Despite the clear legal foundation of refugee freedom of movement at international law, states are also committed to the deterrence of human smuggling and trafficking, to the maintenance of effective general border controls, to safeguarding the critical interests of receiving communities, and to effectuating safe and dignified repatriation when refugee status comes to an end. Legal obligations to respect refugee freedom of movement therefore co-exist with, and must be reconciled to, other important commitments.

Malgré les fondements juridiques clairs, au sein du droit international, de la liberté de circulation des réfugiés, les États sont également tenus de dissuader le trafic et la traite des êtres humains, de maintenir des contrôles globalement effectifs à leurs frontières, de protéger les intérêts des communautés d'accueil et de rapatrier dignement et en sécurité les réfugiés dont le statut a pris fin. Les obligations légales de respecter la liberté de circulation des réfugiés coexistent et doivent être conciliées avec d'autres engagements importants.

A pesar de la clara base legal de la libertad de circulación de los refugiados en el derecho internacional, las naciones también están comprometidas con la disuasión del contrabando y el tráfico de personas, el mantenimiento de controles fronterizos efectivos, la protección de los intereses específicos de las comunidades receptoras y la repatriación digna cuando la condición de refugiado concluya. Por lo tanto, las obligaciones legales de respetar la libertad de circulación de los refugiados coexisten con otros compromisos importantes, y deben conciliarse con ellos.

With a view to promoting a shared understanding of how best to understand the scope of refugee freedom of movement in the modern protection environment we have engaged in sustained collaborative study of, and reflection on, relevant norms and state practice. Our research was debated and refined at the Eighth Colloquium on Challenges in International Refugee Law, convened between March 31 and April 2, 2017, by the University of Michigan's Program in Refugee and Asylum Law. These Guidelines are the product of that endeavor and reflect the consensus of Colloquium participants on how states can best answer the challenges of implementing the right of refugees to freedom of movement in a manner that conforms with international legal principles.

Afin de promouvoir une compréhension commune de l'étendue de la liberté de circulation des réfugiés en tenant compte de ces développements, nous nous sommes engagés dans une étude approfondie et une réflexion commune sur les différentes normes et pratiques des États. Les résultats de notre recherche ont été débattus et affinés à l'occasion du huitième colloque sur les défis du droit international des réfugiés, lequel s'est tenu entre le 31 mars et le 2 avril 2017 au sein du programme de droit des réfugiés et de l'asile de l'université de Michigan. Ces recommandations sont le fruit de cette initiative et reflètent le consensus des participants au colloque, relativement à la question de déterminer comment les États peuvent rencontrer au mieux les défis liés à la mise en œuvre de la liberté de circulation des réfugiés en se conformant aux divers principes de droit international.

Con el objetivo de promover una comprensión compartida sobre la mejor manera de interpretar el alcance de la libertad de circulación de los refugiados en un contexto moderno de protección, hemos participado en un estudio colaborativo sostenido, y en la reflexión sobre las normas y la práctica estatal pertinentes. Nuestra investigación fue debatida y perfeccionada en el Octavo Coloquio sobre Desafíos en el Derecho Internacional de los Refugiados, celebrado entre el 31 de marzo y el 2 de abril de 2017, por el Programa de Legislación en materia de Refugio y Asilo de la Universidad de Michigan. Estas directrices son el producto de ese esfuerzo y reflejan el consenso de los participantes del coloquio sobre cómo las naciones pueden responder mejor a los desafíos de poner en funcionamiento el derecho de los refugiados a la libertad de circulación de manera tal que se ajuste a los principios legales internacionales.

GENERAL PRINCIPLES

1. Refugee status is declaratory. A person becomes a refugee as soon as he or she in fact meets the criteria of the Convention's refugee definition, not when refugee status is formally recognized.

PRINCIPES GÉNÉRAUX

1. Le statut de réfugié a une valeur déclarative. Une personne devient un réfugié dès qu'elle rencontre, de fait, les critères de la définition conventionnelle du réfugié, après que le statut de réfugié lui ait été formellement reconnu.

PRINCIPIOS GENERALES

1. La condición de refugiado es declaratoria. Una persona se convierte en refugiado tan pronto como cumple con los criterios de la definición de refugiado de la Convención, no cuando se reconoce formalmente la condición de refugiado.

Несмотря на четкую правовую основу свободы передвижения беженцев в между-народном праве, государства также заинтересованы в ограничении контрабанды и торговли людьми, обеспечении эффективного общего пограничного контроля, защите важнейших интересов принимающих общин и осуществлению безопасной и достойной репатриации, после завершения действия статуса беженца. Таким образом, юридические обязательства по соблюдению свободы передвижения беженцев сосуществуют с другими важными обязательствами и должны быть с ними согласованы.

وعلى الرغم من أن القانون الدولي وضح الأسس القانونية لحرية تنقل اللاجئين، إلا أن الدول ملتزمة أيضًا مكافحة تهريب البشر والاتجار بهم ورقابة الحدود بشكل فعال وشامل لصون المصالح الحيوية للمجتمعات المضيفة وتيسير عودة اللاجئ إلى دولة الموطن بشكل يحمي كرامته عند انتهاء أسباب اللجوء. لذلك فإن الالتزامات القانونية باحترام حرية اللاجئين في التنقل يجب أن تتماشى مع الالتزامات الهامة الأخرى وأن تتطابق معها.

Стремясь обеспечить понимание того, как лучше всего определять границы свободы передвижения беженцев в современных условиях, мы проводили последовательное совместное изучение и сопоставление соответствующих норм и государственной практики. Эти исследования обсуждались и уточнялись на шестом коллоквиуме по проблемам международного права беженцев, который проходил с 31 марта по 2 апреля 2017 года по Программе Мичиганского уни-верситета по законодательству о правах беженцах и убежищу. Данные Руково-дящие принципы являются результатом указанных усилий и отражают единое мнение участников коллоквиума в том, что лица, принимающие решения, могут наилучшим образом обеспечить применение статьи 1(F)(а) в соответствии с международно-правовыми принципам.

ومن أجل تعزيز فهم مشترك لأفضل طريقة لفهم نطاق حرية اللاجئين في التنقل في بيئة الحماية الحديثة، شاركنا في دراسة تعاونية مستدامة للمعايير ذات الصلة وممارسات الدول والتفكير فيها. وقد نوقش بحثنا وصُقل في الندوة الثامنة حول التحديات التي تواجه قانون اللاجئين الدولي، والتي عقدها برنامج دراسة قانون اللاجئين وطالبي اللجوء بجامعة ميتشغان في الفترة من 31 مارس إلى 2أبريل 2017. والتي ننتج عنها هذه المبادئ التوجيهية، والتي تعكس توافق آراء المشاركين في الندوة حول كيفية ضمان استجابة الدول إلى تحديات تنفيذ حق اللاجئين في حرية التنقل على نحو يتفق مع مبادئ القانون الدولي.

ОБЩИЕ ПРИНЦИПЫ

1. Статус беженца является декларативным. Лицо становится беженцем, как только он или она фактически соответствуют критериям определения беженца согласно Конвенции, а не когда статус беженца признается официально.

المبادئ العامة

1. تمتع الشخص بوضعية اللجوء لا يتطلب تصريح. يصبح الشخص لاجئًا حالما يستوفي صفات تعريف اللاجئين الموضحة بالاتفاقية، وليس عندما تمنح صفة اللاجئ بشكل رسمي.

2. Some Convention rights, including in particular to protection against both *refoulement* and discrimination and to access a state's courts, must be respected as soon as a refugee comes under the jurisdiction of a state party. Other Convention rights are defined to apply only once a refugee enters a state's territory, is lawfully present, is lawfully staying, or durably resides in a state party. Convention rights, once accrued, must be provisionally honored until and unless a final determination is made that the person claiming protection as a refugee is not in fact a refugee.

2. Certains droits conventionnels, en particulier la protection contre le refoulement, l'interdiction des discriminations et le droit d'accéder à un juge, doivent être respectés dès qu'un réfugié relève de la juridiction d'un État partie. D'autres droits conventionnels sont définis comme s'appliquant exclusivement au réfugié qui a pénétré sur le territoire d'un État, qui y séjourne régulièrement, qui y réside régulièrement ou qui y réside durablement. Les droits conventionnels doivent être respectés provisoirement jusqu'à ce qu'une décision finale ait été adoptée, selon laquelle la personne sollicitant la reconnaissance de la qualité de réfugié n'est pas, en réalité, un réfugié.

2. Algunos derechos de la Convención, incluidos, en particular, la protección contra la devolución o *refoulement* y la discriminación, y el acceso a los tribunales de una nación, deben respetarse apenas un refugiado se encuentra bajo la jurisdicción de un estado parte. Otros derechos de la Convención solo se aplican una vez que un refugiado ingresa en el territorio de una nación, se encuentra presente en el territorio de forma legal, permanece allí legalmente, o reside en un estado parte en forma permanente. Una vez acumulados, los derechos de la Convención se deben honrar en forma temporal hasta que, y a menos que, se determine definitivamente que la persona que reclama protección como refugiado no es en realidad un refugiado.

3. International law requires that treaties be interpreted harmoniously if possible. There is no irreconcilable normative conflict between Convention and ICCPR provisions that define the freedom of movement of refugees, in consequence of which refugees are entitled to claim the benefit of both Convention and ICCPR rights.

3. Le droit international requiert que les traités soient, dans la mesure du possible, interprétés harmonieusement. Il n'y a pas de conflit normatif irréconciliable entre la Convention et les dispositions du PIDCP qui définissent la liberté de circulation des réfugiés. En conséquence, les réfugiés peuvent revendiquer le bénéfice à la fois de la Convention et des droits consacrés par le PIDCP.

3. El derecho internacional exige que, de ser posible, los tratados se interpreten de manera armoniosa. No existe un conflicto normativo irreconciliable entre las disposiciones de la Convención y el Pacto Internacional de Derechos Civiles y Políticos que definan la libertad de circulación de los refugiados, por lo cual los refugiados tienen derecho a reclamar los beneficios de los derechos de la Convención y del PIDCP.

DEPARTURE TO SEEK PROTECTION

4. Refugees, like all persons, are free to leave any country pursuant to Art. 12(2) of the ICCPR. In accordance with Art. 12(3), the freedom to depart may be subjected only to limitations provided by law, implemented consistently with other ICCPR rights, and shown to be necessary to safeguard a state's national security, public order (*ordre public*), public health or morals, or the rights and freedoms of others.

LE DÉPART POUR CHERCHER UNE PROTECTION

4. Les réfugiés, comme toute autre personne, sont libres de quitter tout pays conformément à l'article 12, §2, du PIDCP. Conformément à l'article 12, §3, la liberté de quitter ne peut être soumise à des restrictions que si celles-ci sont prévues par la loi, nécessaires pour protéger la sécurité nationale, l'ordre public, la santé ou la moralité publiques, ou les droits et libertés d'autrui, et compatibles avec les autres droits reconnus par le PIDCP.

SALIDA PARA BUSCAR PROTECCIÓN

4. Los refugiados, como todas las personas, son libres de abandonar cualquier país de conformidad con el artículo 12 (2) del PIDCP. De acuerdo con el artículo 12 (3), la libertad para dejar un país puede estar sujeta únicamente a las limitaciones establecidas por la ley, implementadas de manera coherente con otros derechos del PIDCP, y necesarias para proteger la seguridad nacional de una nación, el orden público (*ordre public*), la salud pública o los principios morales, o los derechos y las libertades de otros individuos.

5. A limitation is only necessary if shown to be the least intrusive means to safeguard the protected interest.

5. Une restriction n'est nécessaire que s'il est établi qu'il s'agit de la mesure la moins restrictive possible pour protéger l'intérêt légitime en jeu.

5. Una limitación solo es necesaria si se demuestra que es el medio menos intrusivo para salvaguardar el interés protegido.

2. بعض الحقوق التي تنص عليها الاتفاقية، خاصة الحماية من كلا من الإعادة القسرية والتمييز
والوصول إلى محاكم الدولة، يجب أن يحترم مجرد أن يصبح اللاجئ في نطاق ولاية أحد الدول
الموقعة على الاتفاقية. بعض الحقوق المشار إليها في الاتفاقية لا يمكن إن يتمتع بها اللاجئ إلا بعد
دخوله إقليم الدولة وذلك بأن يكون متواجد على أراضيها بشكل قانوني أو مقيم بها بصورة قانونية
أو أن يكون مقيما بشكل دائم على أراضي إحدى الدول الموقعة على الاتفاقية. يجب أن تُحترم
الحقوق التي تقرها الاتفاقية، مجرد استحقاقها، ما لم يتخذ قرار نهائي بأن الشخص الذي يطلب
الحماية كلاجئ لا يستوفي الشروط المنصوص عليها في الاتفاقية.

2. Некоторые права, указанные в Конвенции, в частности, защита от *депортации*
и дискриминации, а также доступ к судам должны соблюдаться, как только беженец попадает под юрисдикцию государства-участника. Другие права, указанные
в Конвенции, определяются как применимые только после того, как беженец
въезжает на территорию государства, законно находится, законно пребывает или
долгое время проживает в государстве-участнике. Права Конвенции, которые когда-то были применены, должны соблюдаться в предварительном порядке до тех
пор, пока не будет принято окончательное решение о том, что лицо, требующее
защиты в качестве беженца, на самом деле не является беженцем.

3. يتطلب القانون الدولي إن تفسر المعاهدات على نحو متسق إذا أمكن. ولا يوجد تضاد يمنع
التوفيق بين أحكام العهد الدولي الخاص بالحقوق المدنية والسياسية فيما يتعلق بحرية تنقل
اللاجئين، وبالتالي يحق للاجئين أن يطالبوا بالاستفادة من حقوق العهد الدولي الخاص بالحقوق
المدنية والسياسية على حد سواء.

3. Международное право требует, чтобы договоры интерпретировались по возможности гармонично. Не существует непримиримого нормативного конфликта
между Конвенцией и положениями МПГПП, которые определяют свободу передвижения беженцев, в результате чего беженцы имеют право требовать исполнения
прав и Конвенции, а также МПГПП.

المغادرة للبحث عن الحماية

4. اللاجئين، شأنهم شأن جميع الأشخاص، يتمتعون بالحق في مغادرة أي دوله عملًا بالمادة
12(2) من العهد الدولي الخاص بالحقوق المدنية والسياسية. بموجب المادة 12(3)، لا يجوز أن
تخضع حرية المغادرة إلا للقيود التي ينص عليها القانون، والتي تنفذ بشكل متسق مع الحقوق
الأخرى المنصوص عليها في العهد الدولي الخاص بالحقوق المدنية والسياسية، وتبين أنها ضرورية
لحماية الأمن القومي للدولة والنظام العام أو الصحة العامة أو الآداب العامة أو حقوق الآخرين
وحرياتهم.

ВЫЕЗД ДЛЯ ПОИСКА ЗАЩИТЫ

4. Беженцы, как и все люди, могут покинуть любую страну в соответствии со статьей 12(2) Международного пакта о гражданских и политических правах (МПГПП).
В соответствии со статьей 12(3), свобода выезда может подвергаться только ограничениям, предусмотренным законом, реализуемым вместе с другими правами
МПГПП, которые являются обоснованно необходимыми для обеспечения национальной безопасности государства, общественного порядка, общественного
здоровья или нравственности, а также прав и свобод других лиц.

5. ولا يمكن استخدام القيود اللازمة لحماية تلك المصالح إلا إذا تبين أنها الوسيلة الأقل عنفا.

5. Ограничение необходимо только в том случае, если подтверждено, что оно
является наименее ограничительным средством защиты охраняемых интересов.

6. So long as an individual seeking to leave a state's territory does so freely, meaning that he or she has made an autonomous decision to do so, the state of departure may not lawfully restrict the right to leave on the basis of concerns about risk to the individual's life or safety during the process of leaving or traveling.

6. Aussi longtemps qu'un individu cherchant à quitter le territoire d'un État le fait librement, à la suite d'une décision autonome, l'État de départ ne peut pas légalement restreindre son droit de quitter en invoquant des considérations liées aux risques pour la vie ou la sécurité de cet individu résultant du fait même du départ ou du voyage.

6. Siempre que una persona que desee abandonar el territorio de una nación lo haga libremente, lo que significa que ha tomado una decisión autónoma al respecto, la nación de la que parta puede no restringir legalmente el derecho a partir sobre la base de preocupaciones de riesgo para la vida o la seguridad de la persona durante el proceso de abandono del territorio o viaje.

7. International law requires states to prosecute and punish transnational and other organized criminals who engage in human smuggling, that is the procurement of unauthorized entry of a person into another state for a financial or other material benefit. The deterrence of human smuggling may not, however, be invoked to justify a restriction on the right of persons seeking to leave any country. This is because the avoidance of breach of another state's migration laws or policies does not fall within the scope of the public order (*ordre public*) exception authorized by ICCPR Art. 12(3), which speaks to an interest of the state invoking the restriction rather than to an interest of another state.

7. Le droit international requiert des États qu'ils poursuivent et sanctionnent les organisations criminelles transnationales ou autres qui se livrent au trafic d'êtres humains, c'est-à-dire qui permettent à une personne de pénétrer sans autorisation sur le territoire d'un État, en échange d'un avantage financier ou de tout autre avantage matériel. Cependant, la lutte contre le trafic d'êtres humains ne peut être invoquée pour justifier une restriction au droit de toute personne de quitter tout pays. Cela résulte de ce que la prévention de la violation du droit et des politiques migratoires d'autres États ne relève pas de l'exception d'ordre public telle que visée par l'article 12, §3, du PIDCP, lequel concerne l'intérêt de l'État invoquant la restriction et non l'intérêt d'un État tiers.

7. El derecho internacional exige que las naciones procesen y castiguen a los delincuentes transnacionales y otros delincuentes organizados que participen en el tráfico de personas, que consiste en procurar la entrada no autorizada de una persona a otra nación para obtener un beneficio económico u otro beneficio material. No obstante, no se puede invocar la disuasión del tráfico de personas para justificar una restricción del derecho de las personas que deseen abandonar un país. Esto se debe a que evitar el incumplimiento de las leyes o políticas de migración de otra nación no está dentro del alcance de la excepción autorizada del orden público (*ordre public*) por el artículo 12 (3) del PIDCP, que habla de un interés de la nación que invoca la restricción, más que de un interés de otra nación.

8. International law also requires states to combat human trafficking. In contrast to smuggling, human trafficking is by definition an exploitative practice that harms individuals under the departure state's jurisdiction. It may thus *prima facie* engage an interest under ICCPR Art. 12(3). But because the right of everyone to leave a country may only be lawfully restricted if that is the least intrusive means available to pursue even a clearly legitimate interest, state efforts must focus on interrupting the work of traffickers rather than on seeking to stop the departure of would-be refugees and others. This approach aligns with Art. 14 of the UN Trafficking Protocol, requiring anti-trafficking commitments to be pursued in a manner that ensures respect for refugee and other international human rights.

8. Le droit international requiert également des États qu'ils luttent contre la traite des êtres humains. Au contraire du trafic d'êtres humains, la traite est, par définition, l'exploitation d'un individu relevant de la juridiction de l'État de départ. La lutte contre la traite concerne donc, *prima facie,* un intérêt relevant de l'article 12, §3, du PIDCP. Toutefois, étant donné que le droit de toute personne de quitter tout pays ne peut être restreint légalement que s'il s'agit de la mesure la moins restrictive aux fins de protéger un intérêt, fût-il manifestement légitime, les efforts des États doivent être concentrés sur l'arrêt de la traite plutôt que sur l'arrêt de la fuite des potentiels réfugiés et autres victimes. Cette approche rejoint celle de l'article 14 du Protocole des Nations unies sur la traite, lequel requiert des États qu'ils s'engagent contre la traite en respectant le droit des réfugiés et le droit international général des droits de l'homme.

8. El derecho internacional también exige que las naciones combatan la trata de personas. A diferencia del contrabando, la trata de personas es, por definición, una práctica de explotación que perjudica a las personas bajo la jurisdicción de la nación desde la que parten. Por lo tanto, a priori puede captar un interés según el artículo 12 (3) del PIDCP. Pero dado que el derecho de todos a abandonar un país solo puede ser legalmente restringido si ese es el medio menos intrusivo disponible para perseguir incluso un interés claramente legítimo, los esfuerzos de las naciones deben enfocarse en interrumpir el trabajo de los traficantes en lugar de tratar de detener la partida de posibles refugiados y otras personas. Este enfoque se alinea con el artículo 14 del Protocolo de Trata de las Naciones Unidas, que exige que los esfuerzos para combatir la trata de personas se realicen de manera tal que garanticen el respeto por los refugiados y otros derechos humanos internacionales.

6. До тех пор, пока человек, стремящийся покинуть территорию государства, делает это свободно, что означает, что он принял самостоятельное решение по этому вопросу, государство отправления не может законным образом ограничивать право на выезд, исходя из опасений относительно риска для жизни или безопасности человека в процессе отъезда или путешествия.

---

7. ويطالب القانون الدولي الدول بملاحقة وعقاب المجرمين الدوليين وغيرهم من عملاء الجريمة المنظمة الضالعين في جريمة تهريب البشر، أي تسهيل دخول شخص إلى دولة أخرى بشكل غير مصرح به مقابل منفعة مالية ومادية أخرى. غير أنه لا يمكن التذرع بردع تهريب البشر لتبرير تقييد حق الأشخاص الذين يسعون إلى مغادرة أي بلد. وذلك لأن تجنّب انتهاك قوانين أو سياسات الهجرة في دولة أخرى لا يدخل في نطاق استثناء النظام العام المرخص به بموجب المادة 12(3) من العهد الدولي الخاص بالحقوق المدنية والسياسية التي تتحدث عن مصلحة الدولة التي تحتج بالقيود وليس لمصلحة دولة أخرى.

7. Международное право требует от государств преследовать и наказывать транснациональных и других организованных преступников, которые занимаются контрабандой людей, то есть подготовкой несанкционированного проникновения человека в другое государство для получения финансовой или иной материальной выгоды. Однако сдерживание контрабанды людей не может быть использовано для оправдания ограничения этого права для лиц, которые желают покинуть любую страну. Это связано с тем, что отсутствие нарушения законов или политики миграции другого государства не входит в сферу общественного порядка, кроме исключения, разрешенного в статье 12(3) МПГПП, где говорится о заинтересованности государства, ссылающегося на ограничение, а не на интересы другого государства.

---

8. يلزم القانون الدولي بمكافحة الاتجار بالبشر. وعلى النقيض من التهريب، فإن الاتجار بالبشر هو، بحكم تعريفه، ممارسة استغلالية تضر بالأفراد الخاضعين للولاية القضائية لدولة المغادرة. وبالتالي قد يكون من الناحية الشكلية مواجهة مع المادة 12(3) من العهد الدولي الخاص بالحقوق المدنية والسياسية. ولكن نظرًا لأن حق كل شخص في مغادرة بلد ما لا يجوز تقييده قانونًا إلا إذا كان ذلك هو أقل الوسائل تدخلًا والمتاحة لمواصلة تحقيق مصلحة مشروعة بوضوح، يجب أن تركز جهود الدولة على مقاطعة عمل المتاجرين بدلًا من السعي إلى وقف رحيل اللاجئين المرتقبين وغيرهم. يتوافق هذا النهج مع المادة 14 من بروتوكول الأمم المتحدة المتعلق بالاتجار بالبشر، الذي يتطلب الالتزام بمتطلبات مكافحة الاتجار بالبشر بطريقة تكفل احترام حقوق اللاجئين وغيرها من حقوق الإنسان الدولية.

8. Международное право также требует от государств бороться с торговлей людьми. В отличие от контрабанды торговля людьми по определению является эксплуататорской практикой, наносящей вред людям, находящимся под юрисдикцией государства отправления. Таким образом, *прежде всего*, действовать в соответствии с МПГПП статьей 12(3). Но поскольку право каждого покинуть страну может быть ограничено только на законных основаниях, если это наименее ограничительное средство, доступное для достижения даже вполне законных интересов, усилия государства должны сосредоточиться на пресечении работы торговцев людьми, а не на попытке помешать отъезду потенциальных беженцев и других лиц. Этот подход согласуется со статьей 14 Протокола ООН о запрещении торговли людьми, в соответствии с которым обязательства по борьбе с торговлей людьми должны осуществляться таким образом, чтобы обеспечить соблюдение прав беженцев и других международных прав человека.

ACCESS TO PROTECTION

9. The duty of *non-refoulement* set by Art. 33 of the Convention binds a state both inside and at its borders, as well as in any extraterritorial place in which it exercises jurisdiction, whether lawfully or otherwise. The failure of a state agent to hear or to respond to a protection claim made within state jurisdiction that results in a refugee's return to, or remaining in, a place in which there is a real chance of being persecuted, is an act of *refoulement*.

ACCÈS À LA PROTECTION

9. L'obligation de non-refoulement consacrée par l'article 33 de la Convention lie un État tant à l'intérieur de ses frontières qu'à ses frontières, de même que dans toute situation extraterritoriale où il exerce sa juridiction, conformément ou non au droit international. Le fait pour un agent de l'État de ne pas recevoir, ou de ne pas répondre à, une demande de protection réalisée au sein de la juridiction de cet État, est un acte de refoulement lorsqu'il conduit au retour ou au maintien d'un réfugié dans un lieu où il risque réellement une persécution.

ACCESO A LA PROTECCIÓN

9. El deber de no devolución establecido por el artículo. 33 de la Convención vincula a una nación tanto dentro como fuera de sus fronteras, así como en cualquier lugar extraterritorial en el que ejerza jurisdicción, ya sea de modo lícito o de otra manera. El hecho de que un representante estatal no escuche o no responda a un reclamo de protección dentro de la jurisdicción de la nación que resulte en el retorno a, o la permanencia en, un lugar en el que exista una posibilidad real de que el refugiado sea perseguido, es un acto de devolución o *refoulement*.

---

10. A good faith understanding of the duty of *non-refoulement* requires states to provide reasonable access and opportunity for a protection claim to be made. While the mere existence of a natural barrier (eg. a mountain range or river) does not in and of itself amount to an act of *refoulement*, a state may not lawfully construct or maintain a man-made barrier that fails to provide for reasonable access to its territory by refugees.

10. Il résulte d'une interprétation de bonne foi du principe de non-refoulement que les États doivent fournir la possibilité effective et raisonnable d'introduire une demande de protection. Bien que la seule existence d'une barrière naturelle (comme une montagne ou une rivière) ne constitue pas en elle-même un acte de refoulement, un État ne peut légalement construire ou maintenir un obstacle humain qui empêche l'accès raisonnable du réfugié à son territoire.

10. Una comprensión de buena fe del deber de no devolución requiere que las naciones proporcionen acceso y oportunidades razonables para que se realice un reclamo de protección. Si bien la mera existencia de una barrera natural (por ejemplo, una cadena montañosa o un río) no constituye en sí misma un acto de devolución, una nación no puede construir ni mantener legalmente una barrera artificial que no proporcione un acceso razonable a su territorio a los refugiados.

---

11. As more refugees arrive at a state's border, or as those arriving face more imminent risks, access to protection is reasonable only if it is responsive to such additional or more acute needs.

11. Lorsqu'un nombre plus important de réfugiés arrivent à la frontière, ou lorsque ceux qui arrivent à la frontière font face à des risques plus imminents, l'accès à la protection n'est raisonnable que s'il est tenu compte des besoins liés à cette situation.

11. A medida que más refugiados lleguen a la frontera de una nación o que los que arriben enfrenten riesgos más inminentes, el acceso a la protección será razonable solo si responde a esas necesidades adicionales o más imperiosas.

---

12. The existence of a mass influx of refugees – defined as a situation in which the number of refugees arriving at a state's frontiers clearly exceeds the capacity of that state to receive and to protect them – may, in an extreme case, justify derogation from one or more Convention or other rights on the basis of the principle of necessity. Derogation based upon necessity may be invoked only if the state faces a grave and imminent peril and must derogate in order to safeguard an essential interest.

12. L'existence d'un afflux massif de réfugiés – défini comme la situation dans laquelle le nombre de réfugiés arrivant à la frontière d'un État dépasse sans conteste la capacité de cet État en termes d'accueil et de protection – peut, dans des circonstances extrêmes, justifier des dérogations à l'un ou plusieurs des droits conventionnels en vertu d'un état de nécessité. Les dérogations fondées sur cet état de nécessité ne peuvent être invoquées que si l'État fait face à un péril grave et imminent, de sorte qu'il se voit contraint d'appliquer pareilles dérogations aux fins de protéger un intérêt essentiel.

12. La existencia de una afluencia masiva de refugiados, definida como una situación en la que la cantidad de refugiados que llega a las fronteras de una nación excede claramente la capacidad de esa nación para recibirlos y protegerlos, puede, en casos extremos, justificar la derogación de uno o más derechos de la Convención u otros derechos sobre la base del principio de necesidad. La derogación basada en la necesidad puede invocarse solo si la nación enfrenta un peligro grave e inminente y debe derogar para proteger un interés esencial.

ДОСТУП К ЗАЩИТЕ

9. Обязательства, вытекающие из *принципа невысылки*, согласно статьи 33 Конвенции, должны реализовываться государством внутри территории и на его границах, а также экстерриториально, при осуществлении юрисдикции, законным или иным образом. Неспособность государственного должностного лица принять или отреагировать на требование защиты, сделанное в рамках юрисдикции государства, которая приводит к возвращению беженца туда, где есть реальная вероятность его преследования, является случаем *депортации*.

9. تم وضع واجب عدم الإعادة القسرية في المادة 33 من الاتفاقية التي تلزم دولة داخل حدودها، وكذلك في أي مكان خارج الحدود الإقليمية تمارس فيه الولاية القضائية، سواء كانت قانونية أو غير ذلك. إن عدم قيام ممثل الدولة بالاستماع إلى مطلب الحماية الذي قدم في إطار الولاية القضائية أو الاستجابة لها، مما يؤدي إلى عودة اللاجئ إلى مكان يمكن فيه التعرض للاضطهاد أو البقاء فيه، هو فعل من الإعادة القسرية.

10. Должное понимание обязанности *принципа невысылки* требует от государств предоставления разумного доступа и возможности для требования защиты. Хотя само существование естественного барьера (например, горного хребта или реки) само по себе не является случаем *высылки*, государство не может законно строить или поддерживать искусственный барьер, который не может обеспечить разумный доступ беженцев к его территории.

10. إن التفسير الإيجابي لعدم الإعادة القسرية يتطلب من الدول إتاحة الإمكانيات اللازمة لتمكين الأشخاص من المطالبة بالحماية. في حين أن مجرد وجود حاجز طبيعي (على سبيل المثال سلسلة جبال أو نهر) لا يرقى لوحده وفي حد ذاته ليكون من أفعال الإعادة القسرية، لا يجوز للدولة أن تقوم بصورة قانونية ببناء حاجز من صنع الإنسان يمنع وصول اللاجئين إلى أراضيها.

11. По мере того, как все больше беженцев прибывает на государственную границу или когда они сталкиваются с более серьезным риском, доступ к защите разумен, когда она реагирует на эти дополнительные или более острые потребности.

11. مع وصول المزيد من اللاجئين إلى حدود الدولة، أو عندما يواجه أولئك الذين يصلون مخاطر وشيكة، عندها لا يكون الحصول على الحماية ممكنا إلا إذا استجابت الدولة لهذه الاحتياجات الإضافية أو الأكثر حدة.

12. Существование массового притока беженцев определяется ситуацией, при которой количество беженцев, прибывающих на государственные границы, явно превышает способность этого государства принять и защитить их, может, в только крайнем случае, оправдать отступление от одной или более статей Конвенции или других прав на основании принципа необходимости. Отступление, основанное на принципе необходимости, может быть использовано только в том случае, если государство сталкивается с серьезной и неизбежной опасностью и вынуждено частично отменять действие положений для обеспечения существенного интереса.

12. إن حدوث تدفق جماعي للاجئين في أقصى صوره حين يزيد عدد اللاجئين الذين يصلون إلى حدود الدولة قدرة تلك الدولة على تلقيهم وحمايتهم، قد يبرر هذا التدفق عدم التقيد بواحده أو أكثر من الاتفاقيات الدولية أو غيرها عملا بمبدأ الضرورة. ولا يجوز الاحتجاج بهذا المبدأ إلا إذا واجهت الدولة خطرًا وشيكًا يبرر عدم التقيد بالاتفاقيات لحماية أحد المصالح الأساسية.

13. A state may, however, only invoke necessity where it has not contributed to the peril. It must also continuously assess that peril and its response thereto in order to ensure that the derogation undertaken remains necessary. Because derogation is necessary only if it is the least intrusive response capable of safeguarding the essential interest, the *refoulement* of refugees will almost invariably be impermissible. More generally, if and when a dependable system of burden and responsibility sharing as envisaged by the Convention's Preamble is implemented, the conditions precedent for lawful resort to necessity-based derogation are unlikely to be satisfied.

13. Toutefois, un État ne peut invoquer cet état de nécessité que s'il n'a pas lui-même contribué aux circonstances qui ont conduit à cet état de danger. Il doit également réaliser une évaluation continue de ce péril, ainsi que de sa réponse à ce danger, aux fins de s'assurer que les dérogations aux droits conventionnels demeurent nécessaires. Etant donné qu'une dérogation n'est nécessaire que s'il s'agit de la réponse la moins restrictive aux fins de protéger l'intérêt essentiel en cause, le refoulement de réfugiés ne sera presque jamais admis. Plus généralement, si et lorsqu'un système de partage de la charge et de la responsabilité tel qu'annoncé par le préambule de la Convention est mis en œuvre, les conditions énoncées ci-avant pour recourir légalement à une dérogation aux droits conventionnels fondée sur l'état de nécessité sont peu susceptibles d'être rencontrées.

13. No obstante, una nación solo puede invocar la necesidad si no ha contribuido a generar el peligro. También debe evaluar ese peligro y su respuesta al mismo continuamente, a fin de garantizar que la derogación efectuada siga siendo necesaria. Dado que la excepción es necesaria solo si es la respuesta menos intrusiva capaz de proteger el interés esencial, la devolución de los refugiados será casi invariablemente inadmisible. En términos más generales, si se aplica un sistema fiable de reparto de la carga y la responsabilidad, tal como se prevé en el preámbulo de la Convención, es poco probable que se cumplan las condiciones previas para el recurso legal a la derogación basada en la necesidad.

LIBERTY UPON ARRIVAL

14. Refugees entering a state party are immediately entitled to the protection of Art. 9 of the ICCPR, stipulating that everyone has the right to liberty and security of person, and may not be subjected to arbitrary arrest or detention.

LIBERTÉ À L'ARRIVÉE

14. Les réfugiés qui entrent sur le territoire d'un État sont immédiatement bénéficiaires de la protection garantie par l'article 9 du PIDCP, lequel consacre le droit de tout individu à la liberté et à la sécurité de sa personne, de même que l'interdiction d'une arrestation ou d'une détention arbitraire.

LIBERTAD LUEGO DE LA LLEGADA

14. Los refugiados que ingresen a un estado parte tienen derecho inmediato a gozar de la protección del artículo 9 del PIDCP, que estipula que todas las personas tienen derecho a la libertad y la seguridad personal, y que no pueden ser sometidas a arrestos o detenciones arbitrarios.

15. Detention of a refugee during the very earliest moments after arrival is not arbitrary and therefore does not breach ICCPR Art. 9 so long as such detention is prescribed by law and is shown to be the least intrusive means available to achieve a specific and important lawful purpose, such as documenting the refugee's arrival, recording the fact of a claim, or determining the refugee's identity if it is in doubt.

15. La détention d'un réfugié durant la période qui suit immédiatement son arrivée n'est pas arbitraire et, en conséquence, ne viole pas l'article 9 PIDCP, aussi longtemps que cette détention est prévue par la loi et constitue la mesure la moins restrictive possible pour atteindre un objectif légitime, comme l'enregistrement de l'arrivée d'un réfugié et des faits à l'origine de sa demande, ou encore la détermination de l'identité du réfugié en cas de doute.

15. La detención de un refugiado inmediatamente después de su llegada no es arbitraria y, por lo tanto, no infringe el artículo 9 del PIDCP, siempre y cuando dicha detención esté ordenada por ley y se demuestre que es el medio menos intrusivo disponible para lograr un propósito legal específico e importante, tal como documentar la llegada del refugiado, registrar el hecho de un reclamo o determinar la identidad del refugiado, si está en duda.

13. Однако государство может ссылаться на необходимость только, когда оно не способствовало опасности. Опасность и ответ на нее должны постоянно оцениваться, чтобы отмена действия была необходимой. Поскольку отмена действия необходима только в том случае, если это является наименее ограничительным ответом, который способен обеспечить реализацию существенного интереса, *высылка* беженцев практически всегда является недопустимым вариантом. В более общем плане, при условии реализации надежной системы распределения и ответственности, предусмотренной преамбулой Конвенции, предпосылки прецедента для законного использования такого основополагающего прекращения действия вряд ли будут удовлетворены.

СВОБОДА ПО ПРИБЫТИИ

14. Беженцы, въезжающие на территорию государства-участника, немедленно получают право на защиту согласно статье 9 МПГПП, в которой говорится, что каждый человек имеет право на свободу и личную неприкосновенность и не может подвергаться произвольному аресту или задержанию.

15. Задержание беженца сразу по прибытии не является произвольным и, следовательно, не нарушает статью 9, если такое задержание предписано законом и подтверждено, что оно является наименее ограничительным средством, доступным для достижения конкретной, важной и законной цели, например, оформления прибытия беженца, регистрации факта подачи иска или определения личности беженца, если она вызывает сомнения.

16. Any further detention must be continuously justified on an individuated basis. It is not enough for detention to promote a legitimate government objective, such as ensuring national security, public order (*ordre public*), public health or morals, or the rights and freedoms of others. Because any limitation on the right to liberty must be demonstrably the least intrusive means available to secure a permissible objective, detention is lawful only if lesser restrictions on liberty – such as reporting requirements or sureties – are incapable of ensuring the permissible objective.

16. Toute détention au-delà de cette période doit être continuellement justifiée à l'aide d'un examen des circonstances individuelles. Il n'est pas suffisant que la détention promeuve un intérêt légitime comme la protection de la sécurité nationale, de l'ordre public, de la santé ou de la moralité publiques, ou des droits et libertés d'autrui. Étant donné que toute limitation à la liberté n'est admise que s'il s'agit de la mesure la moins restrictive pour atteindre un objectif légitime, la détention n'est conforme au droit international que si d'autres mesures moins restrictives à la liberté – comme une obligation de signalement régulier auprès des autorités ou une caution – ne sont pas en mesure d'atteindre l'objectif légitime.

16. Toda detención adicional debe justificarse continuamente y en forma individual. No es suficiente que la detención promueva un objetivo legítimo del gobierno, como garantizar la seguridad nacional, el orden público (*ordre public*), la salud pública o los principios morales, o los derechos y las libertades de otros individuos. Debido a que cualquier limitación del derecho a la libertad debe ser de manera demostrable el medio menos intrusivo disponible para garantizar un objetivo permisible, la detención es legal solo si menores restricciones a la libertad (como los requisitos de información o las garantías) no pueden garantizar el objetivo permisible.

17. Nor may a state routinely subject all refugees to restrictions on liberty that are less intrusive than detention. Under Convention Art. 31(2), a refugee coming directly from a territory where his or her life or freedom was at risk, who has presented himself or herself without delay to authorities, and who has shown good cause for illegal entry or presence is presumptively exempt from any restriction on freedom of movement unless that restriction is shown to be necessary – that is, that it is the least intrusive means available to secure a permissible objective. The requirements of Art. 31(2) must be interpreted in a broad, non-mechanistic, and purposive way.

17. De même, un État ne peut systématiquement soumettre tous les réfugiés à des restrictions à leur liberté fussent-elles moins restrictives que la détention. Selon l'article 31, §2, de la Convention, un réfugié arrivant directement d'un territoire où sa vie ou sa liberté était menacée, qui s'est présenté sans délai aux autorités et leur a exposé des raisons reconnues valables de son entrée ou de sa présence irrégulières, ne peut, en principe, faire l'objet d'aucune restriction à sa liberté de circulation, à moins que la nécessité de pareille restriction ne soit démontrée – c'est-à-dire à moins qu'il ne s'agisse de la mesure la moins restrictive possible pour atteindre un objectif légitime. Les exigences de l'article 31, §2, doivent être interprétées de manière large, compte tenu des circonstances propres au cas d'espèce et conformément à leur objectif.

17. Una nación tampoco puede someter rutinariamente a todos los refugiados a restricciones a la libertad que sean menos intrusivas que la detención. En virtud del artículo 31 (2) de la Convención, un refugiado que provenga directamente de un territorio donde su vida o libertad estaba en riesgo, que se ha presentado sin demora a las autoridades, y que ha demostrado una buena causa para la entrada o presencia ilegal estará presuntamente exento de cualquier restricción de la libertad de circulación, a menos que se demuestre que esa restricción es necesaria, es decir, que es el medio menos intrusivo disponible para garantizar un objetivo permisible. Los requisitos del artículo 31 (2) deben interpretarse de manera amplia, no mecánica ni intencional.

MOVEMENT AND RESIDENCE

18. A refugee who is lawfully present in a state is entitled under both Convention Art. 26 and ICCPR Art. 12(1) to move freely within that state's territory and to choose his or her place of residence. A refugee is lawfully present (even if not yet lawfully staying) when he or she has been granted provisional admission or some other form of authorization to be present in the state, including for purposes of the assessment of his or her claim to be a refugee.

CIRCULATION ET RÉSIDENCE

18. Conformément tant à l'article 26 de la Convention qu'à l'article 12, §1er, du PIDCP, un réfugié se trouvant régulièrement sur le territoire d'un État a le droit de circuler librement sur le territoire de cet État et d'y choisir son lieu de résidence. Un réfugié se trouve régulièrement sur le territoire (même s'il n'y réside pas encore régulièrement) lorsqu'il bénéficie d'une admission provisoire ou d'un autre type d'autorisation au séjour, en ce compris aux fins d'examiner sa demande d'asile.

CIRCULACIÓN Y RESIDENCIA

18. Conforme a los artículos 26 de la Convención y 12 (1) del PIDCP, un refugiado que esté en una nación de manera legal tiene derecho a circular libremente dentro del territorio de esa nación y elegir su lugar de residencia. Un refugiado está presente en un territorio de manera legal (incluso si aún no reside legalmente) cuando se le ha otorgado la admisión temporaria o alguna otra forma de autorización para permanecer en la nación, incluso a los efectos de la evaluación de su solicitud para ser reconocido como refugiado.

16. ويجب أن يتم دوما توضيح أسباب أي احتجاز آخر على بشكل منفصل. ولا يكفي أن يكون سبب الاحتجاز تعزيز هدف حكومي مشروع، مثل ضمان الأمن القومي والنظام العام أو الصحة العامة أو الآداب العامة أو حقوق الآخرين وحرياتهم. لأن أي قيود على الحق في الحرية يجب أن تكون أقل الوسائل المتاحة عنفا لضمان تحقيق هدف مقبول، لأن الاحتجاز لا يعد إجراء قانوني إلا إذا كان الإجراء الأقل تقيدا للحرية – كأن يطلب من الأشخاص تقديم تقارير أو الضمانات - غير قادرة على ضمان الهدف المسموح به.

16. Любое дальнейшее содержание под стражей должно быть оправдано в каждом конкретном случае. Для задержания недостаточно общей законной правительственной цели, такой как обеспечение национальной безопасности, общественного порядка, общественного здоровья или нравственности, а также прав и свобод других лиц. Поскольку любое ограничение права на свободу должно быть наименее ограничительным средством для обеспечения допустимой цели, задержание является законным только в том случае, если менее ограничительные меры, например, предоставление отчета о месте пребывания или поручительство, неспособны обеспечить ее достижение.

17. ولا يجوز للدولة أن تُخضع جميع اللاجئين بشكل روتيني للقيود المفروضة على الحرية التي تكون أقل عنفا من الاحتجاز. بموجب مادة الاتفاقية رقم (2)31، اللاجئ الذي يأتي مباشرة من إقليم تتعرض فيه حياته أو حريته للخطر، والذي قدم نفسه من دون تأخير إلى السلطات والذي أظهر سببًا وجيهًا للدخول أو الوجود غير القانونيين، معفي من أي تقييد لحرية التنقل ما لم يكن هذا التقييد ضروريًا - أي أنه أقل الوسائل تقييدًا المتاحة لتأمين هدف مسموح به. متطلبات المادة 31(2) يجب أن تُفسر بشكل شامل ومرن.

17. Кроме того, государство не может подвергать всех беженцев средствам ограничения свободы, которые являются менее ограничительными, чем содержание под стражей. В соответствии со статьей 31(2) Конвенции беженец, прибывающий непосредственно с территории, на которой его или ее жизнь или свобода подвергались риску, и который незамедлительно представился властям и продемонстрировал значимые основания для незаконного въезда или присутствия на территории страны, предположительно освобождается от любых ограничений свободы передвижения, если это ограничение не представляется необходимым, то есть, если оно является наименее ограничительным средством для обеспечения допустимой цели. Требования статьи 31(2) должны толковаться в широком и целенаправленном смысле.

التحرك والإقامة

18. يحق للاجئ المقيم بشكل قانوني في دولة ما بموجب المادة رقم٢٦ من الاتفاقية و المادة 12 العهد الدولي الخاص بالحقوق المدنية والسياسية رقم 12(1) التحرك بحرية داخل إقليم تلك الدولة واختيار مكان إقامته. اللاجئ الموجود بصورة قانونية (حتى وإن لم يكن قد أقام بعد بصورة قانونية) عندما يكون قد مُنح حق الدخول المؤقت أو أي شكل آخر من أشكال الإذن بالحضور في الولاية، بما في ذلك لأغراض تقييم ادعائه بأنه لاجئ.

ПЕРЕДВИЖЕНИЕ И ПРОЖИВАНИЕ

18. Беженец, законно находящийся в государстве, имеет право в соответствии со статьей 26 Конвенции и статьей 12(1) МПГПП свободно передвигаться по территории этого государства и выбирать свое местожительство. Нахождение беженца является законныом (даже если данное лицо еще не пребывает на территории законно), когда ему или ей было предоставлено временное разрешение или какая-либо другая форма разрешения на пребывание в государстве, в том числе в целях оценки его или ее требования стать беженцем.

19. Once lawfully present, no refugee-specific restriction on freedom of movement or choice of residence is permissible. Under Convention Art. 26, only restrictions also applicable to aliens generally in the same circumstances are lawful. Even if applicable to aliens generally in the same circumstances, ICCPR Art. 12(3) disallows any restriction on movement or choice of residence that is not provided for by law and shown to be the least intrusive means available to ensure national security, public order (*ordre public*), public health or morals, or the rights and freedoms of others.

19. Dès qu'un réfugié séjourne régulièrement, aucune restriction à sa liberté de circulation et au choix de son lieu de résidence, fondée sur son statut, n'est autorisée. Conformément à l'article 26 de la Convention, seules les restrictions appliquées, dans les mêmes circonstances, aux étrangers en général sont autorisées. Mêmes applicables aux étrangers en général dans les mêmes circonstances, ces restrictions doivent respecter l'article 12, §3, du PIDCP, lequel interdit toute restriction à la liberté de circulation ou au libre choix du lieu de résidence qui n'est pas consacré par la loi et ne constitue pas le moyen le moins restrictif pour protéger la sécurité nationale, l'ordre public, la santé ou la moralité publiques, ou les droits et libertés d'autrui.

19. Una vez que el individuo esté presente en el territorio de manera legal, no se permite aplicar ninguna restricción específica sobre la libertad de circulación ni la elección de la residencia del refugiado. En virtud del artículo 26 de la Convención, solo son legales las restricciones que en general también son aplicables a extranjeros en las mismas circunstancias. Incluso si en general se aplica a extranjeros en las mismas circunstancias, el artículo 12 (3) del PIDCP no permite ninguna restricción de circulación o elección de residencia que no esté prevista por la ley y que se demuestre que es el medio menos intrusivo disponible para garantizar la seguridad nacional, el orden público (*ordre public*), la salud pública o los principios morales, o los derechos y las libertades de otros individuos.

20. It makes no difference whether the restriction on freedom of movement or choice of residence results from direct or indirect state action. If, for example, a state were to provide a refugee with the necessities of life in only a specified location, that decision amounts to a restriction on freedom of movement and choice of residence which is lawful only if it meets the requirements of Convention Art. 26 and ICCPR Art. 12.

20. Il importe peu que la restriction à la liberté de circulation ou au libre choix du lieu de résidence résulte d'un action directe ou indirecte de l'État. Par exemple, si un État ne fournit les besoins essentiels du réfugié que dans un lieu déterminé, cela constitue une restriction à la liberté de circulation et au libre choix du lieu de résidence, qui n'est conforme au droit international que si cette restriction rencontre les critères de l'article 26 de la Convention et de l'article 12 du PIDCP.

20. No importa si la restricción a la libertad de circulación o elección de residencia es producto de una acción estatal directa o indirecta. Si, por ejemplo, una nación proporcionara a un refugiado las necesidades vitales básicas en un lugar específico, esa decisión equivale a una restricción a la libertad de circulación y elección de residencia que es legal solo si cumple con los requisitos de los artículos 26 de la Convención y 12 del PIDCP.

21. ICCPR Art. 12(3) disallows any restriction on movement or choice of residence that infringes any other right in the ICCPR. As such, an otherwise valid restriction that, for example, poses a risk to a refugee's physical security by requiring presence or residence in a dangerous location is not lawful.

21. L'article 12, §3, du PIDCP interdit toute restriction à la liberté de circulation ou au choix du lieu de résidence qui n'est pas compatible avec les autres droits reconnus par le PIDCP. Il en résulte, par exemple, que serait illégale toute restriction rencontrant les critères précédemment énoncés mais entraînant un risque pour la sécurité physique d'un réfugié, en ce qu'elle exige qu'il demeure ou réside dans un lieu dangereux.

21. El artículo 12 (3) del PIDCP no permite ninguna restricción de circulación o elección de residencia que infrinja cualquier otro derecho del PIDCP. Por lo tanto, una restricción válida de otro tipo que, por ejemplo, represente un riesgo para la seguridad física de un refugiado al requerir presencia o residencia en un lugar peligroso, no es legal.

١٩. مجرد وجودهم بصورة قانونية، لا يجوز فرض قيود خاصة بحرية التنقل أو اختيار الإقامة على اللاجئين. حيث يخضع اللاجئين لنفس القيود التي يخضع لها سائر الأجانب بنفس الظروف القانونية وذلك بموجب المادة رقم ٢٦من الاتفاقية. حتى في حالة تطابق الإجراءات مع الأجانب في نفس الظروف، فإن المادة رقم ١٢(٣) من العهد الدولي الخاص بالحقوق المدنية والسياسية لا تُسمح بأي قيود على التنقل أو اختيار الإقامة التي لا ينص عليها القانون وتبين أنها أقل الوسائل المتاحة لضمان الأمن القومي والنظام العام أو الصحة العامة أو الآداب العامة أو حقوق الآخرين وحرياتهم.

19. После получения права на законное нахождение, наложение каких-либо ограничений на свободу передвижения или выбора места жительства не допускается. В соответствии со статьей 26 Конвенции законными являются только ограничения, применимые к иностранцам, как правило, в тех же обстоятельствах. Даже если это применимо к иностранцам, как правило, в тех же обстоятельствах, статья 12(3) МПГПП запрещает любые ограничения на передвижение или выбор места жительства, которые не предусмотрены законом, и указывает, что они являются наименее ограничительными средствами, обеспечивающими национальную безопасность, общественный, общественное здоровье или нравственность, а также права и свободы других лиц.

٢٠. ولا فرق بين ما إذا كان التقييد على حرية التنقل أو اختيار مكان الإقامة ناتجًا عن إجراءات مباشرة أو غير مباشرة من جانب الدولة. على سبيل المثال، إذا كانت الدولة توفر للاجئ الحياة الضرورية في مكان محدد فقط، فإن هذا القرار يرقى إلى تقييد حرية التنقل، واختيار مكان الإقامة الذي لا يكون مشروعًا إلا إذا استوفى متطلبات المادة رقم 26 من الاتفاقية والمادة رقم 12 العهد الدولي الخاص بالحقوق المدنية والسياسية.

20. Не имеет значения, является ли ограничение свободы передвижения или выбора места жительства прямым или косвенным действием государства. Если, например, государство должно было предоставить беженцу предметы первой необходимости только в определенном месте, это решение ограничивает свободу передвижения и выбора места жительства, которое является законным, если оно отвечает требованиям статьи 26 Конвенции и статьи 12 МПГПП.

٢١. فطبقا للمادة رقم ١٢(٣) من العهد الدولي الخاص بالحقوق المدنية والسياسية لا يسمح بوضع أي قيود على التنقل أو اختيار الإقامة التي تنتهك أي حق آخر في العهد الدولي الخاص بالحقوق المدنية والسياسية. على هذا النحو، فإن تقييدًا صالحًا على نحو آخر يشكل، على سبيل المثال، خطرًا على الأمن البدني للاجئين، وذلك من خلال اشتراط وجوده أو إقامته في مكان خطير.

21. Статья 12(3) МПГПП запрещает любые ограничения на передвижение или выбор места жительства, которые нарушают любое другое право согласно МПГПП. Таким образом, любое действующее ограничение, которое создает риск для физической безопасности беженца, которое требуют нахождения или проживания в опасном месте, не является законным.

22. Art. 28 of the Convention authorizes a state to issue a Convention travel document to enable any refugee physically present in its territory to travel abroad. Once a refugee is lawfully staying in a state's territory, including after formal recognition of his or her refugee status, the state of residence is obliged to issue that refugee with a Convention travel document meeting the requirements of the Schedule to the Convention, unless compelling reasons of national security or public order require otherwise.

22. L'article 28 de la Convention autorise un État à délivrer un titre de voyage qui permet à tout réfugié résidant régulièrement sur son territoire de voyager à l'étranger. Lorsqu'un réfugié réside régulièrement sur le territoire d'un État, en ce compris après la reconnaissance formelle de son statut, l'État de résidence est contraint de lui fournir un titre de voyage conforme à l'annexe de la Convention, à moins que des raisons impérieuses de sécurité nationale ou d'ordre public ne s'y opposent.

22. El artículo 28 de la Convención autoriza a una nación a emitir un documento de viaje de la Convención para permitir que cualquier refugiado físicamente presente en su territorio viaje al exterior. Una vez que un refugiado reside legalmente en el territorio de una nación, incluso después de haberse reconocido formalmente su condición de refugiado, la nación de residencia está obligada a emitir un documento de viaje de la Convención que cumpla con los requisitos del Anexo a la Convención, a menos que existan razones persuasivas de seguridad nacional o del orden público que exijan lo contrario.

RETURN TO ONE'S OWN COUNTRY

23. Art. 12(4) of the ICCPR provides that no one may be arbitrarily deprived of the right to enter his or her own country. Because a refugee's "own country" will ordinarily be his or her country of origin, he or she is presumptively entitled to enter that state with a view to attempting voluntary re-establishment there, as well as to be repatriated there consequent to lawful cessation under the Convention.

LE RETOUR DANS SON PROPRE PAYS
23. L'article 12, §4, du PIDCP prévoit que nul ne peut être privé arbitrairement du droit d'entrer dans son propre pays. Etant donné que le « propre pays » d'un réfugié sera généralement son pays d'origine, il est présumé bénéficier du droit d'entrer dans cet État aux fins de tenter de s'y établir à nouveau, de manière volontaire ou à la suite d'un rapatriement résultant d'une cessation du statut de réfugié conformément aux critères établis par la Convention.

REGRESO AL PROPIO PAÍS
23. El artículo 12 (4) del PIDCP establece que ninguna persona puede ser privada arbitrariamente del derecho a ingresar a su propio país. Debido a que el "propio país" de un refugiado normalmente será su país de origen, presuntamente tiene derecho a ingresar en esa nación con el fin de intentar restablecerse allí de manera voluntaria, así como de ser repatriado allí como consecuencia del cese legal en virtud de la Convención.

24. In some circumstances an individual may have more than one "own country." This may be the case for a refugee who has established special ties to a state of refuge, entitling him or her to claim that state as one of his or her "own countries." While this would in principle be grounds for a former refugee subject to repatriation to contest his or her removal from the state of refuge, such a claim should not ordinarily prevail. This is because ICCPR Art. 12(4) only prohibits the *arbitrary* deprivation of the right to enter (and by implication, to remain in) one's own country. The repatriation of a person whose refugee status has ceased in line with the requirements of the Convention is normally not arbitrary, since it is consistent with the Convention's object and purpose of ensuring protection only for the duration of risk in the country of origin.

24. Dans certaines circonstances, un individu peut avoir plus d'un « propre pays ». Cela peut être le cas en ce qui concerne le réfugié qui a construit des liens particuliers avec son pays d'accueil, en manière telle qu'il peut considérer ce pays comme étant son « propre pays ». Bien que, en principe, cela pourrait constituer un motif de contestation du rapatriement du réfugié dont le statut a cessé, ce type de motif ne devrait généralement pas être accepté. Cela résulte de la circonstance que l'article 12, §4, du PIDCP ne prohibe que la privation *arbitraire* du droit de rentrer (et, en conséquence, de rester) dans son propre pays. Le rapatriement d'une personne dont le statut de réfugié a cessé conformément aux critères énoncés par la Convention n'est généralement pas arbitraire, puisqu'il cadre avec l'objet et l'objectif de la Convention, qui entend n'assurer une protection que le temps que le risque perdure dans le pays d'origine.

24. En algunas circunstancias, una persona puede tener más de un "propio país". Este puede ser el caso de un refugiado que ha establecido vínculos especiales con una condición de refugio, lo cual le brinda derecho a reclamar esa nación como uno de sus "propios países". Si bien en principio esto sería motivo para que un ex refugiado sujeto a repatriación impugne el abandono de la nación que le ha brindado refugio, tal reclamo normalmente no debería prevalecer. Esto es porque el artículo 12 (4) del PIDCP solo prohíbe la privación *arbitraria* del derecho a entrar (y, por ende, a permanecer) en el propio país. La repatriación de una persona cuya condición de refugiado haya cesado de conformidad con los requisitos del Convenio normalmente no es arbitraria, ya que es coherente con el objeto y el propósito de la Convención de garantizar la protección solo durante la duración de la situación de riesgo en el país de origen.

22. تسمح المادة 28 من الاتفاقية للدولة بإصدار وثيقة سفر خاصة لتمكين أي لاجئ موجود فعليًّا في إقليمها من السفر إلى الخارج. وبمجرد أن يقيم اللاجئ بصورة قانونية في إقليم الدولة، بما في ذلك بعد الاعتراف الرسمي بوضعه كلاجئ، فإن دولة الإقامة ملزمة بإصدار وثيقة سفر خاصة لهذا اللاجئ تفي بمتطلبات الجدول الزمني للاتفاقية، ما لم تكن هناك أسباب قاهرة مرتبطة بالأمن القومي أو النظام العام تتطلب خلاف ذلك.

22. Статья 28 Конвенции разрешает государству выдавать проездной документ согласно Конвенции, который позволяет любому беженцу, физически присутствующему на его территории, выезжать за границу. После того, как беженец является законно пребывающим на территории государства, в том числе после официального признания его статуса беженца, государство проживания обязано выдать этому беженцу проездной документ согласно Конвенции, соответствующий требованиям Приложения к Конвенции, если только веские причины национальной безопасности или общественного порядка требуют иного.

عودة الشخص إلى موطنه

23. تنص المادة 12(4) من العهد الدولي الخاص بالحقوق المدنية والسياسية على أنه لا يجوز حرمان أي شخص تعسفًا من حقه في دخول بلده. ونظرًا لأن موطن اللاجئ عادة ما يكون دولة المنشاء، فإنه يحق له أن يدخل تلك الدولة كعودة طوعية أو إن يعاد إلي هناك بعد انتفاء صفة اللجوء عنه بموجب الاتفاقية.

ВОЗВРАЩЕНИЕ В СОБСТВЕННУЮ СТРАНУ

23. Статья 12(4) МПГПП предусматривает, что никто не может быть произвольно лишен права на возвращение в свою страну. Поскольку «собственная страна» беженца обычно является страной его происхождения, он или она, предположительно, имеют право вернуться в это государство с целью попыток добровольного обустройства, а также могут быть репатриированы туда в результате законного прекращения своего статуса согласно Конвенции.

---

24. وفي بعض الحالات، قد يكون لدى الفرد أكثر من موطن واحد. قد يكون هذا هو الحال بالنسبة للاجئ الذي أقام علاقات خاصة مع دولة اللجوء، مما يخوله أن يدعي أن الدولة هي أحد دول الموطن. في حين أن هذا من حيث المبدأ يمكن أن يكون سببًا ليعترض لاجئ سابق على عملية الإعادة إلى الوطن على إبعاده من دولة اللجوء، فإن هذا الادعاء لا ينبغي أن يسود عادةً. ويرجع ذلك إلى أن مادة العهد الدولي الخاص بالحقوق المدنية والسياسة رقم 12(4) تحظر فقط الحرمان التعسفي من الحق في الدخول (ومن ضمنه، البقاء في) بلد الموطن. إن إعادة الشخص الذي توقفت صفة اللاجئ عنده بما يتماشى مع مقتضيات الاتفاقية ليست عادة تعسفية، لأنه يتسق مع هدف الاتفاقية والغرض منها ألا يكفل الحماية إلا لمدة الخطر في بلد المنشأ.

24. В некоторых случаях у лица может быть более одной «собственной страны». Такая ситуация может присутствовать для беженца, который установил особые связи с государством, предоставившим ему убежище, которые дают ему право требовать, чтобы это государство было одной из его «собственных стран». Хотя, в принципе, такая ситуация может быть основанием для того, чтобы бывший беженец, подлежащий репатриации, оспаривал свое выдворение из страны, предоставившей убежище, такое требование обычно не должно преобладать. Это связано с тем, что статья 12(4) МПГПП только запрещает *произвольное* лишение права на возвращение (и, следовательно, на пребывание в стране). Репатриация лица, статус беженца которого прекращается в соответствии с требованиями Конвенции, обычно не является произвольной, поскольку она согласуется с объектом и целью Конвенции по обеспечению защиты только в отношении дальнейшего наличия риска в стране происхождения.

25. A (present or former) refugee's 'own country' must ordinarily authorize readmission to its territory. In the rare instance where there is an official declaration by that country that mass return or repatriation poses a threat to the life of the nation – for example, where the state's basic infrastructure has been decimated by war and cannot yet support a major population increase – ICCPR Art. 4(1) allows that state provisionally, without discrimination, and to the extent strictly necessary, to derogate from its duty of readmission. Measures derogating from the provisions of the Covenant must, however, be of an exceptional and temporary nature. As such, derogation will not justify an indefinite bar to entry but only a delay of entry to the extent strictly required by the exigencies of the emergency.

25. Le « propre pays » actuel ou précédent du réfugié doit géné-ralement autoriser la réadmission sur son territoire. Dans les rares hypothèses où ce pays fait une déclaration officielle selon laquelle un retour ou un rapatriement de masse représente une menace pour sa survie – par exemple, lorsque son infrastructure de base a été détruite par la guerre et ne suffit plus, à ce stade, pour faire face à une augmentation majeure de la population – l'article 4, §1er, du PIDCP autorise cet État à déroger provi-soirement à son obligation de réadmission, pour autant que ce soit sans discriminations et dans la stricte mesure où la situation l'exige. En outre, les mesures qui dérogent au Pacte doivent être exceptionnelles et temporaires. En soi, pareille dérogation ne justifierait pas une interdiction d'entrée à durée indéterminée, mais uniquement un report temporaire, dans la stricte mesure nécessitée par l'état d'urgence.

25. El "propio país" de un refugiado (actual o anterior) debe autorizar la readmisión a su territorio. En el caso inusual de que exista una declaración oficial de ese país de que el retorno o la repatriación masivos representen una amenaza para la vida de la nación, por ejemplo, donde la infraestructura básica de la nación haya sido diezmada por la guerra y aún no pueda soportar un aumento importante de la población, el artículo 4 (1) del PIDCP permite que dicha nación de forma temporaria, sin discrimina-ción, y en la medida estrictamente necesaria, derogue su deber de readmisión. Sin embargo, las medidas que permiten excepcio-nes a las disposiciones del Pacto deben ser de naturaleza excep-cional y temporal. En consecuencia, la derogación no justificará una prohibición indefinida de entrada, sino solo un retraso de entrada en la medida estrictamente requerida por las exigencias de la emergencia.

These Guidelines reflect the consensus of the undersigned, each of whom participated in their personal capacity in the Eighth Colloquium on Challenges in International Refugee Law, held at Ann Arbor, Michigan, USA, on March 31–April 2, 2017.

James C. Hathaway
Convener and Chair
University of Michigan

Marjoleine Zieck
Research Director
University of Amsterdam

Ali Bilgic
Bilkent University

Susan Glazebrook
Supreme Court of New Zealand

Yunsong Huang
Sichuan University

Sarah Joseph
Monash University

Satvinder Juss
King's College London

Nora Markard
Hamburg University

Yasuhisa Arai
Student
University of Michigan

Russell Busch
Student
University of Michigan

Erin Collins
Student
University of Michigan

Andrew Fletcher
Student
University of Michigan

Allison Hight
Student
University of Michigan

Dusan Jovanovic
Student
University of Michigan

Melissa Pettit
Student
University of Michigan

Xun Yuan
Student
University of Michigan

Matthew Lind
Co-Rapporteur
University of Michigan

Lauren Nishimura
Co-Rapporteur
University of Michigan

The Colloquium deliberations benefited from the counsel of Madeline Garlick, Chief of Protection Policy and Legal Advice Section, Division of International Protection, United Nations High Commissioner for Refugees.

25. ويتعين على «بلد الموطن» للاجئ (الحالي أو السابق) أن يأذن بإعادة الدخول إلى أراضيه. وفي الحالات النادرة التي يوجد فيها إعلان رسمي من تلك الدولة أن العودة الجماعية أو العودة إلى الوطن تشكل تهديدًا لحياة الأمة - على سبيل المثال، حيث دمرت الحرب البنية التحتية للدولة، ولا يمكنها أن تدعم زيادة سكانية كبيرة - مادة العهد الدولي الخاص بالحقوق المدنية والسياسية رقم٤(١) سمح لتلك الدولة مؤقتًا، ومن دون تمييز، وبالقدر الضروري للغاية، من عدم التقيد بواجب إعادة القبول. بيد أن التدابير التي تتخلى عن أحكام العهد يجب أن تكون ذات طابع استثنائي ومؤقت. على هذا النحو، فإن عدم التقيد لن يبرر وجود حظر غير محدد للدخول، ولكن فقط تأجيل الدخول إلى الحد الذي تفتضيه ضرورات الطوارئ.

25. (Настоящая или прежняя) «собственная страна» беженца должна разрешать возвращение на свою территорию. В редких случаях, когда официальное заявление этой страны о том, что массовое возвращение или репатриация представляет угрозу для жизни нации, например, когда базовая инфраструктура государства была уничтожена войной и не может поддержать значительное увеличение населения, статья 4(1) МПГПП позволяет этому государству временно, без какой-либо дискриминации, и ровно в необходимой степени, отступить от своей обязанности по возвращению своих граждан. Однако меры, отступающие от положений Пакта, должны носить исключительный и временный характер. Таким образом, отступление не будет оправдывать неопределенный барьер для въезда, а лишь его задержку входа, строго необходимую в связи с чрезвычайной ситуацией.

Index

Abbreviations used in the index

CAT   Convention against Torture and Other Cruel, Inhuman or Degrading Treatment or Punishment (1984)

CERD   Committee on the Elimination of Racial Discrimination

CESCR   Committee on Economic, Social and Cultural Rights

CRSR   Refugee Convention (1951)

ICCPR   International Covenant on Civil and Political Rights (1966)

ICESCR   International Covenant on Economic, Social and Cultural Rights (1966)

ICL   International Criminal Law

IHL   International Humanitarian Law

IHRL   International Human Rights Law

ILC   International Law Commission

OAU   Organization of African Unity

PRSR   Refugee Protocol (1967)

RSD   Refugee Status Determination

UNC   UN Charter (1945)

UNHCR   UN High Commissioner for Refugees

VCLT   Vienna Convention on the Law of Treaties (1969)

acquired rights
  accretion of, IV.9
  non-refoulement as, IV.9
  "protection elsewhere" and, IV.8–9
arrest or detention, freedom from (ICCPR 9), VIII.14–17
  national security/public order and, VIII.16

burden-sharing/avoidance of tension between states (CRSR Preamble) and
  mass influx, methods of dealing with, VIII.13
  "protection elsewhere" and, IV Intro

criminals. *See* exclusion for serious international crimes (CRSR 1(F)(a))

self-interest of applicant, relevance,
VII.11
"serious non-political crime"
(CRSR 1(F)(b))
distinguished, VII.13
societal/collective impact, need
for, VII.11
predicament approach vs intention, II.6–
10. *See also* nexus to a Convention
ground (CRSR 1(A)(2))
procedural fairness (international standards
including notification to applicant of
intentions/opportunity to challenge)
internal protection alternative, I.25
"protection elsewhere", IV.12
professions, right to practice (CRSR 19)
lawful presence requirement, IV.5
treatment "as favourable as possible and,
in any event, not less favourable than
that accorded to aliens generally in the
same circumstances", V.9
"protection elsewhere"
burden-sharing/avoidance of tension
between states (CRSR Preamble) and,
IV Intro
definition/examples, IV Intro
expulsion of person/transfer of protective
responsibility prior to establishment
of lawful presence (CRSR 32), IV.5
"lawful presence" in sending state as
impediment
good faith determination by
sending state in accordance
with international law, IV.5
timing of establishment, IV.5
receiving party
non-party to the Convention as,
IV.2
non-state entity, exclusion as, IV.2
respect for CRSR/PRSR rights
requirement, IV.1–11
acquired rights, IV.8–9
level of rights enjoyed by others
in the receiving state as
benchmark, IV.10
refoulement risk (CRSR 33), IV.6–7

sending state's obligations
assurance of receiving state's
intentions regarding refugee
status/guarantee of CRSR
2–34 rights, IV.4
good faith empirical assessment
of likely compliance by
receiving state, IV.3
respect for rights under IHRL/IHL, IV.11
safeguards/rights of transferee
actual or constructive knowledge
of breach of obligations
by receiving state as bar
to further transfers to that
state, IV.15
effective remedy/due process, IV.12
"a reasonable period and all the
necessary facilities to obtain
admission into another
country" (CRSR 31(2)), IV.13
right to contest the legality of
proposed transfer before it is
effected, IV.12
sending state's obligation to
facilitate return of transferee
in the event of its failure to
ensure respect for his/her
rights, IV.14
written agreement between the
two states, desirability/
proposed provisions, IV.16

**"refugee" (CRSR 1[A][2]) ("Convention
refugee")**
definition, III Intro, VI Intro, VII Intro, I.1,
II.1, VI.1
state parties' obligations towards,
limitations, I.1–2
Refugee Convention (1951) (CRSR)
integrity, safeguards, VI.4
interpretation
broad and purposive, VIII.17
good faith obligation, V.7
harmoniously with other treaties,
VIII.3
as part of the IHRL corpus, V.3–4
savings clause (CRSR 5), V.4